Ben-Haim's "theories and presentation of how to calculate what one *needs* to know are, or should be, *must* reading for anyone seriously involved in any aspect of today's economic world, from the trader on a desk to a Central Bank head. It is much too easy, given the stresses of today's world, to skip past missing information so as to act quickly in the market, but that is exactly the path which leads to significant errors, as we have all unfortunately witnessed. *A method of calculating the 'info gap' is certainly vital in setting policy.*" Lew Weston, Retired Partner, Goldman, Sachs & Co.

"In an economic world where complexity defines the system and the underlying models are at best simplistic and incomplete, it is imperative that policy decisions be taken on the assumption of (disappointingly) incomplete knowledge. Now, more than ever, is the economics profession confronted with the truth of it all. *This is the time for info-gap and decisions under fundamental uncertainty.*" Dr Maria Demertzis, Research Department, De Nederlandsche Bank.

"The work by Yakov Ben-Haim is always inspiring. It is impressive how many scientists already apply his theory. With his enthusiasm, Yakov has made uncertainty issues a topic in a variety of disciplines and thus promoted interdisciplinary work, which is most welcome. It is particularly important to consider uncertainty in economic decision-making, as the current financial crisis shows. For me, as a forest scientist and forest economist, uncertainty is a key topic to be addressed by any sustainable management strategy for ecosystems. This book provides an excellent overview on opportunities for economic applications of the Information-Gap Theory. The manifold practical examples make it easy for all to understand and to follow, including persons who are yet not familiar with uncertainty issues." Dr Thomas Knoke, Institute of Forest Management, Technical University of Munich.

"Much of the recent economic crisis can be traced to over-reliance on simple mathematical models that take no account of the fact that real economies are subject to significant Knightian uncertainty. Ben-Haim shows how Info-Gap Theory can be used to model this uncertainty with carefully chosen, relevant and important economic examples. A must-read for serious economic decision makers." Prof. Colin J. Thompson, Maths and Stats Department, University of Melbourne.

Also by Yakov Ben-Haim:

INFO-GAP DECISION THEORY: Decisions Under Severe Uncertainty, 2nd edition

ROBUST RELIABILITY IN THE MECHANICAL SCIENCES

CONVEX MODELS OF UNCERTAINTY IN APPLIED MECHANICS, with I. Elishakoff

THE ASSAY OF SPATIALLY RANDOM MATERIAL

Info-Gap Economics

An Operational Introduction

Yakov Ben-Haim

palgrave
macmillan

First published 2010 by
PALGRAVE MACMILLAN

Palgrave Macmillan in the UK is an imprint of Macmillan Publishers Limited, registered in England, company number 785998, of Houndmills, Basingstoke, Hampshire RG21 6XS.

Palgrave Macmillan in the US is a division of St Martin's Press LLC, 175 Fifth Avenue, New York, NY 10010.

Palgrave Macmillan is the global academic imprint of the above companies and has companies and representatives throughout the world.

Palgrave® and Macmillan® are registered trademarks in the United States, the United Kingdom, Europe and other countries.

ISBN 978–0–230–22804–7 hardback

This book is printed on paper suitable for recycling and made from fully managed and sustained forest sources. Logging, pulping and manufacturing processes are expected to conform to the environmental regulations of the country of origin.

A catalogue record for this book is available from the British Library.

A catalog record for this book is available from the Library of Congress.

10 9 8 7 6 5 4 3 2 1
19 18 17 16 15 14 13 12 11 10

Printed and bound in Great Britain by
CPI Antony Rowe, Chippenham and Eastbourne

To contact the author:

Prof. Yakov Ben-Haim
Yitzhak Moda'i Chair in Technology and Economics
Technion – Israel Institute of Technology
Haifa 32000 Israel
yakov@technion.ac.il
http://info-gap.com

Contents

Preface

The management of surprises is central to the "economic problem", and info-gap theory is a response to this challenge. This book is about how to formulate and evaluate economic decisions under severe uncertainty. The book demonstrates, through numerous examples, the info-gap methodology for reliably managing uncertainty in economic policy analysis and decision making.

Economics has employed quantitative analysis for description of phenomena and prescription of policy more successfully than any other social science. The continual introduction of new mathematical tools to economic analysis has characterized economic research and practice for well over a century. This trend continues as new tools emerge and as their relation to traditional problems is identified.

But can quantitative methods really help in dealing with the severe uncertainty surrounding economic decisions?

This book provides an affirmative answer by responding to a very traditional economic problem: Knightian uncertainty, the lack of even probabilistic knowledge with which to characterize some aspects of a situation. Frank Knight (1921) studied the connection between probabilistic risk (which can be insured against) and what he called "true uncertainty" for which no probabilistic information is available. He identified the central role in economic processes of non-probabilistic uncertainty—of the inability to know all of the past and present or to fathom the future. Foremost, he identified its role in the explanation of profit in competitive entrepreneurship.

Our concern with Knightian uncertainty is in how it can be modelled and managed in the formulation and evaluation of a wide range of economic decisions and policies, in fields as diverse as monetary policy, financial economics and public policy. The challenge is that our data are fragmentary or noisy, our models are inaccurate, our understanding is incomplete, and even when these deficiencies are minor, the future can be very different from the past. These are Knightian uncertainties, what we will refer to as information-gaps: disparities between what we *do know* and what we *need to know* in order to make reliable decisions. The art of info-gap modelling of Knightian uncertainty is a central focus of this book.

Economic decisions can be sorted into two groups. *Strategic decisions* reflect fundamental goals of the organization, entail understanding of the organization in its economic, social or political context, and often have long-term impact. Setting guidelines for interest rates by a monetary authority, or deciding to enter the derivatives market for an investment bank, or choosing a policy format for environmental regulation are all strategic decisions. *Tactical decisions* provide specific details and precise directives for action, and usually operate on a short time scale. Open-market operations by a central bank, selecting the composition of investment portfolios, or determining the tax rate for regulating pollution emissions are examples of tactical decisions. Strategic decisions provide guidelines for tactical decisions, and tactical decisions are the practical attempt to achieve strategic goals.

Professional judgment based on knowledge and experience is essential in both strategic and tactical decision making. Strategic decision making tends to involve more human judgment and less quantitative analysis than tactical decision making. A major exception is when tactical decision making must be both integrative and fast. Nonetheless, the broad scope of strategic thinking tends to limit the practicality of mathematical modelling, while the specific focus of a tactical decision can often be usefully quantified. A central aim of info-gap analysis of decisions is to employ quantitative analysis in the support of strategic decision making, while also using info-gap theory in the formulation and analysis of tactical decisions.

Strategic thinking often involves mental models and intuitive understanding which cannot be precisely quantified because of the essentially linguistic nature of the knowledge involved. The experienced economist grasps the state of a national economy or global market, without being able to reliably quantify the relations among the many variables involved. The gap between mental and quantitative models is an info-gap. Info-gap theory provides a tool for supporting strategic planning and for providing guidelines around which tactical decisions are formed. At the same time, info-gap theory is directly applicable to the formulation of tactical decisions.

Info-gap theory is described in plain English in chapter 1, which is a brief and entirely math-free exposition of the main concepts and implications of an info-gap analysis. Chapter 2 is an info-gap analysis of robustness to uncertainty, and opportuneness from uncertainty, in a simple stylized example. The main features of robustness and opportuneness functions are identified and the types of conclusions which can be drawn are discussed. These two chapters make up Part I, Getting Started, and will interest all readers who are not familiar with info-gap decision theory (Ben-Haim, 2006).

The core of the book is Part II, Economic Decisions, containing four topical chapters that can be read independently. These chapters should be viewed as illustrations of the info-gap analysis of four very different realms of economic decision making. None of these chapters is meant to prescribe specific policy recommendations. The purpose is to demonstrate in detail the method of info-gap analysis of uncertainty, and the way in which the analysis supports the formulation of policy. The goal is to enable the reader to develop his or her own applications.

Chapter 3 deals with *monetary policy*. The emphasis is on policy choices with the aim of confidently achieving specified goals in the face of a range of uncertainties. We start with a simple economic model and consider the choice of Taylor coefficients for controlling inflation and output gap, given uncertainty in the parameters of the economic model. We then extend the model to include public expectations and explore the importance of credibility of the central bank. We then add shocks to the system, in addition to parametric uncertainty in the model. The shocks are defined by probability distributions, but the tails of these distributions are highly uncertain. Finally we introduce central bank uncertainty about public expectations for the future.

Chapter 4 discusses *financial stability* from the perspectives of various risk management decisions. We begin with a simple analysis of structured securities and show how analysis of robustness reveals the impact of uncertain correlations among the underlying securities. We then discuss the concept of value at risk of a portfolio, where the tails of the probability distribution of the returns are highly uncertain. We discuss the stress testing of a financial system based on a suite of models. The chapter concludes with an example of the strategic allocation of assets when the payoffs are uncertain.

Chapter 5 discusses several topics in the economic analysis of *public policy.* We begin with an info-gap robustness analysis of the choice between limiting the emission of pollution or taxing such emissions when the marginal costs and benefits are uncertain. We then study policy choices for enforcing pollution limits when emission permits are traded in a competitive market, and the costs of abatement are uncertain to the regulator. Finally we consider policy choices for managing long-range economic impacts of climate change from industrial emission of greenhouse gases.

Chapter 6 discusses *estimation and forecasting.* Economic data invariably have a random element so statistical tools are highly relevant. However, data also have important non-random info-gaps—errors, omissions, future revisions and so on—which are amenable to an info-gap analysis. We begin by considering an info-gap regression which employs historical observation and contextual economic understanding for predicting future outcomes. We then consider an auto-regression of a single variable, where the data are subject to substantial revision in the future. Finally, we construct a statistical confidence interval and evaluate its robustness to uncertainty in the data upon which the confidence interval is based.

The four chapters in Part II are just a beginning. Many important topics remain untouched. Subjects which are amenable to info-gap analysis include the design of index numbers for comparing prices and quantities in different times and regions, tax structures for efficient achievement of social policy, contract structure for uncertain principal-agent interactions, analysis of incentives for compliance and enforcement of public policies, and many more. The aim of this book is to demonstrate the application and added value of info-gap theory and to enable the reader to apply this methodology to new domains.

The book concludes in Part III, Wrapping Up, with two very different methodological perspectives.

Chapter 7 is a discussion of the *art of uncertainty modelling.* Throughout the book we have formulated info-gap models of uncertainty to represent model and data deficiencies in a wide range of situations. In this chapter we take stock of the processes by which one constructs info-gap models of uncertainty. We also discuss a range of specific models, though this is not an exhaustive discussion. The aim is to help the reader in formulating uncertainty models for his or her own applications.

Chapter 8 is a different methodological perspective on the book. We suggest an info-gap approach to the debate between Friedman and Samuelson on *economic positivism.*

∼ ∼ ∼

Numerous people have contributed to the development of ideas in this book. I especially wish to acknowledge useful comments and criticisms by Micha Ben-Gad, Kerstin Bernoth, Maria Demertzis, L. Joe Moffitt, John K. Stranlund and Ellis W. Tallman.

Yakov Ben-Haim
The Technion
Haifa, Israel
January 2010

Miriam,

For your loving help with all those info-gaps.

Part I

Getting Started

Chapter 1

Info-Gap Theory in Plain English

Info-gap theory is described without using equations. The idea of an information-gap is introduced. The three components of an info-gap analysis are discussed: uncertainty model, system model, and performance requirement. The robustness and opportuneness functions are introduced and their use in decision making is discussed. Robust-satisficing and opportune-windfalling strategies are described. Implications of info-gap theory are outlined. Applications of info-gap theory to a wide range of disciplines are mentioned.

∼ ∼ ∼

1.1 Can Models Help?

After every crisis, large or small, economists, policy analysts, and the public at large ask: can better models help prevent or ameliorate such situations?

This book is an answer to that question. Yes, quantitative models can help if we remember that they are rough approximations to a vastly more complex reality. Models can help if we include realistic representations of uncertainty among our models, recognizing that "realism" means stark simplicity in portraying our ignorance. Yes, models can help if we insist on retaining the pre-eminence of human judgment over the churning of our computers.

Info-gap theory is a methodology for supporting model-based decisions under severe uncertainty (Ben-Haim, 2006). An info-gap is a disparity between what *is known*, and what *needs to be known* in order to make a comprehensive and reliable decision. An info-gap is resolved when a surprise occurs, or a new fact is uncovered, or when our knowledge and understanding improve. We know very little about the substance of an info-gap. For instance, we rarely know what unusual event will delay the completion of a task. Even more strongly, we *cannot* know what is not yet discovered, such as tomorrow's news or fads and fashions, or future scientific theories or technological inventions. The ignorance of these things are info-gaps. An info-gap is a Knightian uncertainty (Knight, 1921) since it is not characterized by a probability distribution.

Policy makers devise plans or strategies for a specific economic, social and historical situation in order to secure a favorable outcome while mitigating risk and uncertainty. Personal judgment is crucial in this process, and info-gap theory does not supplant the decisions made by experienced professionals. In fact info-gap theory augments personal judgment with quantitative tools for managing uncertainty. The policy maker faces a disparity between what is known and what needs to be known in order to attain a favorable policy outcome. Info-gap theory can help deal with this challenge.

Policy makers wish to choose an action with confidence that the consequence will be satisfactory. However, these two attributes of a policy—success and reliability—are different from each other and conflict with each other. Ambitious goals may be risky. The crux of the challenge is uncertainty: fragmentary data, approximate models and imperfect understanding. Choices that exhaustively exploit uncertain knowledge may tend to fall short of the quality of outcome which is predicted by that knowledge, precisely because some of that knowledge is wrong. On the other hand, better-than-anticipated outcomes are also possible when our knowledge is imperfect. Policies must be selected not only according to their predicted outcomes, but also according to the immunity of those outcomes to errors in the knowledge underlying the predictions, and according to the opportunities inherent in the uncertainty. Info-gap decision theory provides a tool for evaluating both the robustness against pernicious uncertainty as well as the opportuneness from propitious uncertainty. Info-gap theory is a methodology for decision under severe uncertainty which has been applied in many disciplines as we will see in section 1.4.

Robustness trades off against quality. If our knowledge were complete and accurate then it would be reliable to select a policy which is predicted to have the best outcome. However, lacunae in information (info-gaps) prevent us from reliably identifying optimal outcomes. But why isn't the best estimate of the *optimal* outcome also necessarily the best bet for an *adequate* outcome? How do we know which estimated outcome is most resistent (robust) to error in the knowledge upon which the estimate is based? How do we know which policy to choose with highest confidence of achieving a satisfactory result?

The answers to these questions depend on deeper understanding of the conflict between the success of an outcome (its quality) and the immunity of that quality to uncertainty in the knowledge on which the quality is predicated.

A basic theorem of info-gap theory asserts that robustness trades off against quality: the immunity to uncertainty of an outcome *increases* as the estimated quality of that outcome *decreases.* The info-gap robustness function quantifies this trade-off. Furthermore, one can talk of a *cost of robustness:* the increment in quality which must be sacrificed in exchange for a positive increment of robustness against uncertainty.

For example, consider a central bank's choice of an interest rate. Given a macro-economic model of the economy and data on the current state of affairs, one can estimate the quality of outcome for any choice of interest rate. However, current data are often wrong and may be substantially revised in the future, and the model is based on assumptions which can be challenged and has been statistically estimated from historical data which may not reflect the future state of the economy. Finally, the outcome may be evaluated in terms of current concerns, such as inflation, which may not reflect future concerns, such as deflation. Small errors in any of these elements can result in diminished satisfaction with the outcome. Quality at a level which is somewhat less than predicted can be guaranteed provided that the data and preferences do not err too much. The more the quality requirement is relaxed, the greater the tolerance to error. The cost of robustness is the rate at which quality must be exchanged for immunity to error. Info-gap theory provides tools for quantitatively assessing this trade-off.

One possible outcome of considering the immunity to uncertainty is that we may actually **reverse our preference among policy options.** Consider two different policies, for instance two different central bank interest rates. Given best estimates of economic data, models, and outcome requirements, one of these policies will, in all likelihood, entail a better predicted outcome than the other. However, we already know that the preference between these policies should not be based on their predicted outcomes since these predictions have no robustness against info-gaps. How should we choose between these policies? One way is to identify an acceptable or required "critical" level of quality, and then to choose the policy which is more robust to uncertainty at this critical quality. If the cost of robustness is the same for the two policies, then the more robust policy will also be the preferred policy based on the estimated outcome. But it can happen that the policy whose estimated outcome is better nonetheless has higher cost of robustness than the other policy. (Recall that quality and robustness are distinct and conflicting attributes.) Thus the second policy may be more robust than the first at the critical level of quality. In short, it can and often does happen that the policy choice for higher quality but lower robustness is different from the lower-quality higher-robustness choice. Preferences can become reversed as outcome requirements change.

Opportuneness trades off against windfall. Our knowledge is uncertain. The opportuneness of a policy is a measure of how much reality must deviate from our knowledge in order for better-than-anticipated outcomes to be possible. Some policies are very opportune: great windfalls are possible (though certainly not guaranteed) if the knowledge errs by only a small amount. Such policies have a low cost of windfall. Other policies have higher windfall costs, requiring greater deviation of reality from prior knowledge in order for wonderful surprises to become possible.

Policy makers are usually and rightfully risk averse, and pay far more attention to robustness than to opportuneness. Nonetheless, opportuneness is sometimes useful, for instance as the deciding vote between two policies whose robustnesses are similar at the required outcome.

In the next section we consider the structure of an info-gap analysis of robustness and opportuneness in more detail.

1.2 Elements of Info-Gap Theory

The info-gap analysis of a decision is based on three elements. The first element is an **info-gap model of uncertainty,** which is a non-probabilistic quantification of uncertainty. The uncertainty may be in the value of a parameter, such as the slope of the Phillips curve, or in a vector such as the future returns on a portfolio of investments. An info-gap may be in the shape of a function, such as demand vs. price, or the shape of the tail of the probability density function (pdf) of extreme financial loss. An info-gap may be in the size and shape of a set of such entities, such as the set of possible pdf's or the set of possible Phillips curves. We will encounter many examples of info-gap models of uncertainty. In all cases an info-gap model is an unbounded family of nested sets of possible realizations. For instance, if the uncertain entity is a function then the info-gap model is an unbounded family of nested sets of realizations of this function. An info-gap model does not posit a worst case or most extreme uncertainty.[1] Chapter 7 presents an overview of the art of formulating an info-gap model of uncertainty.

The second element of an info-gap analysis is a **model of the system,** such as a macro-economic model, or a capital asset pricing model, or a model of financial stability. The model expresses our knowledge about the system, and may also depend on uncertain elements whose uncertainty is represented by an info-gap model of uncertainty. The system model may be probabilistic, such as a model of the financial value at risk which evaluates quantiles of a probability distribution. In this case the probability distribution may be info-gap-uncertain. The system model also depends on the decisions to be made, and quantifies the outcomes of those decisions given specific realizations of the uncertainties. For instance, the model may express macro-economic outcomes such as inflation, unemployment, growth of the GDP, and so on.

The third element of an info-gap analysis is a set of **performance requirements.** These specify values of the outcomes which the decision maker requires or aspires to achieve. These values may constitute success of the decision, or at least minimally acceptable values. For instance, inflation targeting is sometimes formulated as a range of inflation values which are acceptable. Performance requirements can embody the concept of satisficing: doing well enough or meeting critical requirements. Alternatively, the performance requirements can express windfall aspirations for better-than-anticipated

[1]Sometimes the family of sets is bounded by virtue of the definition of the uncertain entity. For instance, a probability must be between zero and one, so the family of nested sets of possible probability values is bounded. However, this bound does not derive from knowledge about the event whose probability is uncertain, but only from the mathematical definition of probability. Such an info-gap model is unbounded in the universe of probability values.

outcomes. We will encounter examples of both satisficing and windfalling requirements, though satisficing requirements are the most common.

These three components—uncertainty model, system model, and performance requirements—are combined in formulating two *decision functions* which support the choice of a course of action.

The **robustness function** assesses the greatest tolerable horizon of uncertainty. The robustness function is a quantitative answer to the question: how wrong can we be in our data, models and understanding, before the action we are considering leads to an unacceptable outcome. The robustness function is based on a satisficing performance requirement. When operating under severe uncertainty, a decision which is guaranteed to achieve an acceptable outcome throughout a large range of uncertain realizations is preferable to a decision which can fail to achieve an acceptable outcome even under small error. In this way the robustness function generates preferences among available decisions. When choosing between two options, the *robust-satisficing* decision strategy selects the more robust option.

The **opportuneness function** assesses the lowest horizon of uncertainty which is necessary for better-than-anticipated outcomes to be possible (though not guaranteed). The windfalling decision maker asks: how wrong must we be in order for attractive but unexpected outcomes to be possible? The opportuneness function is based on windfalling rather than satisficing. When operating under severe uncertainty it is possible that best-model anticipations are overly pessimistic. The windfaller seeks to exploit the ambient uncertainty. A decision which would result in a really wonderful outcome if we err only slightly is preferred (by the windfaller) over a decision which requires great deviation in order to enable the same outcome. The opportuneness function generates preferences among the available decisions. These preferences may not agree with the preferences generated by the robustness function. When considering the choice between two options, the *opportune-windfalling* decision strategy chooses the more opportune strategy, recognizing that it may be less robust.

1.3 Implications of Info-Gap Theory

This book is motivated by the conflict between respect for, and scepticism about, economic models. As William Poole put it in the specific context of central bank policy (2004):

> The true art of good monetary policy is in managing forecast surprises and not in doing the obvious things implied by the baseline forecast. (p.1) ... [P]olicy needs to be informed by the best guesses incorporated in forecasts and by knowledge of forecast errors. Forecast errors create risk, and that risk needs to be managed as efficiently as possible. (p.5)

This book presents a specific methodological response to the challenge of surprise, based on info-gap theory which is a quantitative methodology for analysis and design of policy with severe uncertainty.

Following are some implications and attributes of info-gap decision theory:

1. Do not attempt to exhaustively list adverse events. Surprises by their nature cannot be anticipated.

2. While we cannot forecast surprises, info-gap theory enables one to model one's ignorance of those surprises.

3. Strategic decisions are sometimes based on mental models and intuitive understanding which are not mathematical. An info-gap model of uncertainty can quantify the disparity between the intuition and the math. An info-gap analysis can support strategic decision making by formalizing the uncertainty surrounding the intuitive understanding.

4. Info-gap theory is not a worst-case analysis. While there may be a worst case, one cannot know what it is and one should not base one's policy upon guesses of what it might be. Info-gap theory is related to robust-control and min-max methods, but nonetheless different from them. The strategy advocated here is *not* the amelioration of purportedly worst cases.

5. The basic tool of info-gap policy analysis is a quantitative answer to the **robustness question:** For a specified policy, how wrong can our models and data be, without jeopardizing the

achievement of critical or necessary outcomes of that policy? The answer is provided by the info-gap robustness function. The difference from min-max approaches is that we are able to select a policy without ever specifying how wrong the model actually is. Min-max and info-gap robust-satisficing strategies will sometimes agree and sometimes differ.

6. The main supplementary tool in info-gap policy analysis is a quantitative answer to the **opportuneness question:** for a specified policy, how wrong must our models and data be in order to enable (though not guarantee) a windfall outcome, much better than anticipated? The answer is provided by the info-gap opportuneness function.

7. A policy which is robust to surprises is preferable to a vulnerable policy. A policy which is opportune to surprises is preferable to a non-opportune policy. Robustness is usually the more important criterion. Opportuneness resolves ambiguities in robustness.

8. Highly ambitious policy is more vulnerable to surprises than a policy aimed at modest goals. That is, policy goals trade off against immunity to uncertainty. The robustness function quantifies this trade-off.

9. Optimization of policy goals (e.g., optimizing inflation stability or output gap or capital adequacy, etc.) is equivalent to minimizing the immunity to uncertainty.

10. From items 8 and 9 we conclude that policy goals should be "good enough" but not necessarily optimal, in order to obtain robustness against surprises. That is, policy should be chosen to **satisfice** the goals and not to optimize them.

11. Goals which are satisficed (sub-optimal but good enough) can be achieved by many alternative policies. Choose the most robust from among these alternatives.

12. In some situations the robust-satisficing and optimizing strategies are the same.

13. When robustness and opportuneness trade-off against each other (which is not always the case), explore the exchange of some robustness against failure in return for substantial opportuneness for windfall.

In summary, info-gap theory provides a quantitative tool for policy formulation and evaluation which is based on Knight's uncertainty and Simon's bounded rationality. We cannot predict surprises, but info-gap theory enables us to model and manage our ignorance of those surprises. Info-gap policy analysis is particularly suited to situations in which surprises are critically important.

1.4 Applications of Info-Gap Theory

Info-gap theory originated in engineering and has since been applied to a wide range of disciplines (Ben-Haim, 1996, 2006).[2]

There have been many applications of info-gap theory to planning and decision problems in biological conservation. Levy *et al.* (2000) use info-gap theory in the analysis of policy alternatives for biological conservation. Burgman (2005) devotes a chapter to info-gap theory as a tool for biological conservation and environmental management. Regan *et al.* (2005) use info-gap theory to devise a preservation program for an endangered rare species. Moilanen *et al.* (2006a, b, c) use info-gap theory for designing multi-site nature reserves. Moilanen *et al.* (2009) use info-gap theory for evaluating economic compensation to land developers for preserving bio-diversity. Nicholson and Possingham (2007) use info-gap theory in designing strategies for bio-diversity preservation. Halpern *et al.* (2006) use info-gap theory in design of a marine nature reserve. Crone *et al.* (2007) use info-gap theory for formulating conservation strategies for a rare butterfly. Moffitt *et al.* (2008) use info-gap theory for designing detection protocols for uncertain introductions of invasive species. Carmel and Ben-Haim (2005) use info-gap theory in a theoretical study of foraging behavior of animals.

Info-gap theory has been used in explaining economic behavior and in analyzing economic policy. Ben-Haim and Jeske (2003) use info-gap theory to explain the home-bias paradox. Ben-Haim (2006) uses info-gap theory to study the equity premium puzzle (Mehra and Prescott, 1985) and the paradoxes of Ellsberg and Allais (see Mas-Colell, Whinston and Green, 1995). Beresford-Smith and Thompson (2007) use info-gap theory for managing financial credit risk. Akram *et al.* (2006) use info-gap theory in formulating monetary policy. McCarthy and Lindenmayer (2007) use info-gap theory to manage commercial timber harvesting that competes with urban water re-

[2]See also http://info-gap.com.

quirements. Knoke (2008) and Hildebrandt and Knoke (2009) use info-gap theory in a financial model for forest management. Cheong *et al.* (2004) use info-gap theory in strategic bidding in competitive electricity markets. Zare *et al.* (2010) study energy-market bidding with info-gap uncertainties. Berleant *et al.* (2008) use info-gap theory in the study of portfolio management under epistemic uncertainty. Stranlund and Ben-Haim (2008) perform an info-gap analysis of price-based vs. quantity-based environmental regulation. Ben-Haim and Demertzis (2008) use info-gap theory in exploring central bank confidence in monetary policy.

There have been a number of applications of info-gap theory to statistical decision problems. Fox *et al.* (2007) study the choice of the size of a statistical sample when the sampling distribution is uncertain. Zacksenhouse *et al.* (2009) study linear regression with info-gap-uncertain data, employing both the robustness and the opportuneness functions. Ben-Haim (2009) applies info-gap theory to the design of forecasting algorithms for linear systems with uncertain dynamics. Klir (2006) discusses the relation between info-gap models of uncertainty and a broad taxonomy of measure-theoretic models of probability, likelihood, plausibility and so on. Moffitt *et al.* (2005) employ info-gap theory in designing container-inspection strategies for homeland security of shipping ports.

A broad spectrum of engineering problems have been studied with info-gap theory (Ben-Haim, 1996). Duncan *et al.* (2007, 2008) use info-gap theory for designing industrial remanufacturing processes. Hall and Solomatine (2008) discuss info-gap theory and other methods for uncertainty analysis in flood risk management. Similarly, info-gap theory has been used in the preliminary design analysis of the Thames 2100 flood protection project (University of Newcastle and Halcrow, 2006). Vinot *et al.* (2005) use info-gap theory for designing test strategies for technological systems. Pierce *et al.* (2006a, b) use info-gap theory to design artificial neural networks for technological fault diagnosis. Kanno and Takewaki (2006a, b) use info-gap theory in the analysis and design of civil engineering structures. Matsuda and Kanno (2008) employ info-gap theory in the analysis of nonlinear mechanical systems subject to uncertain loads. Pantelides and Ganzerli (1998) study the design of trusses and Ganzerli and Pantelides (2000) study the optimization of civil engineering structures. Wang (2005) uses info-gap theory for damage analysis of uncertain flexural-torsional vibration of cracked beams.

Info-gap theory has been applied to project management and related strategic planning problems. Ben-Haim and Laufer (1998) and Regev *et al.* (2006) apply info-gap theory for managing uncertain task-times in projects. Tahan and Ben-Asher (2005) use info-gap theory for analysis and design integration of engineering systems. Ben-Haim and Hipel (2002) use info-gap theory in a game-theoretic study of conflict resolution.

Info-gap decision theory has been used productively to model and manage circumstances of extreme uncertainty in a wide variety of contexts and disciplines. In the remainder of the book we study a range of economic applications. The purpose is to demonstrate how one performs an info-gap analysis of decisions using economic models, and how this analysis supports the decision-making process.

Chapter 2

A First Look: Stylized Example

A very simplistic example gives a preliminary feel for info-gap analysis: how it is done, what one can learn, and how it supports decision making. The system and uncertainty models and the satisficing and windfalling performance requirements are formulated. The robustness function is derived, the robust-satisficing decision strategy is discussed, and three properties are studied: trade-off between robustness and performance, zeroing of the robustness at the anticipated outcome, and crossing of robustness curves leading to reversal of preferences between alternative actions. The opportuneness function is formulated and derived, and how it supplements the robustness function is demonstrated. The opportune-windfalling decision strategy is discussed.

∼ ∼ ∼

Quantitative formulation and evaluation of economic policy uses models and data to choose actions which reliably achieve specified goals. In this chapter we consider a single control variable and a single outcome variable which are related by an equation with uncertain coefficients. This is a simplified prototype of many model-based decision analyses. The control variable could, for instance, be an interest rate or a resource allocation, while the outcome could be inflation, or profit or capital adequacy. In subsequent chapters we will consider more specific and realistic economic models and other types of uncertainties. In this chapter we aim only to illustrate the main features of an info-gap analysis.

2.1 Problem Formulation

Our analysis begins with identifying three components: a system model, an uncertainty model, and a performance requirement or aspiration.

System model. Consider a 1-dimensional system whose outcome, y, is influenced by a control parameter x, which are related by:

$$y = ax + b \tag{2.1}$$

The model coefficients a and b are uncertain scalars. Our goal is to bring the outcome close to the target value y_{T}.

Uncertainty model. Our best estimates of a and b are $\widetilde{a}$ and $\widetilde{b}$, with rough error-estimates σ_a and σ_b. Perhaps these are means and standard errors of an historical sample. Or perhaps they are an expert's educated guesses. We have no knowledge of a probability distribution for a and b, nor any knowledge of a worst or most extreme case.

Consider the absolute fractional error of these estimates, each calibrated by its own error estimate:

$$\left|\frac{a-\widetilde{a}}{\sigma_a}\right| \le h, \quad \left|\frac{b-\widetilde{b}}{\sigma_b}\right| \le h \tag{2.2}$$

These errors are undoubtedly bounded by *some* number, h, but we don't know its value. As far as our knowledge goes[1] h could be any non-negative number. We will call h the *horizon of uncertainty.*

In this situation we adopt a fractional-error info-gap model for uncertainty in the model coefficients:

$$\mathcal{U}(h) = \left\{ (a,b) : \left|\frac{a-\widetilde{a}}{\sigma_a}\right| \le h, \quad \left|\frac{b-\widetilde{b}}{\sigma_b}\right| \le h \right\}, \quad h \ge 0 \tag{2.3}$$

Like all info-gap models, this is an unbounded family of nested sets. In the present example these are sets of model coefficients (a, b). When the horizon of uncertainty, h, is zero, then $\mathcal{U}(0)$ contains only the estimated values, $(\widetilde{a}, \widetilde{b})$. As the horizon of uncertainty increases,

[1] In many cases we might know more, as we will see in later chapters.

the sets $\mathcal{U}(h)$ become more inclusive. There is no known worst case because the value of h is unknown.

Performance requirement. The error of the outcome is the difference between the actual outcome, y, and the target value y_{T}. We require that this error be no greater than a critical value ε_{c}:

$$|y - y_{\text{T}}| \le \varepsilon_{\text{c}} \tag{2.4}$$

We will use the robustness function to explore the feasibility of different critical values, ε_{c}.

ε_{c} is the critical outcome error: any larger error would be unacceptable. However, it would be wonderful if the outcome error is less than a much smaller value, ε_{w}. The windfall aspiration is:

$$|y - y_{\text{T}}| \le \varepsilon_{\text{w}} \tag{2.5}$$

The opportuneness function will reveal the feasibility of different windfall aspirations, ε_{w}.

The inequalities in relations (2.4) and (2.5) have the same mathematical form, but they have very different meaning. Eq.(2.4) is a requirement; "failure" is defined as any violation of this inequality. We will refer to this as a *satisficing requirement.* In contrast, eq.(2.5) is an aspiration for a better-than-anticipated outcome. We may be disappointed if the inequality in eq.(2.5) is violated, but we won't be fired. We will refer to eq.(2.5) as a *windfalling aspiration.*

In section 2.2 we consider the choice of the control value, x, for robustly satisfying the critical requirement in eq.(2.4). In section 2.3 we study the windfall aspiration in eq.(2.5) by using the opportuneness function.

2.2 Robustness

2.2.1 Formulation and Derivation

We must choose the value of the control variable x. The robustness of any choice, x, is the greatest horizon of uncertainty, h, up to which we are sure to satisfy the critical outcome requirement, eq.(2.4), for all realizations of a and b in $\mathcal{U}(h)$:

$$\widehat{h}(x, \varepsilon_{\text{c}}) = \max \left\{ h : \left(\max_{a,b \in \mathcal{U}(h)} |y - y_{\text{T}}| \right) \le \varepsilon_{\text{c}} \right\} \tag{2.6}$$

Large robustness of action x implies that the outcome will satisfy the critical requirement even if the model errs greatly. In contrast, low robustness implies that an adequate outcome is highly vulnerable to uncertainty in the model. Given two different options for the control variable, x_1 and x_2, the *robust-satisficing* choice between them is for the more robust option.

Let $M(h)$ denote the inner maximum in eq.(2.6). $M(h)$ is a *monotonically increasing function* of the horizon of uncertainty, h. This is because the uncertainty sets, $\mathcal{U}(h)$, are nested: they become more inclusive as h increases. The maximum value of $|y-y_{\rm T}|$ cannot decrease as one searches on more inclusive sets.

We will now see that $M(h)$ is the *inverse of the robustness*, $\widehat{h}(x,\varepsilon_{\rm c})$. From the definition in eq.(2.6) we see that the robustness, $\widehat{h}(x,\varepsilon_{\rm c})$, is the greatest value of h at which $M(h)$ is no larger than $\varepsilon_{\rm c}$. Since $M(h)$ increases monotonically as h increases, we see that the robustness is the greatest value of h at which $M(h)=\varepsilon_{\rm c}$. That is:

$$M(h)=\varepsilon_{\rm c} \quad \text{implies} \quad \widehat{h}(x,\varepsilon_{\rm c})=h \tag{2.7}$$

In other words, a plot of $M(h)$ (horizontally) vs. h (vertically) is exactly the same as a plot of $\varepsilon_{\rm c}$ (horizontally) vs. $\widehat{h}(x,\varepsilon_{\rm c})$ (vertically). In short, $M(h)$ is the inverse of $\widehat{h}(x,\varepsilon_{\rm c})$ at fixed x.

We now derive $M(h)$ and then invert it to obtain the robustness.

Define the anticipated response to x as $\widetilde{y}=\widetilde{a}x+\widetilde{b}$. We will consider the special case that $\widetilde{y}$ exceeds the target:

$$\widetilde{y}>y_{\rm T} \tag{2.8}$$

This means that the system must be restrained with respect to its anticipated behavior.

The anticipated gap, $\widetilde{y}-y_{\rm T}$, is positive. Hence the maximum of $|y-y_{\rm T}|$ occurs when y is as large as possible at horizon of uncertainty h. The info-gap model, eq.(2.3), implies that the model coefficients at horizon of uncertainty h can take any values in the intervals:

$$\widetilde{a}-\sigma_a h\le a\le \widetilde{a}+\sigma_a h, \quad \widetilde{b}-\sigma_b h\le b\le \widetilde{b}+\sigma_b h \tag{2.9}$$

Since x can be either positive or negative, but σ_a and σ_b are positive, the maximum of $|y-y_{\rm T}|$ occurs when:

$$a=\widetilde{a}+\sigma_a\,\mathrm{sgn}(x)h, \quad b=\widetilde{b}+\sigma_b h \tag{2.10}$$

where $\mathrm{sgn}(\cdot)$ is the algebraic sign of its argument.

Putting this together we find the inner maximum in eq.(2.6) is:

$$M(h) = \widetilde{a}x + \sigma_a |x| h + \widetilde{b} + \sigma_b h - y_T \quad (2.11)$$

$$= \widetilde{y} + (\sigma_a |x| + \sigma_b) h - y_T \quad (2.12)$$

As explained in eq.(2.7), equating this to ε_c and solving for h gives the robustness function:[2]

$$\widehat{h}(x, \varepsilon_c) = \frac{\varepsilon_c - (\widetilde{y} - y_T)}{\sigma_a |x| + \sigma_b} \quad (2.13)$$

or zero if this is negative.

2.2.2 Trade-Off and Zeroing

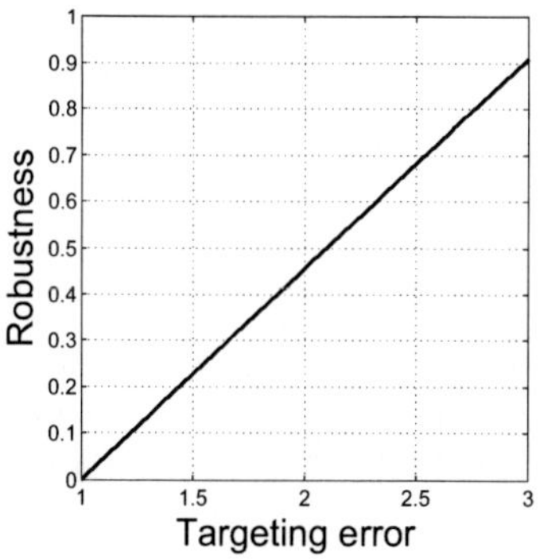

Figure 2.1: Robustness curve, eq.(2.13), $x = -1$.

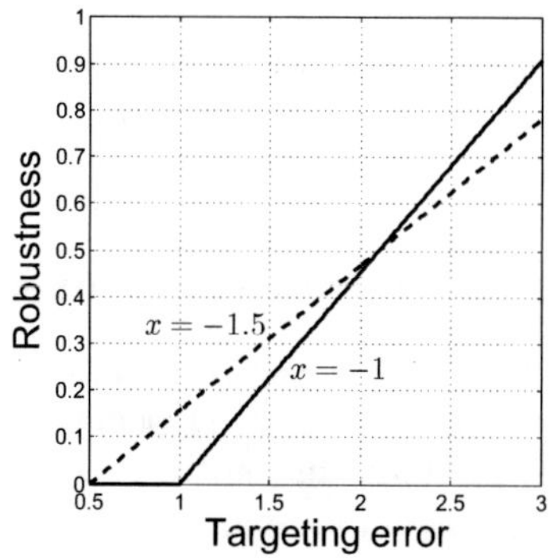

Figure 2.2: Robustness curves, eq.(2.13), for $x = -1$ (solid) and -1.5 (dash).

Fig. 2.1 shows the robustness function in eq.(2.13), displaying two key characteristics of all robustness curves.[3]

Trade-off. First, the positive slope indicates that the *robustness trades off against the performance:* smaller critical error, ε_c, entails

---

[2]Eq.(2.13) assumes eq.(2.8). The general result, for any y_T and $\widetilde{y}$, is: $\widehat{h}(x, \varepsilon_c) = (\varepsilon_c - |\widetilde{y} - y_T|)/(\sigma_a |x| + \sigma_b)$.

[3]Figs. 2.1 and 2.2 are calculated with the parameters: $\widetilde{a} = 1$, $\sigma_a = 2$, $\widetilde{b} = 5$, $\sigma_b = 0.2$, $y_T = 3$. The large value of $\sigma_a / \widetilde{a}$ means that the impact of action x is highly uncertain.

smaller robustness against uncertainty in the model coefficients.[4] The slope of the robustness curve has units, $\Delta\widehat{h}/\Delta\varepsilon_c$, and equals the increment of robustness obtained by giving up a unit of performance. A large slope means that the robustness can be increased with only small loss of performance. Small slope means that robustness is "purchased" by greatly reducing the performance.

Zeroing. The second point to observe in fig. 2.1 is the value at which the *robustness equals zero*. The curve shows the robustness of a particular choice of control, x. The curve reaches the horizontal axis at the anticipated targeting error for this value of x, $\widetilde{y} - y_T$. In other words, the anticipated response to action x has no robustness to uncertainty in the model upon which that anticipation is based. This is important since it implies that one should not evaluate x in terms of its predicted impact, even though this prediction is based on the best estimates, $\widetilde{a}$ and $\widetilde{b}$. Even if the anticipated targeting error is small, the actual error may be large if the robustness is small. One must evaluate a proposed action in terms of its entire robustness curve, not just the intersection of that curve with the performance axis.

2.2.3 Preference Reversal

Fig. 2.2 compares two alternative choices of the control value, x. Both are negative, $x_1 = -1$ being less negative than $x_2 = -1.5$. Because $\widetilde{a}$ is positive, this means that the anticipated targeting error for x_1 is larger than for x_2:

$$\widetilde{y}(x_1) - y_T > \widetilde{y}(x_2) - y_T \qquad (2.14)$$

This inequality is expressed in fig. 2.2 by the dashed curve hitting the horizontal axis at a smaller targeting error than the solid curve. This is the zeroing property. Based on anticipated targeting error one would prefer x_2 over x_1.

However, the very fact ($x_2 < x_1 < 0$) that results in eq.(2.14), also causes the slope of the robustness curve for x_1 to be larger than for x_2:

$$\frac{1}{\sigma_a|x_1| + \sigma_b} > \frac{1}{\sigma_a|x_2| + \sigma_b} \qquad (2.15)$$

[4] All robustness curves are monotonic. The slope is positive if small values of the performance are desirable, as in the present example. The slope is negative if large values (like profits) are desirable. The trade-off between robustness and performance holds in all cases.

As explained in section 2.2.2, a large slope of the robustness curve means that the robustness can be substantially increased in exchange for small loss of performance. Thus robustness is "less expensive" with x_1 than with x_2. The graphical manifestation is that the solid curve is steeper than the dashed curve, so the curves for these two alternatives cross one another.

Let $\varepsilon_\times$ denote the value of critical targeting error at which the robustness curves cross each other in fig. 2.2. If the analyst can tolerate error as large or larger than $\varepsilon_\times$, then x_1 is more robust than x_2 for satisfying the performance requirement. This suggests that x_1 should probably be preferred.[5] If the analyst requires critical error less than $\varepsilon_\times$ then x_2 is more robust, so x_2 should be preferred, recalling that the robustness is now lower.

The situation in fig. 2.2 shows the important situation of *preference reversal.* x_2 is preferred over x_1 based on the anticipated outcomes, eq.(2.14). This preference holds also for relatively demanding performance requirements: x_2 is more robust for values of $\varepsilon_{\rm c}$ less than the crossing value, $\varepsilon_\times$. However, these outcomes may have low robustness, depending on where the curve-crossing occurs. For less demanding requirements, $\varepsilon_{\rm c} > \varepsilon_\times$, which are achieved more robustly, the preference is reversed and favors x_1 because it is more robust than x_2.

2.2.4 What Do the Numbers Mean?

Let's return to fig. 2.1 and ask: what do the numbers mean? The horizontal axis is the critical targeting error, $\varepsilon_{\rm c}$: the greatest acceptable difference between the target value, $y_{\rm T}$, and the actual outcome, y (see eq.(2.4) on p.17). The target value is 3 in the numerical example, so a critical error of 1.5, for example, would mean that an outcome between 1.5 and 4.5 is acceptable.

From fig. 2.1 we see that the robustness for this choice of the control value, $x = -1$, and this satisficing requirement, $\varepsilon_{\rm c} = 1.5$, is $\widehat{h}(-1, 1.5) = 0.23$. This means that each model coefficient, a and b, can deviate from its estimated value, $\widetilde{a}$ and $\widetilde{b}$, up to 23% (in units of estimated error σ_a or σ_b) without violating the performance requirement. Any larger deviation may violate the requirement, but does

[5] Additional information, if it were available, might nonetheless indicate otherwise. For instance, if the analyst has Bayesian or other probabilistic beliefs about likelihoods of (a, b) values, then this would be relevant. In other examples we will consider such situations.

not necessarily do so.

The slope of the robustness curve in fig. 2.1 is 0.45. This means that the robustness improves by 0.45 for each unit increase in the critical error. For instance, the robustness at $\varepsilon_c = 2.5$ is $\widehat{h} = 0.68$.

Now consider the two robustness curves in fig. 2.2, for control values $x = -1$ and $x = -1.5$. The latter has better estimated targeting error: 0.5 rather than 1 (both at zero robustness). However, the slope of the robustness curve for $x = -1.5$ is 0.31, rather than 0.45 for $x = -1$. In other words $x = -1.5$ has a higher cost for robustness in units of lost performance. Consequently the robustness curves cross one another at $(\varepsilon_\times, \widehat{h}_\times) = (2.1, 0.5)$. This means that $x = -1.5$ is more robust for targeting errors between 0.5 and 2.1, but its robustness is only 50% at $\varepsilon_c = 2.1$ and it has no robustness at $\varepsilon_c = 0.5$. Unless a targeting error less than 2.1 is essential (which it might be), the robust-satisficing preference (between these two alternatives) is for $x = -1$.

2.3 Opportuneness

2.3.1 Formulation

The estimated targeting error is $|\widetilde{y} - y_T|$. We learned in section 2.2.2 that if we adopt this estimated value as the critical requirement, ε_c in eq.(2.4), the resulting robustness is precisely zero. Anticipated outcomes have no robustness against error in the data and models upon which the estimates are based.

However, that does not mean that the targeting error must exceed the estimated error. It is possible for the targeting error to be less than $|\widetilde{y} - y_T|$. Let ε_w be a value less than $|\widetilde{y} - y_T|$. Achieving better-than-anticipated targeting error as small as ε_w would be a windfall, as in eq.(2.5). Of course, in order for a windfall to happen it is necessary for one or both of the actual model coefficients, a and b, to differ from the estimated values $\widetilde{a}$ and $\widetilde{b}$. Windfalls require favorable surprises, and surprises require uncertainty. Any given choice of the control variable x is "opportune" if great windfall (very small targeting error) is possible (though not guaranteed) even at small horizon of uncertainty.

We formally define the opportuneness of intervention x as the lowest horizon of uncertainty at which windfall $\varepsilon_{\rm w}$ is possible:

$$\widehat{\beta}(x, \varepsilon_{\rm w}) = \min \left\{ h : \left(\min_{a,b \in \mathcal{U}(h)} |y - y_{\rm T}| \right) \leq \varepsilon_{\rm w} \right\} \tag{2.16}$$

Comparing this definition of opportuneness to the definition of robustness in eq.(2.6) on p.17, we see that $\widehat{\beta}(x, \varepsilon_{\rm w})$ is the mathematical dual of $\widehat{h}(x, \varepsilon_{\rm c})$. Each "max" operator in eq.(2.6) is inverted to a "min" operator in eq.(2.16). This inversion has a potent effect on the meaning of these functions. While the robustness is the *maximum* uncertainty at which *failure cannot occur*, the opportuneness is the *minimum* uncertainty at which *windfall can occur.*[6]

One can derive an expression for the opportuneness function by a method similar to that used in section 2.2.1. The general result for the example discussed in this chapter, without the assumption in eq.(2.8), is:

$$\widehat{\beta}(x, \varepsilon_{\rm w}) = \frac{|\widetilde{y} - y_{\rm T}| - \varepsilon_{\rm w}}{|\sigma_a x| + \sigma_b} \tag{2.17}$$

or zero if this is negative.

2.3.2 Interpretation

The opportuneness function is the lowest horizon of uncertainty which enables better-than-anticipated results, $\varepsilon_{\rm w}$. If this horizon of uncertainty is large, then better-than-anticipated results (windfalls) will require extraordinary circumstances; if this horizon of uncertainty is small, then windfall is possible (though not guaranteed) even in nearly ordinary situations. Thus, a small value of $\widehat{\beta}(x, \varepsilon_{\rm w})$ means that windfall is feasible, and decision x is opportune. A large value of $\widehat{\beta}(x, \varepsilon_{\rm w})$ means that great uncertainty is needed in order to enable windfall as good as $\varepsilon_{\rm w}$. We can summarize this by saying that $\widehat{\beta}(x, \varepsilon_{\rm w})$ assesses the degree to which intervention x is immune to windfall outcomes: large $\widehat{\beta}(x, \varepsilon_{\rm w})$ implies high immunity to windfall and low opportuneness; small $\widehat{\beta}(x, \varepsilon_{\rm w})$ implies low immunity to windfall and high opportuneness.

In short, the opportuneness function, $\widehat{\beta}(x, \varepsilon_{\rm w})$, is the *immunity against windfall.* Since windfall is desirable, small values of $\widehat{\beta}(x, \varepsilon_{\rm w})$

[6] In subsequent chapters we will encounter situations where the inner operator in the robustness is "min". We will find that the corresponding opportuneness function has "max" as its inner operator. The mathematical and semantic inversion between robustness and opportuneness is retained.

(low immunity to windfall) are preferable over large values. Given the choice between two options, the *opportune-windfalling* strategy is to choose the option which is more opportune for windfall, namely, the option whose opportuneness function has a smaller value.

The opportuneness function, $\widehat{\beta}(x, \varepsilon_{\rm w})$ in eq.(2.17), decreases (gets better) as the windfall aspiration for small targeting error, $\varepsilon_{\rm w}$, gets larger (less ambitious). Thus the opportuneness of intervention x trades off against the windfall: good opportuneness (small $\widehat{\beta}$) entails modest aspiration (large $\varepsilon_{\rm w}$). This is the windfalling analog of the trade-off between robustness and performance discussed in section 2.2.2.

We also see from eq.(2.17) that the opportuneness function equals zero when the windfall aspiration $\varepsilon_{\rm w}$ equals the anticipated targeting error. No surprise or uncertainty is needed in order to enable the anticipated outcome. This is the windfalling analog of the robustness-zeroing discussed in section 2.2.2.

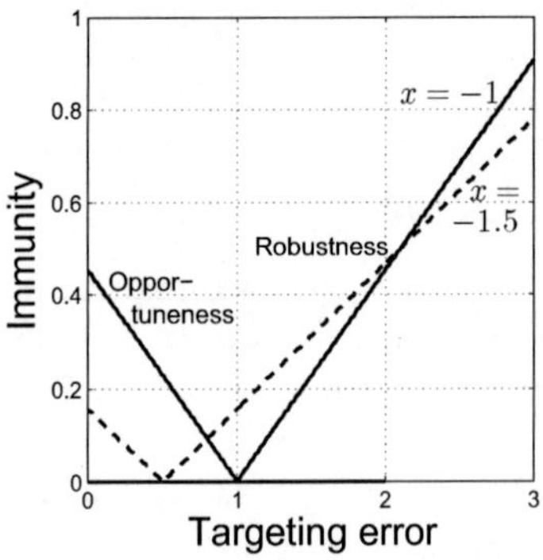

Figure 2.3: Robustness and opportuneness curves, eqs.(2.13) and (2.17), for $x = -1$ (solid) and -1.5 (dash).

Fig. 2.3 shows robustness and opportuneness curves for the same numerical example presented in figs. 2.1 and 2.2. The robustness curves here are the same as in fig. 2.2.

The opportuneness curves in fig. 2.3 show the trade-off and zeroing properties discussed above. They also indicate that the more aggressive intervention, $x_2 = -1.5$, is more opportune than $x_1 = -1$.

The most salient feature of the opportuneness curves in fig. 2.3 is that they do *not* cross one another, unlike the robustness curves. This is important because it means that the opportuneness analysis can resolve ambiguity in the robustness analysis. If the analyst requires critical targeting error around 2.1 (where the robustness curves cross), the robustness analysis does not entail a clear recommendation; the analyst is indifferent between x_1 and x_2. However, because x_2 is more opportune than x_1, this can "break the tie" between these two control values.

Part II

Economic Decisions

Chapter 3

Monetary Policy

We consider a sequence of monetary policy analyses with progressively more and different aspects. We start in section 3.1 with selecting an interest rate based on a Taylor rule, given uncertainty in the parameters of the macro-economic model. In section 3.2 we include public expectations about inflation and output gap, and consider both the choice of the interest rate and the choice of the degree of credibility of the central bank's announced goals. In section 3.3 we add shocks to inflation and output gap, while the tails of the probability distributions of these shocks may differ substantially from what is anticipated. In section 3.4 we consider an uncertain economic model subject to shocks, in an economy with heterogeneous sectors whose beliefs about central bank credibility are uncertain to the bank.

~ ~ ~

3.1 Taylor Rule for Interest Rates

Inflation targeting has become a common goal of central banks, whereby the bank uses monetary policy to keep the inflation within specified bounds. This section illustrates the evaluation and formulation of a Taylor rule by which a central bank chooses its interest rate in attempting to keep inflation below an upper bound and above a lower bound. We use the Rudebusch-Svensson (1999) model of the US economy. We ignore shocks at this stage and only consider uncertainty in the parameters of the macro-economic model. The consideration of inflation and output shocks is introduced in section 3.3.

3.1.1 Policy Preview

The policy maker will use robustness functions to evaluate alternative choices of the Taylor coefficients. Robustness will be evaluated for both lower- and upper-target bounds on both inflation and output gap.

The plot of robustness vs. the lower- or upper-target bound for either inflation or output gap is strictly monotonic. Lower- and upper-target robustness curves have opposite slopes, but in both cases the slope expresses the usual trade-off: higher aspirations are more vulnerable to uncertainty than lower aspirations, as discussed in section 2.2.2. The lower-target robustness decreases as the value of the lower target bound *increases.* The upper-target robustness decreases as the upper target bound *decreases.*

We also observe that the robustness equals zero when the target bound equals the value predicted by the estimated model. This means that the estimated outcome of a policy is not a good basis for evaluating that policy; one should consider the entire robustness curve.

In some situations the policy preference for the lower-target bound conflicts with the policy preference for the upper-target bound. Intuitively, robustifying against one side causes increased vulnerability on the other side.

However, this is not invariable. The robustness curves for two policy alternatives can cross each other, resulting in a reversal of preference, and consequently in policy agreement between lower- and upper-target bounds.

The intersection between robustness curves may occur when considering different periods in the future. In some cases the robustness decreases as the time horizon increases, as one might intuitively expect. However, the conflict between lower-target and upper-target robustnesses can reverse this, causing later time horizons to be more robust than near times. But then the intersection of robustness curves can reverse this again. In short, the evaluation of a policy over time should use the time-evolution of the robustness curves, and not only the dynamics of the anticipated responses (at which the robustness is zero).

3.1.2 Operational Preview

All robustness analyses depend on the same components, which we outline here for the current example.

System model. The macro-economic dynamics for inflation and output gap are specified in eqs.(3.1)–(3.4). The central bank's Taylor rule for inflation is eq.(3.5). The dynamics can be represented more compactly and generically with the auto-regressive relations of eq.(3.7).

Performance requirements. We consider three different requirements on the inflation and output gap: an upper bound, a lower bound, and a combination of both. These are specified in eqs.(3.10)–(3.12).

Uncertainty model. The coefficients of the dynamic model are uncertain, which is quantified in the info-gap model in eq.(3.9). This model requires estimates of the coefficients, and errors of these estimates. However, the disparity between the true and the estimated values is unknown. Consequently the info-gap model is an unbounded family of nested sets of model coefficients. There is no known worst case.

Decision variables. In this example the only decision variables are the Taylor coefficients, $g = (g_\pi, g_y)$, in the interest rate rule, eq.(3.5).

Robustness functions. We can now formulate the robustness functions for each state variable and each performance requirement, as presented in eqs.(3.13)–(3.15). The two-sided robustness, eq.(3.15), is simply related to the two one-sided robustness functions as shown in eq.(3.16).

3.1.3 Formulation

Economic formulation. The Rudebusch-Svensson model for inflation and output gap (1999) (see also Onatski and Stock (2000)) is specified by eqs.(3.1)–(3.5):

$$\pi_{t+1} = a_0\pi_t + a_1\pi_{t-1} + a_2\pi_{t-2} + a_3\pi_{t-3} + by_t \qquad (3.1)$$

$$y_{t+1} = c_0 y_t + c_1 y_{t-1} + d(\bar{\imath}_t - \bar{\pi}_t) \qquad (3.2)$$

t is the time step in quarters. π_t is the deviation of the inflation from a target value (or the inflation itself), in the tth quarter. y_t is the output gap at time t, measured as 100 times the log ratio of the actual real output to the potential output. i_t is the Federal funds interest rate at an annual rate, and $\bar{\imath}_t$ is the 4-quarter average Federal funds rate:

$$\bar{\imath}_t = 0.25(i_t + i_{t-1} + i_{t-2} + i_{t-3}) \qquad (3.3)$$

Likewise, $\overline{\pi}_t$ is the 4-quarter average of the inflation variable:

$$\overline{\pi}_t = 0.25(\pi_t + \pi_{t-1} + \pi_{t-2} + \pi_{t-3}) \tag{3.4}$$

The Federal funds rate is regulated by a Taylor rule, which prescribes the monetary policy reaction in response to the inflation rate and the output gap:

$$i_t = g_\pi \overline{\pi}_t + g_y y_t \tag{3.5}$$

where g_π and g_y are decision variables to be chosen by the policy maker. The original model of Rudebusch and Svensson includes zero-mean shocks $\varepsilon_{\pi,t+1}$ and $\varepsilon_{y,t+1}$ in eqs.(3.1) and (3.2) respectively. In this section we model shocks and surprises by considering uncertainty in the coefficients of the model. Additive shocks are considered in section 3.3. The eight coefficients in eqs.(3.1) and (3.2) have been estimated by Rudebusch and Svensson (1999). Their values, with standard errors, are shown in table 3.1.

Table 3.1: Mean and standard error of coefficients in eqs.(3.1) and (3.2), Rudebusch and Svensson (1999).

	a_0	a_1	a_2	a_3
Mean	0.07	−0.10	0.28	0.12
Standard Error	0.08	0.10	0.10	0.08

	b	c_0	c_1	d
Mean	0.14	1.16	−0.25	−0.10
Standard Error	0.03	0.08	0.08	0.03

Auto-regressive formulation. It is useful to recast the Rudebusch-Svensson model in a more generic formulation in order to appreciate how our analysis can be applied to other models as well. The state vector at time step t is an M-dimensional vector x_t. In the Rudebusch-Svensson case:

$$x_t = \begin{pmatrix} \pi_t \\ y_t \end{pmatrix} \tag{3.6}$$

The dynamics are defined by the auto-regressive relations:

$$x_{t+1} = \sum_{j=0}^{J} C_j x_{t-j}, \quad t = 0,\ 1,\ 2,\ \ldots \tag{3.7}$$

where each C_j is an $M \times M$ matrix which is constant over time, but some of whose elements are uncertain. Some elements of the C_j's contain control variables (Taylor coefficients) which we denote collectively by g. The value of x_t is known for times prior to and including $t = 0$. The representation of the Rudebusch-Svensson model, eqs.(3.1)–(3.5), in the auto-regressive format of eq.(3.7), is presented in the appendix, section 3.6.

3.1.4 Uncertainty, Performance and Robustness

Uncertainty model. Let $c = (a_0, \ldots, a_3, b, c_0, c_1, d)$ denote the model coefficients in eqs.(3.1) and (3.2). The basic idea of the info-gap model of uncertainty is that the actual values of the model coefficients, c_i, can deviate by an unknown amount from the estimated values, $\widetilde{c}_i$, fractionally in units of uncertainty weights, w_i:

$$\left| \frac{c_i - \widetilde{c}_i}{w_i} \right| \le h \tag{3.8}$$

The horizon of uncertainty, h, is unknown so this relation represents unknown and unbounded potential difference between estimated and realized values of the model coefficient.

We express this precisely as a symmetric interval info-gap model for uncertainty in the model coefficients:

$$\mathcal{U}(h) = \left\{ c : \ |c_i - \widetilde{c}_i| \le w_i h, \ \ i = 1, \ldots, 8 \right\}, \quad h \ge 0 \tag{3.9}$$

We have put the uncertainty weight, w_i, on the right-hand side of the inequality, rather than in the denominator as in eq.(3.8), in order to handle the special case of zero error: a coefficient whose value is certain.

In subsequent numerical calculations we choose the center point values, $\widetilde{c}_i$, as the estimated mean values in table 3.1. The standard errors in that table are used for the uncertainty weights, w_i.

In the Rudebusch-Svensson model the Taylor coefficients, g_π and g_y, and the model coefficients, c, are embedded in some of the estimated matrix elements derived in section 3.6.

Performance requirements. We will consider three different satisficing requirements for the ℓth element of the state vector at time step θ in the future. Let $x_{\theta,\ell}$ denote the ℓth state variable at time θ. Let $\widetilde{x}_{\theta,\ell}$ denote the best estimate of $x_{\theta,\ell}$ at time θ, calculated with eq.(3.7) using the estimated matrices $\widetilde{C}$. We consider three requirements:

$$x_{\theta,\ell} \le x_{\mathrm{u}} \tag{3.10}$$

$$x_{\mathrm{l}} \le x_{\theta,\ell} \tag{3.11}$$

$$\widetilde{x}_{\theta,\ell} - \Delta x \le x_{\theta,\ell} \le \widetilde{x}_{\theta,\ell} + \Delta x \tag{3.12}$$

Eq.(3.10) is the requirement that the ℓth state variable (e.g. inflation or output gap) not exceed the upper bound, x_{u}, at time θ in the future. Eq.(3.11) imposes a lower bound, x_{l}, on the same state variable. Eq.(3.12), in which Δx is non-negative, is a combination of the previous two requirements, and requires that the state variable be within a symmetric interval around its anticipated value.[1]

Robustness functions. We now formulate the robustness function for each of these three performance requirements. The robustness of any choice of Taylor coefficients, $g = (g_\pi, g_y)$, is the greatest horizon of uncertainty, h, up to which we are sure to satisfy the outcome requirement, one of eqs.(3.10), (3.11) or (3.12), for all realizations of the c_j's in $\mathcal{U}(h)$. We define three different robustness functions, corresponding to the three different performance requirements:

$$\widehat{h}_{\mathrm{u}}(g, x_{\mathrm{u}}, \ell) = \max\left\{h : \left(\max_{c\in\mathcal{U}(h)} x_{\theta,\ell}\right) \le x_{\mathrm{u}}\right\} \tag{3.13}$$

$$\widehat{h}_{\ell}(g, x_{\mathrm{l}}, \ell) = \max\left\{h : \left(\min_{c\in\mathcal{U}(h)} x_{\theta,\ell}\right) \ge x_{\mathrm{l}}\right\} \tag{3.14}$$

$$\widehat{h}(g, \Delta x, \ell) = \max\left\{ h : \left(\min_{c\in\mathcal{U}(h)} x_{\theta,\ell}\right) \ge \widetilde{x}_{\theta,\ell} - \Delta x, \left(\max_{c\in\mathcal{U}(h)} x_{\theta,\ell}\right) \le \widetilde{x}_{\theta,\ell} + \Delta x \right\} \tag{3.15}$$

$$= \min[\widehat{h}_{\ell}(g, \widetilde{x}_{\theta,\ell} - \Delta x, \ell),\ \widehat{h}_{\mathrm{u}}(g, \widetilde{x}_{\theta,\ell} + \Delta x, \ell)] \tag{3.16}$$

$\widehat{h}_{\mathrm{u}}(g, x_{\mathrm{u}})$ is the greatest horizon of uncertainty up to which the Taylor coefficients g guarantee that the ℓth state variable at time θ will not exceed x_{u}. $\widehat{h}_{\mathrm{u}}(g, x_{\mathrm{l}})$ is defined similarly with respect to the lower bound x_{l}, and $\widehat{h}(g, \Delta x)$ relates to the two-sided requirement.

[1] One could consider an asymmetric performance requirement instead of eq.(3.12), namely: $x_{\mathrm{l}} \le x_{\theta,\ell} \le x_{\mathrm{u}}$. Its robustness is the minimum of the robustnesses of the requirements in eqs.(3.10) and (3.11).

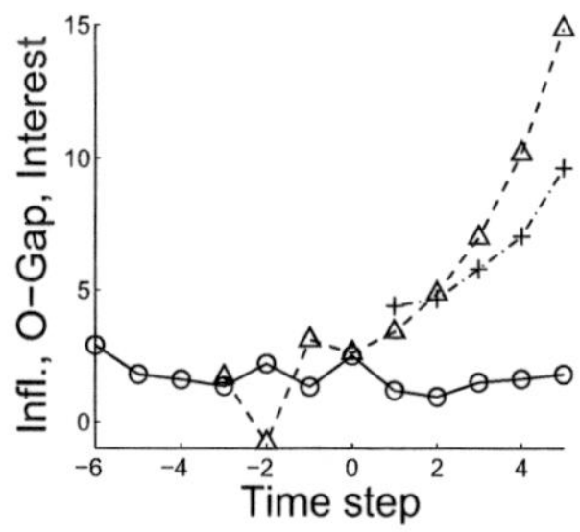

Figure 3.1: Estimated inflation (o), output gap (Δ) and interest rate (+). $(g_\pi, g_y) = (1.5, 0.5)$. $\theta = 5$.

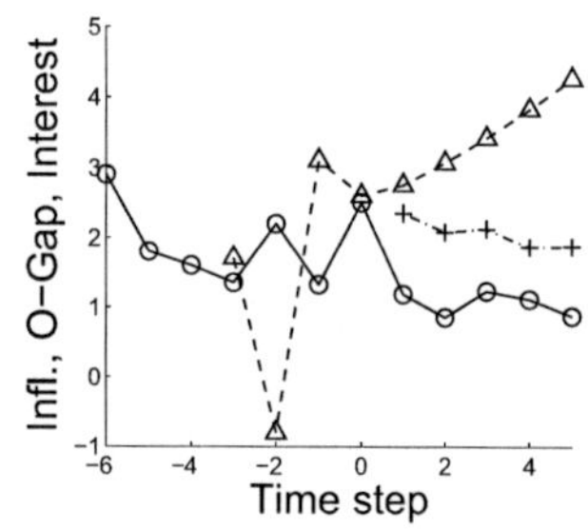

Figure 3.2: Estimated inflation (o), output gap (Δ) and interest rate (+). $(g_\pi, g_y) = (1, 0.2)$. $\theta = 5$.

3.1.5 Policy Exploration

In this section we explore Taylor rules for controlling the inflation and the output gap. The purpose is to illustrate the insight which is obtained from the robustness functions. This is the basis of a systematic and exhaustive examination, which we do not pursue here.

From eqs.(3.1)–(3.5) one sees that, in order to predict the inflation and output gap at time step $t+1$, the Rudebusch-Svensson model requires 7 measurements of past inflation, $\pi_t, \ldots, \pi_{t-6}$, and 4 measurements of past output gap, $y_t, \ldots, y_{t-3}$. Given these data one can calculate the future impact of any choice of Taylor coefficients g_π and g_y, as well as the robustness to model uncertainty.[2]

Figs. 3.1 and 3.2 show the simulated historical data and the anticipated outcomes (inflation and output gap) and Taylor-based interest rates up to five quarters in the future ($\theta = 5$) for two different choices of the Taylor coefficients.[3] The Taylor coefficients in fig. 3.1, $g_\pi = 1.5$ and $g_y = 0.5$, are values suggested by Taylor (Onatski and Stock 2000, p.6). The Taylor coefficients for fig. 3.2 are smaller than for fig. 3.1. Fig. 3.2 shows substantially lower predicted values of inflation and output gap at time steps $t = 1, \ldots, 5$, and much lower interest rates.

[2] In the subsequent numerical example we use the following simulated historical data: $\pi_0, \ldots, \pi_{-6} = 2.5, 1.32, 2.2, 1.35, 1.6, 1.8, 2.9$ and $y_0, \ldots, y_{-3} = 2.6, 3.1, -0.8, 1.7$.

[3] The anticipated outcomes and interest rates are calculated with eqs.(3.1)–(3.5), using the estimated coefficients in table 3.1. Equivalently, one could use eq.(3.7) with the estimated transition matrices $\widetilde{C}$.

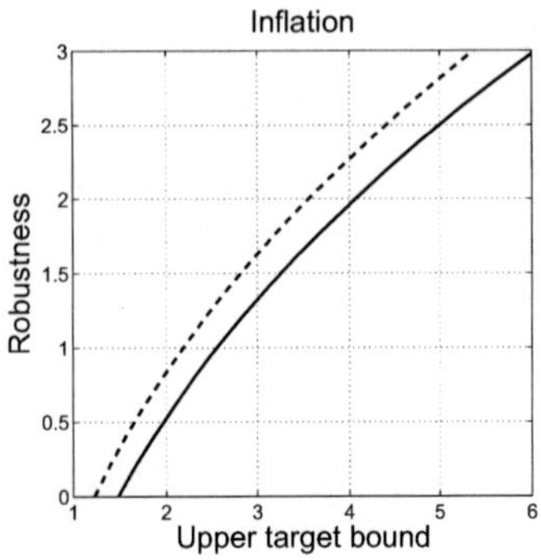

Figure 3.3: Upper-target robustness of inflation, $\widehat{h}_{\rm u}(g, x_{\rm u}, 1)$. $(g_\pi, g_y) = (1.5, 0.5)$ (solid) and $(1, 0.2)$ (dash). $\theta = 3$.

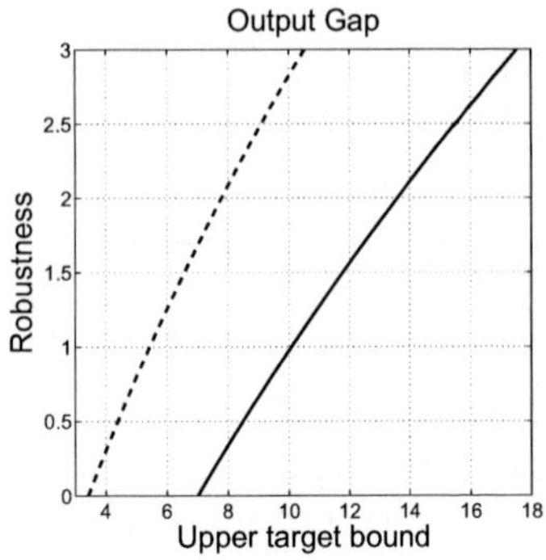

Figure 3.4: Upper-target robustness of output gap, $\widehat{h}_{\rm u}(g, x_{\rm u}, 2)$. $(g_\pi, g_y) = (1.5, 0.5)$ (solid) and $(1, 0.2)$ (dash). $\theta = 3$.

Upper-target robustness. Figs. 3.3 and 3.4 show the upper-target robustness of inflation and output gap, respectively. All calculations in this section employ the info-gap model of eq.(3.9), where the center point values, $\widetilde{c}_i$, and the uncertainty weights, w_i, are the mean and standard error values in table 3.1.

These figures display the zeroing and trade-off properties introduced in section 2.2.2, which we now discuss.[4]

Zeroing. Fig. 3.3 shows that the estimated inflation is smaller when using the smaller Taylor coefficients (dashed curve) as seen by the fact that the dashed curve hits the horizontal axis to the left of the solid curve. However, the robustness to model uncertainty is zero at these estimated values. The same zeroing is seen in fig. 3.4 for the output gap: the estimated output gap is lower with the smaller Taylor coefficients.

Trade-off. The positive slopes of the upper-target robustness curves in figs. 3.3 and 3.4 express the trade-off between robustness and performance: larger robustness is attained by allowing larger output gap or larger inflation. The cost—in terms of lost performance—of increasing the robustness is substantial in both figures. For instance,

[4]This system also displays the preference-reversal property discussed in section 2.2.3, as manifested in intersection between robustness curves, but only with larger Taylor coefficients, associated with larger interest rates. We will encounter an example later.

in the solid curve of fig. 3.3 the robustness is increased from 0 to 2 by increasing the critical inflation from 1.5 to 4.1. From the info-gap model of eq.(3.9) we see that a robustness of 2 means that each model coefficient can deviate from its estimated value by as much as 2 standard errors without violating the performance requirement. Given the large uncertainty in the model coefficients, a robustness of 2 is not excessive. However, the change in critical inflation from 1.5 to 4.1 is substantial. We see on the same curve that robustness of 3 is obtained by allowing the critical inflation to equal 6.0.

We note from figs. 3.3 and 3.4 that the smaller Taylor coefficients (dashed curves) provide greater upper-target robustness for both the inflation and the output gap. This means that the same choice of Taylor coefficients (from between the two sets of coefficients considered here) is made for robustifying both inflation and output gap.

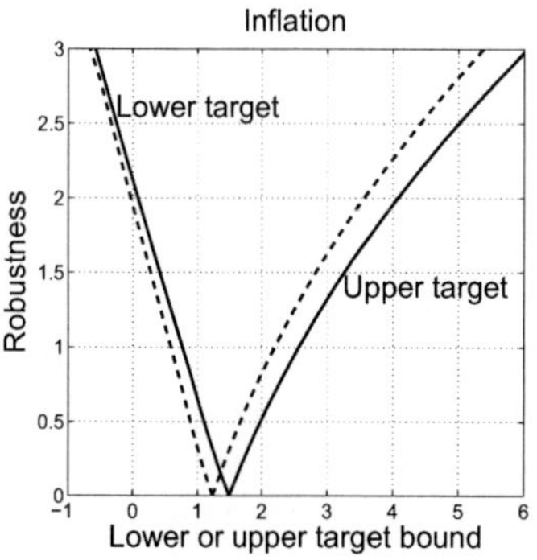

Figure 3.5: Lower- and upper-target robustness of inflation. $(g_\pi, g_y) = (1.5, 0.5)$ (solid) and $(1, 0.2)$ (dash). $\theta = 3$.

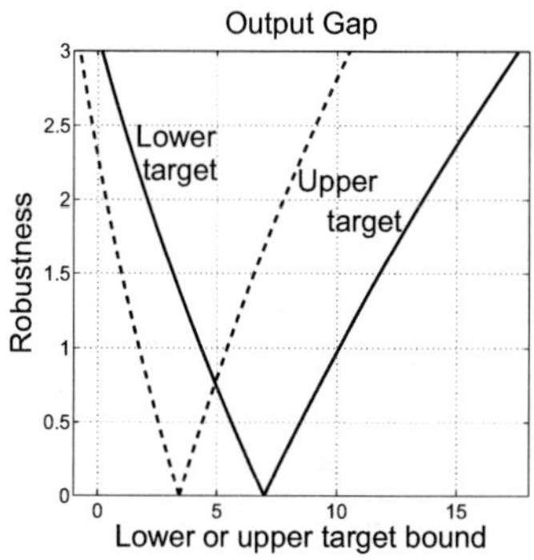

Figure 3.6: Lower- and upper-target robustness of output gap. $(g_\pi, g_y) = (1.5, 0.5)$ (solid) and $(1, 0.2)$ (dash). $\theta = 3$.

Lower-target robustness. Up to now we have only considered the robustness of the upper target bound, $\widehat{h}_{\mathrm{u}}(g, x_{\mathrm{u}}, \ell)$ in eq.(3.13). In figs. 3.5 and 3.6 we include the robustness of the lower target bound, $\widehat{h}_{\ell}(g, x_{\mathrm{l}}, \ell)$ in eq.(3.14). The curves with positive slope in figs. 3.5 and 3.6 are reproduced from figs. 3.3 and 3.4, showing the upper-target robustnesses for inflation and output gap. The curves with negative slope are the lower-target robustnesses.

The negative slope of the lower-target robustness, $\widehat{h}_{\ell}(g, x_{\mathrm{l}}, \ell)$ vs. x_{l}, expresses the trade-off between robustness and performance:

greater robustness is obtained only by allowing a smaller (less restrictive) lower-target bound.

A policy conflict. We noted earlier, in connection with the upper target bound in figs. 3.3 and 3.4, that the smaller Taylor coefficients (dashed curves) are more robust for both inflation and output gap. This means that the policy preference between these two sets of Taylor coefficients is the same when considering either inflation or output gap.

The robustness curves for the lower target bound in figs. 3.5 and 3.6 again show that inflation and output gap are both more robust with the same Taylor coefficients. However, now the larger coefficients (solid curves) are more robust.

We have encountered a policy conflict in the choice between the two sets of Taylor coefficients under consideration. The Taylor coefficients which are robust-preferred for the upper target bound are not robust-preferred for the lower target bound, and vice versa.

A simple intuitive explanation is that a policy which robustifies against the upper target bound will become vulnerable against the lower target bound. It makes sense that a policy which "backs away" from one bound in order to be robust, will encroach on the other bound and thereby lose robustness at this other bound.[5] However, this is not inevitable; curve-crossing and preference reversal can change the situation, as we will now see in figs. 3.7 and 3.8.

Preference reversal and policy agreement. Figs. 3.7 and 3.8 show lower- and upper-target robustness functions for larger Taylor coefficients than we considered before. The interest rates are somewhat high.[6] However, we will observe preference reversal due to crossing of robustness curves, which results in policy agreement between output gap and inflation.

First consider the upper-target robustness curves for output gap, fig. 3.8, which cross each other at robustness of about 0.5, entailing the possibility of preference reversal between these two sets of Taylor coefficients, as discussed in section 2.2.3. Robustness of 0.5 means that each model coefficient can err by as much as 50% of its standard error, and the output gap will not exceed the corresponding value. Half of a standard error is not very much, so this is probably not sufficiently large robustness. If any value of robustness greater than 0.5 is deemed necessary, then the smaller Taylor coefficients (solid

[5]From the frying pan into the fire.

[6]For the smaller of these sets of coefficients the interest rates up to 3 quarters are 8 to 9%. The larger set of coefficients result in interest rates from 15 to 17%.

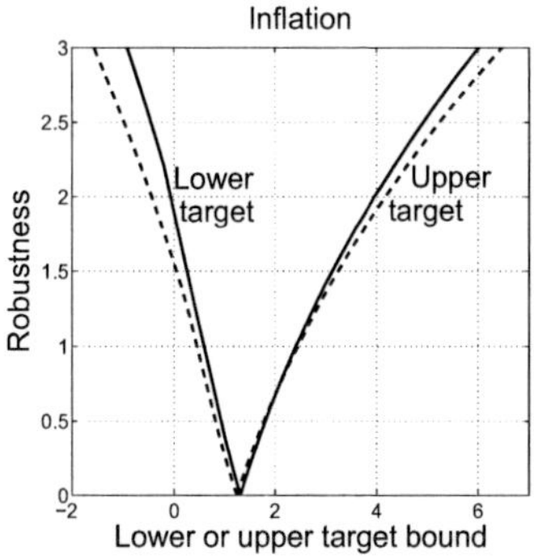

Figure 3.7: Lower- and upper-target robustness of inflation. $(g_\pi, g_y) = (4, 0.5)$ (solid) and $(8, 0.7)$ (dash). $\theta = 3$.

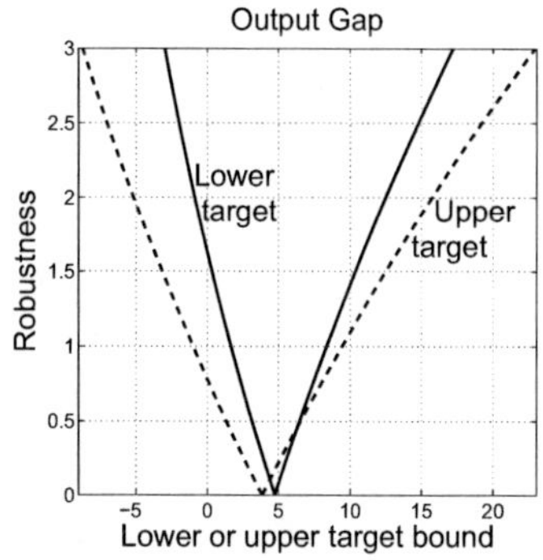

Figure 3.8: Lower- and upper-target robustness of output gap. $(g_\pi, g_y) = (4, 0.5)$ (solid) and $(8, 0.7)$ (dash). $\theta = 3$.

curve) are preferred.[7] Note that, due to the curve crossing, this is the reverse of the best-estimated preference. For instance, at an output gap of 15, the smaller coefficients (solid curve) have robustness of 2.6, as compared with robustness of 1.8 for the larger coefficients (dashed). This is in contrast to the situation at an output gap of 4.9, where the smaller Taylor coefficients have robustness of 0.044, while the larger coefficients have robustness of 0.20 which is greater but still quite small.

The upper robustness curves for inflation in fig. 3.7 show similar curve crossing and preference reversal between the two sets of Taylor coefficients. However, the robustness advantage of the preferred strategy is far weaker than in fig. 3.8.

We see that the lower-target robustness curves in figs. 3.7 and 3.8 do not cross each other, unlike the upper-target robustnesses. Thus there is no reversal of preference between the two sets of Taylor coefficients, when considering the lower-target bound.

This creates an interesting and highly significant policy agreement between the lower- and upper-target performance requirements. In figs. 3.7 and 3.8 we find that the same Taylor coefficients are robust-preferred for both the lower- and upper-target bounds, given

[7] An important judgment is being made here: that robustness of 0.5 is insufficient. However, in order to choose between these two sets of Taylor coefficients we do *not* need to decide how much robustness is necessary. Any choice of robustness in excess of 0.5 leads to the same preference between these options.

reasonable robustness levels. This is unlike the situation in figs. 3.5 and 3.6. Graphically, policy conflict in figs. 3.5 and 3.6 arises because the robustness curves *do not cross* each other. The policy agreement in figs. 3.7 and 3.8 arises because robustness curves *cross in one but not both* cases.

We see the importance, for policy analysis and selection, of the crossing of robustness curves and the resulting reversal of preferences.

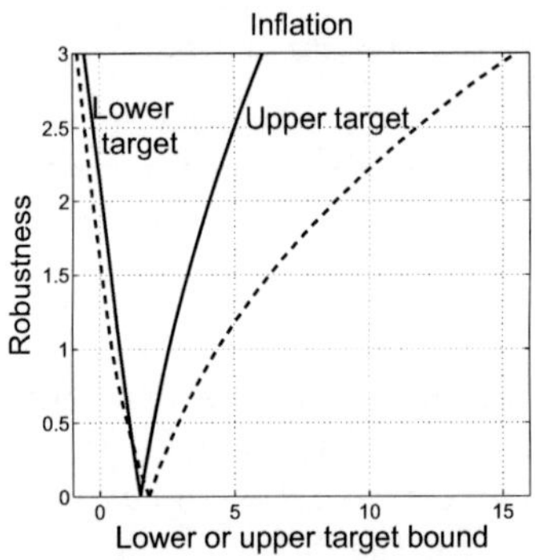

Figure 3.9: Lower- and upper-target robustness of inflation. $\theta = 3$ (solid) and $\theta = 5$ (dash). $(g_\pi, g_y) = (1.5, 0.5)$.

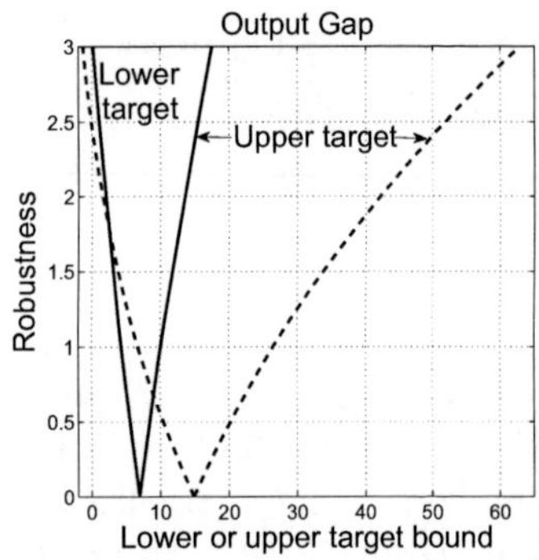

Figure 3.10: Lower- and upper-target robustness of output gap. $\theta = 3$ (solid) and $\theta = 5$ (dash). $(g_\pi, g_y) = (1.5, 0.5)$.

Time horizon. We now consider the effect of the time horizon. Figs. 3.9 and 3.10 show lower- and upper-target robustnesses for $\theta = 3$ and $\theta = 5$ quarters in the future. Fig. 3.9 shows that the upper-target robustness for inflation is far greater for the 3-quarter horizon (solid) than for the 5-quarter horizon (dashed). Not surprising; one would expect that the far future is more difficult to control. The 5-quarter robustness (dashed) is shifted farther to the right (hence lower robustness at any value of the target bound) and also has lower slope (hence higher cost of robustness) than the 3-quarter robustness.

This shifting to the right of the upper-target dashed curve in fig. 3.9 should cause greater lower target robustness at 5 quarters (dashed) than at 3 quarters (solid). This is indeed the case, but only at very low robustness. The lower-target robustness curves cross one another, resulting from slightly lower cost of robustness at 3 quarters (solid). Thus the 3-quarter robustness is greater both in the lower-

and upper-target cases over most of the range (though the lower-target robustness advantage is small).

A similar effect is seen in fig. 3.10 though the lower-target curve crossing occurs further from the horizontal axis. This means that in the output-gap case, the 5-quarter lower-target robustness exceeds the 3-quarter robustness over much of the range.

We see once again the significance of the crossing of robustness curves and the resulting reversal of preferences.

3.2 Expectations, Communication and Credibility

A major task of central banks is the management of public expectations about economic developments. The management of expectations has become "a key instrument in the central banker's toolkit" (Blinder *et al.*, 2008, p.912). Communications by central banks are the subject of intense public scrutiny and constitute newsworthy economic events in their own right. Central banks can use this to inform and educate the public and to reduce the public's uncertainty about the future. Blanchard (2009) notes that "Crises feed uncertainty. And uncertainty affects behaviour, which feeds the crisis." So, especially during crises, policy makers should "First and foremost, reduce uncertainty."

However, central banks themselves face great uncertainties. Clarida, Galí and Gertler (1999, p.1671) note that "the models we use are nowhere near the point where it is possible to obtain a tightly specified policy rule that could be recommended for practical use with great confidence." Consequently, a bank's pronouncements may induce erroneous public beliefs. Credible communication by a central bank may in fact exacerbate rather than reduce the impact of uncertainty.

Finally, the public learns about the economy both from central bank communication and by direct observation. This learning takes place on two levels: about the state of the economy, and about the credibility of central bank pronouncements. Thus a central bank must consider not only what statements to make and how to make them, but also how they will be received.

Many of the decisions which are made by central banks about their communication with the public are difficult to analyze quantitatively, and require considered qualitative judgment by experienced individuals. For instance, should detailed minutes of monetary policy committee meetings be published, or only summaries? Should debate and dispute within the committee be reported? Should the chairperson or bank president make the announcement or should this be relegated to a lower official?

Nonetheless, quantitative analysis is useful in evaluating the impact of communication and credibility on the reliability of achieving specified goals (Ben-Haim and Demertzis, 2008). We will consider a central bank that uses the short term interest rate in trying to keep inflation and output gap within specified bounds. If the bank announces its goals, and if the announcement is credible in the eyes of the public, then the public's expectations of future inflation and output gap will be guided by the bank's goals. On the other hand, if the bank does not announce its intentions, or if its announcements are not credible, then the public will form expectations based solely on observed variables. The question facing the bank is whether to communicate its goals and whether to establish and maintain its credibility. We evaluate the robustness of these alternatives.

We will develop a simple example of the info-gap robustness analysis of a central bank's decisions regarding credible announcement of its goals, and related policy instruments. We will introduce a macroeconomic model whose coefficients are uncertain. We will add three different models for the formation of expectations by the public about inflation and output gap. In one model the expectations adapt around the bank's announced targets for these variables, while in the second model the expectations are formed adaptively from observation alone. The third model for expectation formation combines the previous two models by weighting them according to the public credibility of the bank. We will explore the robustness to model uncertainty as a function of the credibility. Thus, the bank should consider adopting a policy of credible communication of its goals if robustness is increased by increasing the credibility.

The example and its models are not meant to be definitive, but rather to illustrate a methodology which can be applied to diverse models and situations. In the present example we consider a specific point in time, with a specific history, and use the dynamic models to predict the robustness of attaining future goals. A different analysis would be to evaluate the robustness by simulating the evolution of the public's models for forming expectations. Also, we are considering a single representative agent, while other realizations might consider the heterogeneity of public opinion. In subsequent sections of this chapter we explore other variations.

3.2.1 Policy Preview

The policy maker must choose lower- and upper-target values for both inflation and output gap, as well as deciding on the level of credibility to maintain. We will evaluate the robustness to uncertainty as a function of these decisions.

We will see that the robustness is invariably zero when the bank aspires to the outcomes which are predicted by the estimated, baseline model. Since zero robustness means that the anticipated outcome cannot be depended on to occur in practice, this implies that policy options should not be evaluated only with respect to outcomes predicted with the estimated model. Rather, robustness to uncertainty should be incorporated in policy selection.

We will see that robustness *usually* decreases as the upper target for either inflation or output gap is reduced: more demanding performance is more vulnerable to uncertainty. Similarly, robustness decreases as either lower target is increased. This is the usual trade-off between robustness and performance, as discussed in section 2.2.2. However, we will find that the incorporation of expectations can cause deviation from the common rule that robustness decreases as aspirations rise. Expectations will sometimes feed back into the outcomes to result in higher robustness associated with better outcomes. Identifying this reversal in the slope of the robustness curve is useful in policy analysis.

We will find that the robustness to model uncertainty can either increase or decrease as the bank's credibility increases. It is not true that more credibility always enhances robustness to uncertainty, and the ability to quantify this has policy implications. Furthermore, we will observe a conflict between robustness of upper-target and lower-target values. A change in credibility which enhances one of these robustnesses will diminish the other robustness, though not necessarily by a large amount.

We will find that robustness to uncertainty varies strongly over time, and that the temporal dynamics of the robustness is strongly influenced by the bank's credibility. More credibility will tend to reduce the variability of the robustness.

Finally, we will observe situations in which the robustness curves for two different policies cross one another as discussed in section 2.2.3. If the policy maker prioritizes the policies according to their robustness, then preferences among the policies will change as the policy maker's requirements on the outcomes change. The quantification of this preference reversal supports the selection of a policy.

3.2.2 Operational Preview

System model. The system model in this example entails the macro-economic dynamics, eqs.(3.17) and (3.18), the interest rate policy rule, eq.(3.19), and the rule by which the public forms its expectations about inflation and output gap, eqs.(3.26) and (3.27). These expectation-formulation equations represent partial credibility of the central bank, and are the weighted combinations of full credibility, eqs.(3.22) and (3.23), and complete non-credibility, eqs.(3.24) and (3.25).

Performance requirements. The bank's performance requirements, eqs.(3.20) and (3.21), specify intervals within which the inflation and output gap must remain. The target bounds could be specified to change over time, for instance if the bank wanted to gradually maneuver the economy to a tighter regime. However in our example we will consider target bounds which are fixed.

Uncertainty model. The coefficients of the macro-economic model are estimated, and errors of these estimates are available, but the difference between the estimated and the actual values is unknown. This is specified in the info-gap model of eq.(3.28). We are focussing on parametric uncertainty in the model, and not considering uncertain shocks, which will be considered in section 3.3. Uncertainty about the public's expectations is explored in section 3.4.

Decision variables. The central bank's decision variables concern its goals, its credibility, and the interest rate rule. These decision variables are of qualitatively different types. They are all unknown at the start of the analysis, but we do not consider them as uncertain since they are under the policy maker's control. The purpose of the analysis is to support the decision-making process.

Target bounds. The bank must choose lower-target and upper-target bounds for inflation, $\pi_{\rm l}$ and $\pi_{\rm u}$, and for output gap, $y_{\rm l}$ and $y_{\rm u}$. The purpose of the robustness analysis is to identify values of these target bounds which are both economically desirable and robust to model uncertainty and hence feasible or realistic.

Credibility. The public's formation of expectations about future inflation and output gap is modelled as a weighted combination of two algorithms, one which adapts around the central bank's announced goals and the other which adapts entirely from observation. We are proxying the bank's credibility by the weighting parameter, κ, which is between zero and one. κ near zero represents low credibility, while κ near one means high credibility. We treat κ as a decision parameter, on the presumption that the central bank can take actions to influence its credibility as reflected in the public's formation of expectations.

Interest rate. The central bank must choose the coefficients $g = (g_\pi, g_y)$ of its Taylor-like interest rate rule.

Robustness functions. We are now able to formulate the robustness functions, eqs.(3.29) and (3.30), which depend on the decision variables and which combine the system models, performance requirements, and uncertainty models.

3.2.3 Dynamics and Expectations

We consider a simple model based on Clarida, Galí and Gertler (1999):

$$\pi_{t+1} = \lambda y_t + \beta \mathrm{E}_t \pi_{t+1} \quad (3.17)$$

$$y_{t+1} = -\phi(i_t - \mathrm{E}_t \pi_{t+1}) + \mathrm{E}_t y_{t+1} \quad (3.18)$$

ϕ, λ and β are parameters. π_t is the inflation in period t defined as the percent change in the price level from $t-1$ to t. y_t is the output gap, defined as 100 times the difference between the actual and potential output, both expressed in logs, after removal of the long-run trend. i_t is the nominal interest rate. Both π_t and i_t are evaluated after removal of the long-run trend. E_t is the expectation operator for the representative agent based on information available at time t.[8] We concentrate on the average behavior under uncertainty in the parameters ϕ, λ and β, and ignore zero-mean shocks. We will consider shocks in section 3.3.

The central bank will use a Taylor rule to choose the interest rate at each period:

$$i_t = g_\pi \pi_t + g_y y_t \quad (3.19)$$

The bank must choose the vector $g = (g_\pi, g_y)$.

We focus on the impact of credible communication of the central bank with the representative agent in eqs.(3.17) and (3.18). How does this communication influence the confidence with which the bank achieves its goals? Since the bank forms its requirements and

[8] At time t the available data are $\pi_t, \pi_{t-1}, \ldots$ and $y_t, y_{t-1}, \ldots$.

policies with an uncertain model, its communication with the public may mislead and distract attention from actual developments in the economy.

The central bank, if it chooses to do so, announces its intention to use the interest rate in attempting to maintain inflation and output gap within the following intervals:

$$\pi_{\rm l} \le \quad \pi_t \quad \le \pi_{\rm u} \tag{3.20}$$

$$y_{\rm l} \le \quad y_t \quad \le y_{\rm u} \tag{3.21}$$

The public observes inflation and output gap (π_i, y_i) for periods $i = 0, \ldots, t$ and hears the central bank announcement of its goals. The public forms expectations about future inflation and output gap based on this information together with much additional information. Models for learning and the formation of expectations are numerous. Evans and Honkapohja (2001) discuss many models, including static, adaptive and rational expectation models of various sorts. We employ three plausible adaptive models of learning: credible, not credible, and partially credible bank communication. The last model is a weighted combination of the first two.

If the bank's announcement of its goals is **credible** then the public's expectations are formed to converge on the center of the bank's target intervals:

$$\mathrm{E}_t\pi_{t+1} = \pi_t - \psi_\pi(\pi_t - \pi_{\rm m}) \tag{3.22}$$

$$\mathrm{E}_t y_{t+1} = y_t - \psi_y(y_t - y_{\rm m}) \tag{3.23}$$

where $\pi_{\rm m} = (\pi_{\rm u} + \pi_{\rm l})/2$ and $y_{\rm m} = (y_{\rm l} + y_{\rm u})/2$. The coefficients ψ_π and ψ_y are estimated from the observations by minimizing the squared error of the anticipations, as explained in appendix 3.7.

If the bank's announcement of its goals is **not credible** then the public's expectations are formed by regressing on the observations:

$$\mathrm{E}_t\pi_{t+1} = \sum_{i=0}^{K} b_i \pi_{t-i} \tag{3.24}$$

$$\mathrm{E}_t y_{t+1} = \sum_{i=0}^{J} a_i y_{t-i} \tag{3.25}$$

The coefficient vectors b and a are chosen to minimize the squared errors, as explained in appendix 3.7.

Finally, credibility may not be absolute. If the bank is **partially credible** then the public's expectations are formed as a weighted combination of eq.(3.22) with (3.24), and eq.(3.23) with (3.25):

$$\mathrm{E}_t \pi_{t+1} = \kappa[\pi_t - \psi_\pi(\pi_t - \pi_{\mathrm{m}})] + (1-\kappa) b' \pi_{t(K)} \quad (3.26)$$

$$\mathrm{E}_t y_{t+1} = \kappa[y_t - \psi_y(y_t - y_{\mathrm{m}})] + (1-\kappa) a' y_{t(J)} \quad (3.27)$$

where $0 \le \kappa \le 1$. Clearly "credibility" is a subtle qualitative attribute. However, when κ is large (near one) then expectations are formed primarily based on adaptation around the bank's announcements. In contrast, when κ is small (near zero) then expectations are formed primarily by adapting to the data with little direct influence of the bank's announcements. Extreme values of κ represent extremes of credibility.

3.2.4 Uncertainty and Robustness

Uncertainty. The economic model in eqs.(3.17) and (3.18) has 3 coefficients which we denote with the vector $c = (\phi, \lambda, \beta)$. The best estimates and standard errors of these coefficients are $\widetilde{c} = (\widetilde{\phi}, \widetilde{\lambda}, \widetilde{\beta})$ and $s = (s_\phi, s_\lambda, s_\beta)$. The model is formulated so that the model coefficients must be between zero and one.

However, the actual values of these coefficients are highly uncertain. This uncertainty is even greater than the uncertainty of the model coefficients which we considered in section 3.1. In the present situation one might suspect that the model coefficients will be influenced indirectly by the credibility. Credibility influences expectations through eqs.(3.26) and (3.27), which in turn influence inflation and output gap through the dynamics, eqs.(3.17) and (3.18). However, the model coefficients might also have a direct dependence on the credibility. We have no idea about the form of this dependence. This is an info-gap, a Knightian uncertainty: a severe uncertainty about which we have no probabilistic information. The robustness analysis focusses on the question: how wrong can the model coefficients be (where their error derives in part from the unknown impact of the endogenous credibility) and the bank's policy will still yield adequate results?

We use a fractional-error info-gap model which is similar to the model in eq.(3.9) on p.33:[9]

$$\mathcal{U}(h) = \left\{ c : \ c_i \in [0,\ 1],\ |c_i - \widetilde{c}_i| \le s_i h,\ i = 1,\ 2,\ 3 \right\}, \quad h \ge 0 \quad (3.28)$$

[9] We are simplifying the notation a bit, so that $\widetilde{c}_1 = \widetilde{\phi}$ and $s_1 = s_\phi$, etc.

Robustness. The public observes the bank's announced target bounds for inflation and output gap, as well as the actual inflation and output gap (π_i, y_i) for periods $i = 0, \ldots, t$. With these observations, the public forms expectations for future inflation and output gap. The robustness of any choice of Taylor coefficients, g, and credibility, κ, at period $\theta > t$, is the greatest horizon of uncertainty, h, up to which we are sure to satisfy the critical outcome requirements at period θ, either eq.(3.20) or (3.21), for all realizations of the c_j's in $\mathcal{U}(h)$. Let "x" denote either "π" or "y", so that x_θ denotes the corresponding economic variable at period θ in the future. Likewise x_l and x_u denote the lower and upper target values for either π or y. We define the lower-target and upper-target robustness functions:

$$\widehat{h}_{\mathrm{l}x}(g, \kappa, \pi_\mathrm{m}, y_\mathrm{m}, x_\mathrm{l}, \theta) = \max \left\{ h : \left(\min_{c \in \mathcal{U}(h)} x_\theta \right) \geq x_\mathrm{l} \right\} \quad (3.29)$$

$$\widehat{h}_{\mathrm{u}x}(g, \kappa, \pi_\mathrm{m}, y_\mathrm{m}, x_\mathrm{u}, \theta) = \max \left\{ h : \left(\max_{c \in \mathcal{U}(h)} x_\theta \right) \leq x_\mathrm{u} \right\} \quad (3.30)$$

When "x" is "π" then eqs.(3.29) and (3.30) represent lower-target and upper-target robustness for inflation. When "x" is "y" then we have lower-target and upper-target robustness for output gap.

The critical target value, x_l or x_u, appears on both sides of the inequalities in eqs.(3.29) and (3.30). This is not the usual situation, and results from formation of expectations with a credible bank, as we now explain. When the bank is at least partly credible, so that $\kappa > 0$, public expectations include eqs.(3.22) and (3.23). Consequently, when the bank is at least partly credible, x_θ in the inner optimizations of eqs.(3.29) and (3.30) depends on both π_m and y_m. Also, in eq.(3.29), π_m and y_m depend on π_l and y_l respectively, while in eq.(3.30), π_m and y_m depend on π_u and y_u respectively. Thus the performance requirements, x_l and x_u, appear on *both* sides of the inequalities in eqs.(3.29) and (3.30). This results from credible expectation formation and can have surprising impact, as we will see.

The expectation coefficients for a credible bank, ψ_π and ψ_y in eqs.(3.22) and (3.23), depend on the bank's announced target values through π_m and y_m, though they only depend on historical data. Thus ψ_y and ψ_π do not depend on the uncertain future model coefficients.

The expectation vectors for a non-credible bank, b and a appearing in eqs.(3.24) and (3.25), do not depend on the bank's announced target values or on π_m and y_m. Also, they only depend on historical data, so they do not depend on the uncertain future model coefficients.

3.2.5 Policy Exploration

The central bank must decide on its lower and upper target values for inflation, π_{l} and π_{u}, and output gap, y_{l} and y_{u}, in eqs.(3.20) and (3.21), and its Taylor coefficients, g, in eq.(3.19). In addition, the bank must decide whether to announce its target values and to invest effort in establishing and maintaining the credibility, κ, of these announcements, as discussed in connection with eqs.(3.26) and (3.27). We will use the robustness function to explore these policy decisions.

Fig. 3.11 shows lower- and upper-target robustness curves for inflation for three quarters in the future ($\theta = 3$) with Taylor coefficients $(g_\pi, g_y) = (1.5, 0.5)$.[10] The lower-target robustness for inflation, $\widehat{h}_{\mathrm{l}\pi}$, is plotted vs. π_{l}, and the upper-target robustness, $\widehat{h}_{\mathrm{u}\pi}$, is plotted vs. π_{u}. In each case, lower- and upper-target bounds are related by $\pi_{\mathrm{u}} = \pi_{\mathrm{l}} + \delta_\pi$, where $\delta_\pi = 2$. The midpoint of the lower and upper inflation targets is denoted π_{m}, as defined following eq.(3.23) on p.46. The value of π_{m} enters the credible-bank expectation formation. The bank also chooses lower and upper targets for the output gap, whose midpoint, y_{m}, also appears in the credible-bank expectation formation. $y_{\mathrm{m}} = 1.1$ in these calculations.

Trade-off. Looking at fig. 3.11 we see that the lower-target robustness decreases as the lower-target bound, π_{l}, increases. This is the usual trade-off: as the lower aspiration for inflation becomes more demanding (larger π_{l}), the robustness decreases. In the same figure we see the same trade-off in the upper-target robustness: larger π_{u} (less ambitious aspirations) entails larger robustness.[11]

The upper-target robustness curve in fig. 3.11 is much steeper in absolute magnitude than the lower-target curve. This results from the asymmetry of the info-gap model. The slope represents

[10] We use the following values in all examples in this section. The synthetic historical data are $\pi_{t(6)} = (2.5, 1.32, 2.2, 1.35, 1.6, 1.8, 2.9)$ and $y_{t(6)} = (2.6, 3.1, -0.8, 1.7, 1.0, -0.5, 0.6)$. The estimated coefficients and their standard errors are $(\widetilde{\phi}, \widetilde{\lambda}, \widetilde{\beta}) = (0.5, 0.14, 0.9)$ and $(s_\phi, s_\lambda, s_\beta) = (0.1, 0.05, 0.3)$. The regression lags in eqs.(3.24) and (3.25) are $J = K = 2$.

[11] This trade-off is a necessary consequence of the nesting of the sets of the info-gap model, as explained in section 2.2.2. However, the argument there depended on the system model (x_θ here) being *independent* of the performance requirement (x_{l} or x_{u}). In fact, due to expectations, x_θ *depends* on x_{l} and x_{u}, which can cause violation of this trade-off, as we will see in fig. 3.13 and elsewhere.

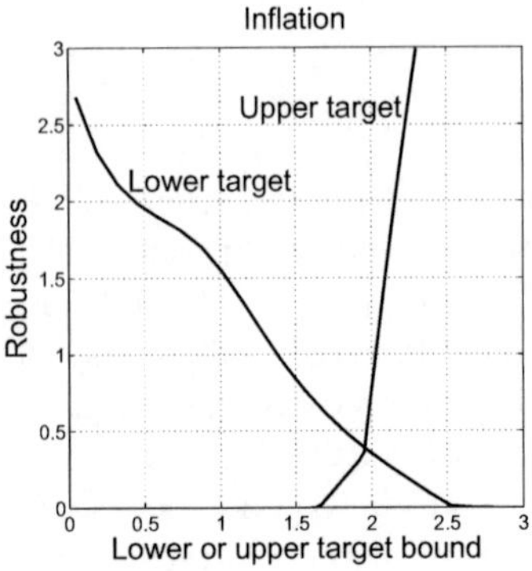

Figure 3.11: Lower- and upper-target robustness of inflation. $\theta = 3$ and $\kappa = 0.8$.

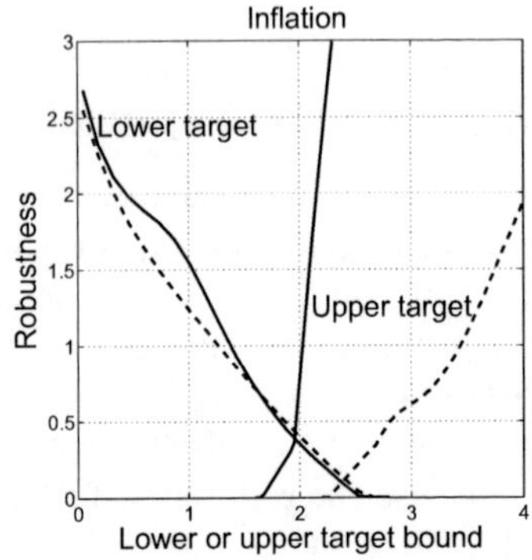

Figure 3.12: Lower- and upper-target robustness of inflation. $\theta = 3$. $\kappa = 0.2$ (dash) and $\kappa = 0.8$ (solid).

the performance-cost of robustness: how much performance must be foregone in exchange for improving the robustness. The upper-target robustness is less "expensive" in units of $\pi_{\rm u}$, than the lower-target robustness in units of $\pi_{\rm l}$.

Zeroing. The lower- and upper-target robustness curves shown in fig. 3.11 reach zero robustness at different points on the horizontal axis, causing these curves to cross each other. This is unlike all the lower- and upper-target robustness curves in section 3.1, such as figs. 3.5 and 3.6 on p.37, which form nice "V" shapes with the apex at zero robustness. This intersection of the robustness curves is the first manifestation, in this example, of expectation formation with a credible central bank. The inner optimizations in the robustness functions, eqs.(3.29) and (3.30), depend on the target values (via the target midpoint values $\pi_{\rm m}$ and $y_{\rm m}$). As a result, the value of $\pi_{\rm l}$ at which the lower-target robustness, $\widehat{h}_{{\rm l}\pi}$, reaches zero, is greater than the value of $\pi_{\rm u}$ at which the upper-target robustness, $\widehat{h}_{{\rm u}\pi}$, reaches zero. Hence these curves cross each other. The distance between these two zeroing points is not equal to $\pi_{\rm u} - \pi_{\rm l}$.[12]

This intersection of lower- and upper-target robustness curves—which results from credible expectation formation—has an impact on

[12] Expectation formation with a credible bank can cause the robustness curves to shift so that they don't intersect at all, as we will see in fig. 3.14.

policy selection.

In fig. 3.11 the upper-target robustness vanishes at $\pi_u = 1.7$, while the lower-target robustness remains positive up to a larger value, $\pi_l = 2.5$:

$$\widehat{h}_{u\pi} = 0 \text{ at } \pi_u \leq 1.7 \quad \text{while} \quad \widehat{h}_{l\pi} = 0 \text{ at } \pi_l \geq 2.5. \tag{3.31}$$

In the absence of expectations, we have "V" shaped robustness-function pairs as in figs. 3.5 and 3.6, so that these zero robustnesses must occur together at $\pi_u = \pi_l$. Credible-bank expectation formation causes the robustness curves to shift, changing the "V" into an "X". Since policy selection depends on the location of the robustness curves, this shifting of the curves can alter the bank's policy decisions.

Central bank credibility. Fig. 3.11 shows results with substantial central-bank credibility: $\kappa = 0.8$ in eqs.(3.26) and (3.27). In fig. 3.12 we compare these results with those for low credibility, $\kappa = 0.2$. Three observations are notable.

First, the upper-target robustness is very sensitive to credibility, and decreases drastically with decrease in bank credibility.

Second, the lower-target robustness is almost entirely insensitive to credibility. The lower-target robustness is simply insensitive to how expectations are formed, unlike the case of upper-target robustness. This is not a universal phenomenon, as we will see when we consider the output gap. The important point is the implication for policy selection. For the specific configuration in fig. 3.12, the policy maker should be quite concerned about credibility as far as upper inflation-targets are concerned, but not at all when considering only lower inflation-targets.

The third point to note in fig. 3.12 is that the crossing of the low-credibility curves (dashed) is much less of an "X", and more like a "V", than the crossing of the high-credibility curves (solid). When expectations are formed only from observations, the pair of robustness curves would be a "V" shape with its apex at zero robustness, and the transition from high to low credibility shows the move in that direction.

Output gap. Up to now we have considered the robustness for inflation. Figs. 3.13 and 3.14 show lower- and upper-target robustness functions for the output gap.[13] We see similar characteristics to those

[13] We use the values in footnote 10 on p.49. The value of π_m is 2.0. The upper and lower targets are related as $y_u = y_l + \delta_y$ where $\delta_y = 2$.

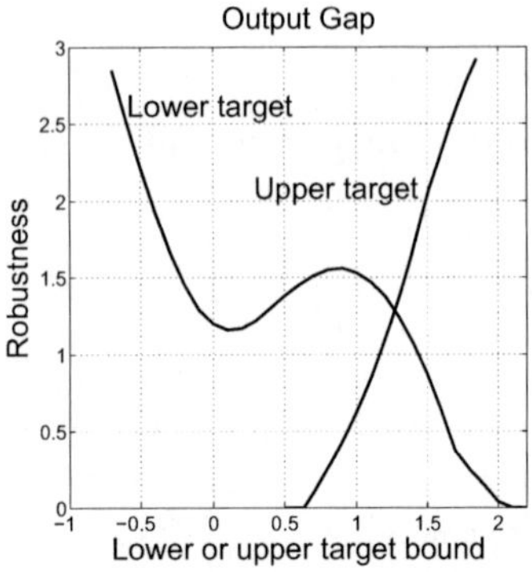

Figure 3.13: Lower- and upper-target robustness of output gap. $\theta = 3$ and $\kappa = 0.8$.

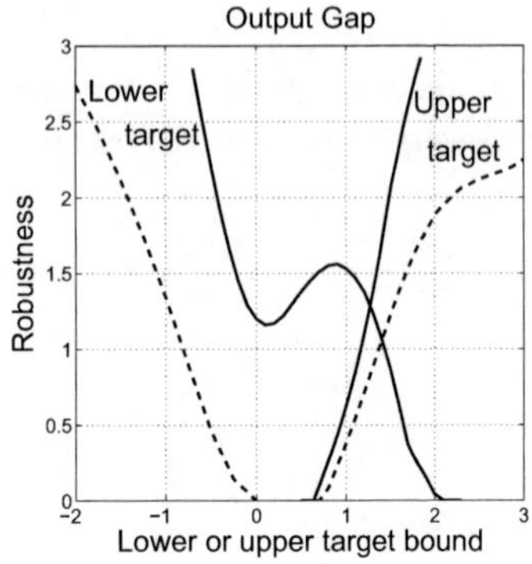

Figure 3.14: Lower- and upper-target robustness of output gap. $\theta = 3$. $\kappa = 0.2$ (dash) and $\kappa = 0.8$ (solid).

displayed in figs. 3.11 and 3.12: (1) trade-off between performance requirement and robustness; (2) crossing of lower- and upper-target robustness curves. However two differences appear.

First, in fig. 3.14 we see that it is now the lower-target robustness which is dramatically sensitive to credibility. Nonetheless we see that the upper-target robustness also is reduced at low credibility.

Second, we see that the lower-target robustness in fig. 3.13 is *not* monotonic in y_l. There is an intermediate hump in the lower-target robustness curve. This is a distinctive manifestation of expectation formation with a credible bank. Due to credible-bank expectation formation, the bank's announced aspirations, x_l and x_u, appear in x_θ and on the right-hand side of the performance-requirement inequalities in the definitions of the robustness, eqs.(3.29) and (3.30) as explained in the paragraph following these equations. If the expectations are formed independently of the bank (e.g., the bank is not credible) then x_θ does not depend on x_l or x_u, and the bank's aspirations appear only on the right-hand side. In the absence of credible-bank expectations, $\widehat{h}_{ly}$ must decrease as y_l increases.[14] However, when expectations are based at least in part on the bank's announcement, then the inner minimum in $\widehat{h}_{ly}$ depends on the bank announcements and the monotonic trade-off between y_l and $\widehat{h}_{ly}$ can be disrupted, as

[14]Strictly speaking, $\widehat{h}_{ly}$ cannot increase as y_l increases. See also footnote 11 on p.49.

we see in fig. 3.13. The non-monotonicity is not overwhelming in this example, and the overall tendency is for trade-off between requirement and robustness. Nonetheless, the slope-reversal does "delay" the fall in robustness with increase in y_l.

This has an implication for policy selection. When a hump appears in a robustness curve as in fig. 3.13, the policy maker can achieve the same robustness at two or three different values of the choice parameter (y_l in the present case). It would be inefficient to choose any but the largest value which is consistent with the required robustness. The non-monotonicity of the robustness curve allows the choice of a more desirable policy—larger y_l—without relinquishing robustness. Furthermore, the policy choice may jump discontinuously as the required robustness changes, if required robustness is near the top of the hump. The broad span of the hump and dip is significant here.

Time horizon. So far, all the examples in this section have studied the robustness at 3 periods in the future. We now consider the temporal variation of the robustness which results from the economic dynamics. Figs. 3.15 and 3.16 show the upper-target robustness for output gap from 1 up to 7 periods in the future. Fig. 3.15 shows the case of low credibility of the bank ($\kappa = 0.2$) and fig. 3.16 shows high bank credibility ($\kappa = 0.8$). Three conclusions are striking.

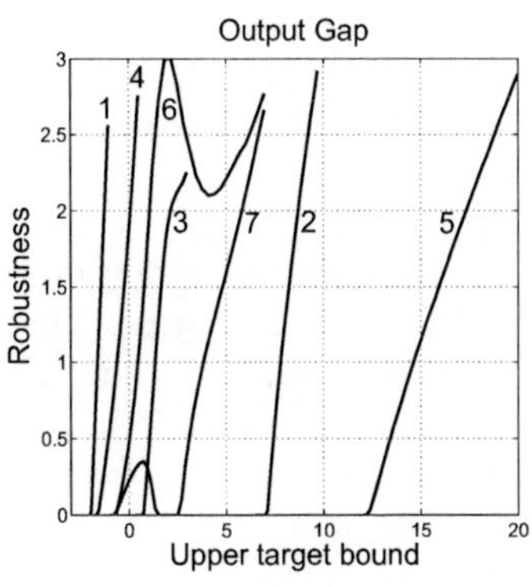

Figure 3.15: Upper-target robustness of output gap. $\theta = 1, \ldots, 7$ and $\kappa = 0.2$.

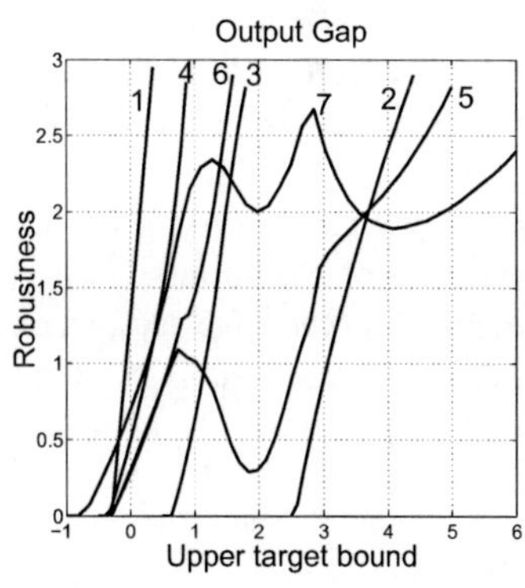

Figure 3.16: Upper-target robustness of output gap. $\theta = 1, \ldots, 7$ and $\kappa = 0.8$.

First consider fig. 3.15, for low credibility of the central bank. One might have anticipated that periods which are in the near future would be more robust to model uncertainty than later periods. However, this is not correct. While some periods are vastly more robust than others, robustness is not ranked according to period. It is true that the nearest period, $\theta = 1$, is more robust than all later periods shown, but the least robust period is $\theta = 5$ which is not the latest period in the figure. But also, the robustness at $\theta = 4$ and at $\theta = 6$ both exceed the robustness at $\theta = 3$, and $\theta = 3$ itself is vastly more robust than $\theta = 2$. In short, in this specific example we see that, with low bank credibility, the robustness for achieving the bank's aspirations varies greatly with time and shows complicated dynamics.

Second, now considering fig. 3.16 with high bank credibility, we note that robustness curves for different periods cross one another. Most dramatically, the curves for $\theta = 1$ and $\theta = 7$ cross each other, as do $\theta = 4$ and $\theta = 7$ as well as $\theta = 3$ and $\theta = 5$. Curve crossing is an important phenomenon. The value of y_{u} at which each robustness curve meets the horizontal axis is the value of output gap which is predicted by the estimated model for that period, given the corresponding bank announcement. Comparing periods $\theta = 1$ and $\theta = 7$ on the horizontal axis of fig. 3.16, the estimated model predicts that $\theta = 7$ can attain lower output gap than $\theta = 1$. However, the robustness is zero for these predictions and, most importantly, these two robustness curves cross one another. This crossing means that $\theta = 1$ is in fact more robust than $\theta = 7$ over most of the range of y_{u}.

Third, the degree of dispersion is quite different in figs. 3.15 ($\kappa = 0.2$) and 3.16 ($\kappa = 0.8$)[15]: the high credibility case, fig. 3.16, has more stable (though still variable) robustness, which incidentally causes more curve crossing in this case. For instance, at robustness of 2, the range of y_{u} values is about 20 for $\kappa = 0.2$ and only about 3.5 for $\kappa = 0.8$. Even excluding the case of $\theta = 5$, the range of y_{u} values at robustness of 2 is about 11 with $\kappa = 0.2$. The dynamics is complicated and can produce surprises, so caution is needed in generalization. The point of the analysis is to identify, for a specific situation facing the policy maker, which strategy—credible communication or reticence—is consistently robust to uncertainty in the available economic model. In the present case it is evident that credible communication by the central bank entails more stable robustness over time.

Preference reversal. We now consider a situation in which the central bank must choose both its Taylor coefficients (which determine the interest rate) as well as its credibility (where moderate credibility requires more effort than no credibility at all). We will

[15]Note the different horizontal scales in these figures.

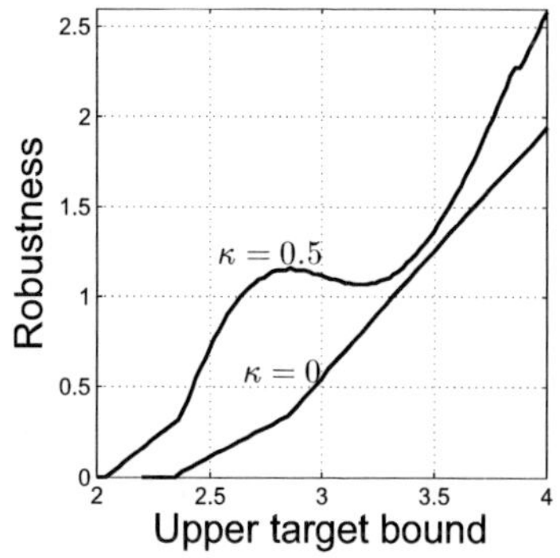

Figure 3.17: Upper-target robustness of inflation with *larger* Taylor coefficients: $(g_\pi, g_y) = (1.5, 0.5)$. $\theta = 3$.

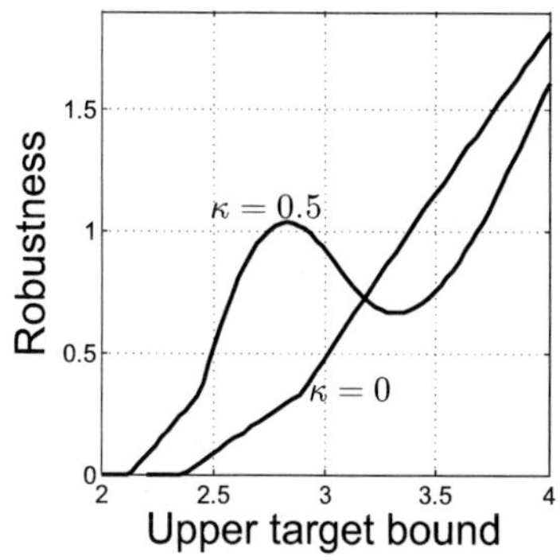

Figure 3.18: Upper-target robustness of inflation with *smaller* Taylor coefficients: $(g_\pi, g_y) = (0.5, 0.5)$. $\theta = 3$.

encounter robustness curves which cross one another, entailing a reversal of preference between the corresponding policy options.

Fig. 3.17 shows upper-target robustness curves for inflation with moderate credibility ($\kappa = 0.5$) and no credibility ($\kappa = 0$). In both cases the bank adopts a fairly strong Taylor rule, $(g_\pi, g_y) = (1.5, 0.5)$, resulting in rather high interest rates during the 3 future periods (3–5% with $\kappa = 0.5$, 2–8% with $\kappa = 0$). Fig. 3.17 suggests a preference for moderate credibility, whose robustness curve dominates the no-credibility case. The effort required to establish and maintain the credibility is rewarded with greater robustness to uncertainty throughout the range of upper-target bounds. The moderate-credibility option is preferred regardless of the bank's choice of the upper target for inflation.[16]

Fig. 3.18 shows the same levels of credibility, but now with less aggressive Taylor coefficients, $(g_\pi, g_y) = (0.5, 0.5)$, and consequently substantially lower interest rates.[17] We now see that the robustness curves cross one another; neither is dominant in robustness throughout the range of π_u values. The decision whether or not to invest in obtaining and maintaining moderate credibility depends on the

[16] The bank must announce its upper and lower targets in order for its credibility to be translated by the public into expectations. However, the bank's preference for moderate credibility is independent of the choice of specific target values.

[17] From the Taylor rule in eq.(3.19), p.45, we see that reducing g_π by 1 causes a reduction in interest by an increment equal to the inflation, *ceteris paribus*.

inflation target which the central bank adopts.

If the central bank determines an upper target for inflation, π_u, which is no greater than 3.2 (the value at which the curves in fig. 3.18 cross), then the preference is for moderate credibility. The robustness advantage of moderate credibility can be substantial. For instance, at $\pi_u = 2.8$ the additional robustness is about 0.7, or immunity to an additional 70% fractional error in the model coefficients. On the other hand, if an upper target in excess of 3.2 is desired, then this is more robustly achieved with no credibility at all. Once again the robustness advantage can be substantial, though not quite as large: at $\pi_u = 3.5$ the no-credibility option has immunity to an additional 40% fractional error.

This example illustrates that the choice between policy alternatives depends on examining the entire robustness curves. It is not sufficient to evaluate a policy only in terms of the outcome which is predicted by the estimated baseline model. The possibility of preference reversal arises when the robustness curves of the different policy options cross one another, as discussed earlier in section 2.2.3.

3.3 Shocks, Expectations and Credibility

In this section we extend the model used in section 3.2 by including inflation and output shocks. We will study the impact of highly uncertain tails on the probability distributions of these shocks, together with uncertainty in the parameters of the economic model. That is, we will consider a hybrid uncertainty model: the decision maker faces info-gaps about the probabilistic model, in addition to "ordinary" info-gap uncertainty in model parameters. Moreover, the hybrid uncertainty will deal with uncertainty in the *shape* of the probability density function, as distinct from the uncertainty in the *values* of model parameters. We will include public expectations about inflation and output gap, and study the impact, on the reliability of outcomes, of central bank credibility. In the next section we consider uncertainty in the central bank's knowledge of public expectations.

3.3.1 Policy Preview

The policy maker must choose values of the lower- and upper-target bounds for both inflation and output gap, as well as the level of credibility which the central bank wishes to maintain. The parameters of the macro-economic model are uncertain and the economy is subject to random shocks with uncertain probability distributions. We evaluate the robustness to model uncertainty vs. the probability of satisfying each target bound. We consider a high level of uncertainty in the tails of the probability distributions of the shocks, allowing for the possibility of tails which are much fatter, or thinner, than anticipated.

We observe the usual trade-off between robustness and performance: high probability of satisfying a target bound entails low robustness to uncertainty in the macro-economic model.

The slope of a robustness curve reflects the cost of robustness in units of probability of success. In some cases the slope is very steep, implying that robustness can be obtained by foregoing only a small increment in probability. In other situations the slope is very shallow, implying a high cost of robustness.

We observe a conflicting impact of central bank credibility. When the robustness of the upper-target bound, for either inflation or output gap, is *enhanced* by increasing the credibility, the lower-target robustness is *reduced.* And vice versa: enhancing lower-target robustness causes a reduction in upper-target robustness.

The robustness to model uncertainty can be strongly influenced by changing the interest rates, which are determined by the bank's choice of the Taylor coefficients. Likewise, in some cases the robustness is quite sensitive to the range between the lower and the upper target.

3.3.2 Operational Preview

System model. The system model employs the inflation and output gap relations in eqs.(3.32) and (3.33), which are the same as those in section 3.2.3 with the addition of random shocks. These equations depend on the public's expectations about inflation and output gap which we used earlier, eqs.(3.26) and (3.27), which reflect the degree of credibility of the central bank's announcements. The bank's policy instrument is a one-step Taylor rule, eq.(3.34).

Performance requirements. The central bank desires to keep the inflation and output gap within specified intervals as before, eqs.(3.20) and (3.21). However, in the presence of random shocks, these aspirations are expressed by requiring specified probability, P_{c}, of satisfying the target bounds, eqs.(3.35) and (3.36).

Uncertainty models. We consider two types of uncertainty: in the model coefficients and in the probability density functions (pdf's) of the shocks. The model-coefficient uncertainty is represented with the fractional-error info-gap model that we used earlier, eq.(3.28) on p.47. Regarding the shocks, we consider uncertainty in the shape of their pdf's. The info-gap model of eq.(3.37) allows for the possibility that the tails of the distributions are either much thinner or much fatter than anticipated.

Decision variables. As in section 3.2, we are interested in selecting realistic target bounds ($\pi_{\rm l}$ and $\pi_{\rm u}$ for inflation; $y_{\rm l}$ and $y_{\rm u}$ for output gap), choosing the Taylor coefficients of the interest rate rule, g_π and g_y, and deciding on the level of central bank credibility, κ. The added dimension here—due to the uncertain random shocks—is to evaluate these decisions in light of the robustness of the probabilities of success.

Robustness functions. The robustness functions, eqs.(3.39) and (3.40), combine the system model, performance requirements and uncertainty models. They provide the basis for decisions since they depend on all the quantities of interest.

3.3.3 Dynamics and Expectations

We now restore the additive shock terms to the Clarida, Galí and Gertler (1999) model which were absent from eqs.(3.17) and (3.18) on p.45. As before in eq.(3.19), a no-lag Taylor rule is used to set interest rates:

$$\pi_{t+1} = \lambda y_t + \beta \mathrm{E}_t \pi_{t+1} + \varepsilon_{\pi t} \tag{3.32}$$
$$y_{t+1} = -\phi(i_t - \mathrm{E}_t \pi_{t+1}) + \mathrm{E}_t y_{t+1} + \varepsilon_{yt} \tag{3.33}$$
$$i_t = g_\pi \pi_t + g_y y_t \tag{3.34}$$

$\varepsilon_{\pi t}$ and ε_{yt} are thought to be zero-mean i.i.d. random variables. However, it is recognized that the processes which produce these shocks may themselves contain considerable surprises. In particular, the shapes of the probability density functions (pdf's) of $\varepsilon_{\pi t}$ and ε_{yt} are uncertain and may contain much fatter or thinner tails than anticipated.

The central bank wants the future values of inflation and output gap to fall within specified intervals, as stated in eqs.(3.20) and (3.21) on p.46. However, since the shocks are random, the bank expresses its aspirations in terms of the probability that the target bounds will be satisfied. We will consider the robustness of these probabilities because the pdf's themselves are uncertain.

Let x denote either π or y. The bank requires that the probabilities that x obeys its lower- and upper-target bounds at period θ in the future, be no less than a critical value, $P_{\rm c}$:

$$\mathrm{Prob}(x_\theta \ge x_{\rm l}|p,c) \ \ge \ P_{\rm c} \tag{3.35}$$

$$\mathrm{Prob}(x_\theta \le x_{\rm u}|p,c) \ \ge \ P_{\rm c} \tag{3.36}$$

These probabilities depend on the pdf's of the inflation and output shocks, $p = [p_\pi(\varepsilon_{\pi t}), p_y(\varepsilon_{yt})]$, and on the model coefficients, $c = (\lambda, \beta, \phi)$, all of which are uncertain.

The public forms expectations about future inflation and output gap. We will use the model of partial credibility of the central bank, eqs.(3.26) and (3.27) on p.47.

3.3.4 Uncertainty and Robustness

We now confront two very different info-gap uncertainty models, one for the coefficients of the macro-economic model and one for the pdf's of the shocks.

Model-coefficient uncertainty. The 3 coefficients of the economic model, eqs.(3.32) and (3.33), are denoted with the vector $c = (\phi, \lambda, \beta)$. The best estimates and standard errors of these coefficients are $\widetilde{c} = (\widetilde{\phi}, \widetilde{\lambda}, \widetilde{\beta})$ and $s = (s_\phi, s_\lambda, s_\beta)$. We use the info-gap model of eq.(3.28) to represent the uncertainty in these coefficients. The horizon of uncertainty, h, represents the unknown fractional error in these coefficients.

Uncertainty in the shock pdf's. Let x denote either π or y. The anticipated or estimated distribution of ε_{xt} is the zero-mean normal distribution with variance σ_x^2, and is denoted $\widetilde{p}_x(\varepsilon_{xt})$. The actual pdf of ε_{xt} is an uncertain distribution whose tails may be much fatter or thinner than anticipated. We will use the following info-gap model to represent uncertainty in $p_x(\varepsilon_{xt})$:

$$\mathcal{U}_p(h_p) = \left\{ p_\pi, p_y : \begin{array}{rcl} p_x(\varepsilon_{xt}) & \ge & 0, \ \displaystyle\int_{-\infty}^{\infty} p_x(\varepsilon_{xt})\,\mathrm{d}\varepsilon_{xt} = 1, \\ p_x(\varepsilon_{xt}) & = & \nu \widetilde{p}_x(\varepsilon_{xt}), \ \text{for } |\varepsilon_{xt}| \le \varepsilon_{\star x} \\ p_x(\varepsilon_{xt}) & \le & \dfrac{h_p}{\varepsilon_{xt}^2}, \ \text{for } |\varepsilon_{xt}| > \varepsilon_{\star x} \end{array} \right\}, \quad h_p \ge 0 \tag{3.37}$$

We are using a different horizon of uncertainty, h_p, for this info-gap model than for eq.(3.28), to reflect that these are very different and unrelated uncertainties.

The first line of eq.(3.37) states the $p_x(\varepsilon_{xt})$ is a mathematically legitimate pdf: non-negative and normalized. The second line states that $p_x(\varepsilon_{xt})$ is proportional to the anticipated pdf for ε_{xt} between $-\varepsilon_{\star x}$ and $+\varepsilon_{\star x}$, where ν is a constant which is determined by the normalization requirement, and differs between different realizations of $p_x(\varepsilon_{xt})$. $\varepsilon_{\star x}$ is a positive constant and is chosen by the analyst so that the uncertain distortion of the distribution appears far out on the tails of $\widetilde{p}_x(\varepsilon_{xt})$, typically at 3 or 4 times σ_x.[18]

Now consider the third line, which applies to the far tails of the pdf. The function $1/\varepsilon_{xt}^2$ decays much more slowly than the anticipated pdf, which is normal and decays in proportion to $\mathrm{e}^{-\varepsilon_{xt}^2/2\sigma_x^2}$. Thus the third line states that the tails of the distribution may decay rapidly or even vanish, or they may decay much more slowly than the exponential decay of the anticipated normal distribution.

The info-gap model of eq.(3.37) allows the pdf to be a mixture of the estimated distribution, $\widetilde{p}_x(\varepsilon_{xt})$, with a distribution whose far tails are uncertain and much different from what is anticipated. To get a feeling for the impact of the heavy tails allowed by this info-gap model, consider the following pdf:

$$p_2(\varepsilon_{xt}) = \left\{ \begin{array}{ll} 0, & |\varepsilon_{xt}| \le \varepsilon_{\star x} \\ \dfrac{\varepsilon_{\star x}}{2\varepsilon_{xt}^2}, & |\varepsilon_{xt}| > \varepsilon_{\star x} \end{array} \right. \tag{3.38}$$

This is a normalized, zero-mean distribution whose tails decay slowly enough so that its variance is infinite! Any sample from this distribution will of course have a finite sample variance, but the population variance is unbounded. $p_2(\varepsilon_{xt})$ is a heavy-tailed distribution which, when mixed with any other distribution, distorts only the far tails. All the pdf's in eq.(3.37) are normalized, but many of the pdf's have infinite variance due to fat far tails.

Robustness functions. The public observes inflation and output gap (π_i, y_i) for periods $i = 0, \ldots, t$, and forms expectations with some level of confidence, κ, in the central bank.

In the info-gap model of eq.(3.37) we are using a different horizon of uncertainty, h_p, than for the model-coefficient uncertainty in eq.(3.28). This will cause the robustness function to be a surface rather than a line.

At any specified horizon of uncertainty, h_p, in the pdf's of the shocks, the robustness to model uncertainty is the greatest horizon

[18] We could consider uncertainty in $\varepsilon_{\star x}$, though we will not pursue that here.

of uncertainty in the model, h, up to which we are sure to satisfy the probabilistic outcome requirements at period θ, for all realizations of $c \in \mathcal{U}(h)$ and $p \in \mathcal{U}_p(h_p)$. Let x denote either π or y. The lower-target and upper-target robustness functions for x are:

$$\widehat{h}_{\mathrm{l}x}(h_p) = \max\left\{ h : \left(\min_{\substack{c\in\mathcal{U}(h) \\ p\in\mathcal{U}_p(h_p)}} \mathrm{Prob}(x_\theta \geq x_\mathrm{l} | p, c) \right) \geq P_\mathrm{c} \right\} \quad (3.39)$$

$$\widehat{h}_{\mathrm{u}x}(h_p) = \max\left\{ h : \left(\min_{\substack{c\in\mathcal{U}(h) \\ p\in\mathcal{U}_p(h_p)}} \mathrm{Prob}(x_\theta \leq x_\mathrm{u} | p, c) \right) \geq P_\mathrm{c} \right\} \quad (3.40)$$

$\widehat{h}_{\mathrm{l}x}(h_p)$ is the robustness of the lower-target bound to model uncertainty, when the horizon of pdf uncertainty equals h_p. This function will decrease monotonically as h_p increases. Consequently, this can also be interpreted as the robustness to pdf uncertainty. Specifically, the robustness to pdf uncertainty equals h_p when the model uncertainty equals $\widehat{h}_{\mathrm{l}x}(h_p)$. We can also think of $\widehat{h}_{\mathrm{l}x}(h_p)$ as a surface plotted over the 2-dimensional plane of P_c vs. h_p.

The upper-target robustness, $\widehat{h}_{\mathrm{u}x}$, has the analogous dual interpretation.

3.3.5 Policy Exploration

We now begin our policy exploration of the robustness functions, eqs.(3.39) and (3.40), for 1 period in the future, so $\theta = t + 1$. The inverses of these robustnesses are derived in appendix 3.8.

Inflation robustness. Fig. 3.19 shows lower- and upper-target robustnesses for inflation.[19] The vertical axis is the robustness to uncertainty in the model parameters, $\widehat{h}_{\mathrm{l}\pi}$ or $\widehat{h}_{\mathrm{u}\pi}$, at uncertainty $h_p = 0.5$ in the pdf's of the shocks. This value of h_p entails the potential for very much heavier tails than anticipated, though these tails first appear far from the anticipated mean.[20] The horizontal axis is the probability, P_c, that the target bound will be obeyed. The negative

[19] The parameters for all calculations in this section, unless indicated otherwise, are $\sigma_\pi = 1$, $\sigma_y = 3$, $\varepsilon_{\star\pi} = 3$, $\varepsilon_{\star y} = 9$, $\pi_\mathrm{l} = 1$, $\pi_\mathrm{u} = 3$, $y_\mathrm{l} = 0$ and $y_\mathrm{u} = 4$. Other data appear in footnote 10 on p.49.

[20] For instance, for $\varepsilon_{\star\pi} = 3$ and $\sigma_\pi = 1$, the weight of the potentially heaviest tail is $\int_{\varepsilon_{\star\pi}}^{\infty} h_p/\varepsilon_{\pi t}^2 \,\mathrm{d}t = h_p/\varepsilon_{\star\pi} \approx 0.17$. The weight of the anticipated tail is $1 - \Phi(\varepsilon_{\star\pi}/\sigma_\pi) \approx 0.0013$.

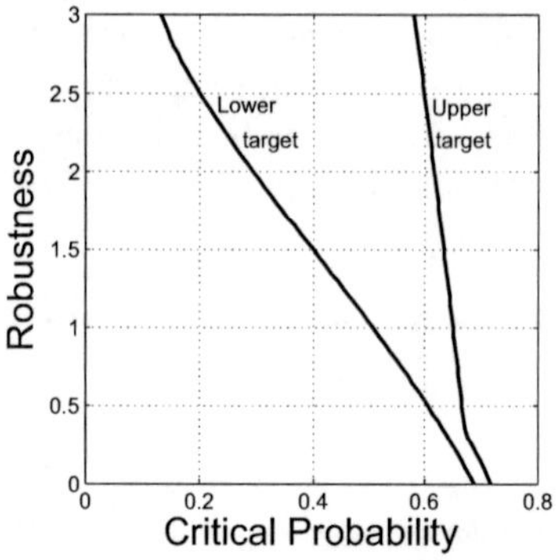

Figure 3.19: Lower- and upper-target robustness for inflation. $\kappa = 0.8$.

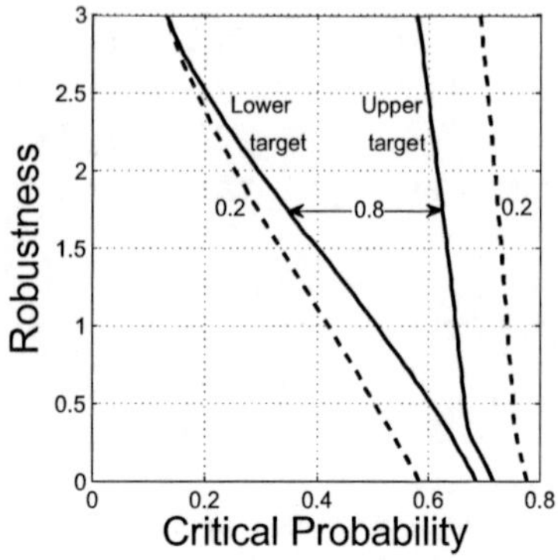

Figure 3.20: Lower- and upper-target robustness for inflation. $\kappa = 0.2$ and 0.8.

slopes express the usual trade-off between robustness-to-uncertainty and performance: high probability of obeying the target entails low robustness to uncertainty.

The upper-target robustness curve is quite steep, implying a low performance-cost for robustness: $\widehat{h}_{\mathrm{u}\pi}$ can be increased significantly without substantially reducing P_{c}. The estimated probability of obeying the upper target is 0.72, at which $\widehat{h}_{\mathrm{u}\pi} = 0$. At $\widehat{h}_{\mathrm{u}\pi} = 2$ the probability has fallen to 0.62, not a large price to pay for significant immunity to uncertainty. The "kink" in the upper-target curve results from hitting the upper constraint on β in the info-gap model.

The lower-target robustness curve is less steep, so it has greater performance-cost for robustness. The estimated probability of obeying the lower target is 0.69, at which $\widehat{h}_{\mathrm{l}\pi} = 0$. However, at $\widehat{h}_{\mathrm{l}\pi} = 2$ the probability has fallen to 0.29, quite a large price to pay for robustness.

Inflation robustness: effect of credibility. Fig. 3.20 shows lower- and upper-target robustness for inflation for two different levels of credibility of the central bank. The solid curves are reproduced from fig. 3.19, with $\kappa = 0.8$ corresponding to high credibility. The dashed curves have $\kappa = 0.2$, representing low credibility.

The interesting thing to note in fig. 3.20 is the opposite impact of credibility on lower- and upper-target inflation. The lower-target robustness is *reduced* when the credibility goes down, while the upper-target robustness in *enhanced* by a reduction in credibility. The effect on upper-target robustness is enormous because the upper-target curves are so steep.

The explanation resides in the specific changes of the public's expectations. With high credibility ($\kappa = 0.8$) the expectation for inflation at the next period is $E_t\pi_{t+1} = 1.74$. At low credibility ($\kappa = 0.2$) the expectation is for lower inflation: $E_t\pi_{t+1} = 1.29$. The lower expected inflation in fact reduces the inflation in the next period, as we see in eq.(3.32), moving the value away from (and further below) the upper target value of $\pi_u = 3$. However, this moves the inflation towards (or even below) the lower target value of $\pi_l = 1$.

The generalization is that upper-target and lower-target aspirations may conflict with one another. A policy change which strengthens one will tend to weaken the other. We encountered a similar policy conflict earlier, on p.38. The utility of the quantitative analysis, such as in fig. 3.20, is in evaluating this conflict. In the specific configuration which we are considering, enhancing the bank's credibility is to the detriment of the upper-target robustness. However, the upper-target robustness is already large and remains large. The enhanced credibility bolsters the less robust lower-target robustness, and therefore may be considered worth the loss of upper-target robustness. The judgment depends on the specific robustness values which are revealed by the quantitative analysis and on the risk-sensitivity of the decision maker.

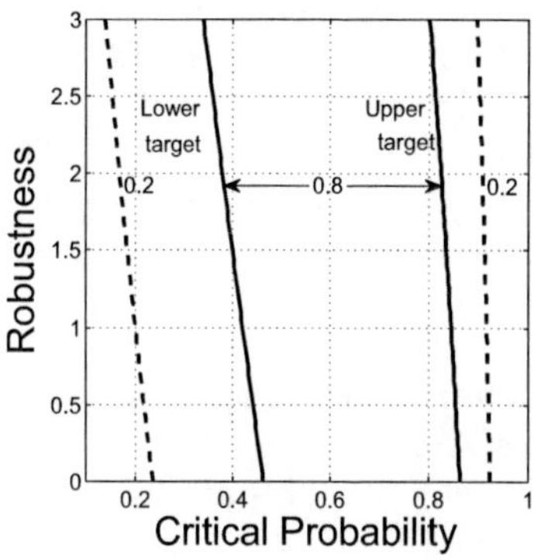

Figure 3.21: Lower- and upper-target robustness for output gap. $\kappa = 0.2$ and 0.8. $(g_\pi, g_y) = (1.5, 0.5)$.

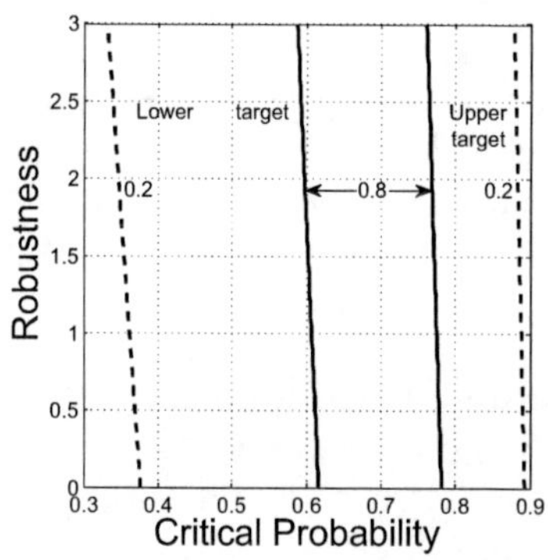

Figure 3.22: Lower- and upper-target robustness for output gap. $\kappa = 0.2$ and 0.8. $(g_\pi, g_y) = (0.5, 0.5)$.

Output gap robustness. Fig. 3.21 shows lower- and upper-target robustness curves for the output gap, at both low credibility ($\kappa = 0.2$) and high credibility ($\kappa = 0.8$). This is the output-gap analog of fig. 3.20 for inflation. A similar disposition of the curves is observed in both cases: lower-target robustness is below the upper-target robustness, and lower and upper aspirations conflict when considering credibility. However, an important difference is that the lower-target robustness is quite a bit lower in the output-gap case. In fact, the lower-target curves sprout off the P_c axis at quite low values of probability of obeying the target. The lower-target robustness is enhanced substantially by raising the bank's credibility: the lower-target curve shifts considerably to the right. Nonetheless the actual robustness is still small or even zero for values of P_c which might reasonably be deemed necessary.

The situation can be ameliorated by altering the bank's interest rate. A smaller Taylor coefficient on inflation, g_π, will reduce the interest rate, eq.(3.34), and thereby augment the output gap, eq.(3.33). This will tend to enhance the lower-target robustness for output gap while, as we have already seen, also tend to reduce the upper-target robustness for output gap. This effect is seen in fig. 3.22, which is the same as fig. 3.21 except for the change in g_π. The upper-target robustness is indeed reduced (though it is still large), and the impact of credibility is stronger than before. However, the lower-target robustness at high credibility has substantial robustness at probabilities of success which are at least approaching what one might require.

Eq.(3.32) shows that the inflation one period in the future is not influenced by the bank's interest rate. Thus the robustness curves for inflation, fig. 3.20, are unaffected by this change in the Taylor coefficients, since we are considering only one period in the future.

Output gap: enhancing lower-target robustness. Returning to fig. 3.21 we note that the lower-target robustness is positive only for unacceptably low probability of satisfying the target. For instance, with credibility of $\kappa = 0.8$, the robustness is $\widehat{h}_{ly} = 1.5$ at 40% probability, which is not very satisfactory.

This can be ameliorated by broadening the output gap target range. As indicated in footnote 19 on p.61, the lower and upper target bounds for the output gap are $y_l = 0$ and $y_u = 4$ in the calculations up to now. Fig. 3.23 shows the robustness of the lower-target bound, $\widehat{h}_{ly}$, for three values of the lower target. The curve for $y_l = 0$ is reproduced from fig. 3.21. We see that the robustness curve shifts to the right as y_l is reduced, reflecting substantial improvement in robustness.

Fig. 3.24 shows the upper-target robustness, $\widehat{h}_{uy}$, for the same lower-target bounds. The curve for $y_l = 0$ is reproduced from fig. 3.22.

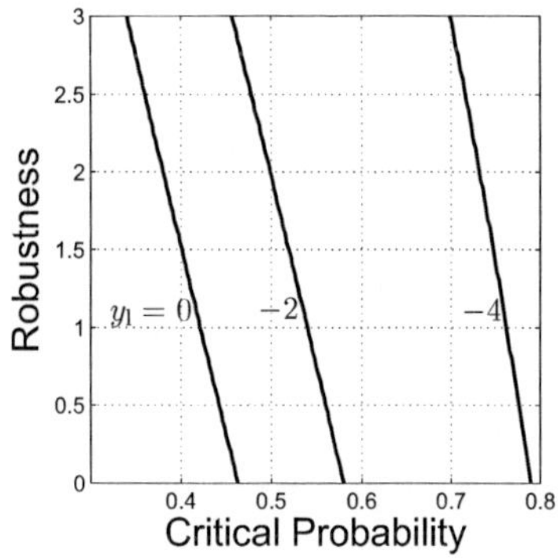

Figure 3.23: Lower-target robustness for output gap with several values of y_l. $\kappa = 0.8$. $(g_\pi, g_y) = (1.5, 0.5)$.

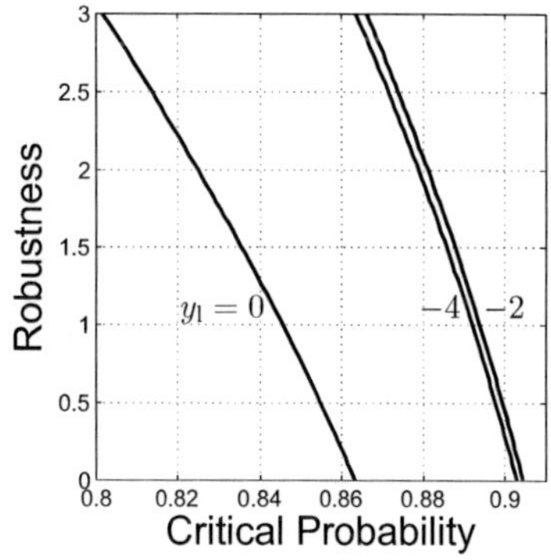

Figure 3.24: Upper-target robustness for output gap with several values of y_l. $\kappa = 0.8$. $(g_\pi, g_y) = (1.5, 0.5)$.

The upper-target robustness is influenced by the lower-target bound since the robustness depends on the expectations which depend on the mid-point of the upper and lower targets. The upper-target robustness improves as y_l changes from 0 to -2. Further reduction of y_l to -4 causes a slight deterioration of the robustness.[21] Nonetheless, the upper-target robustness is still large at quite acceptable values of the probability of success. The choice of $y_l = -4$ would seem to provide acceptable lower- and upper-target robustness.

3.4 Credibility and Interacting Agents

The interaction between agents is an important element in economic dynamics. Individuals and organizations revise their expectations based both on observing economic outcomes and on learning the opinions of other agents. In this section we illustrate an info-gap analysis of uncertainty in the mechanism by which agents revise their beliefs

[21] The explanation is as follows. The expectation coefficient ψ_y for credible expectations (see eq.(3.23) on p.46) is larger with $y_l = -2$ than with $y_l = -4$. Given the algebraic signs of the terms involved, this causes slightly smaller expected output gap at $y_l = -2$ than at $y_l = -4$, contrary to what one would expect given the larger midpoint of the target range with $y_l = -2$. This results in a slightly more negative maximum model-based anticipation of the output gap (eq.(3.96), p.86), with $y_l = -2$. The result is slight reduction in robustness in going from $y_l = -2$ to $y_l = -4$.

about the credibility of the central bank's goals. There are many worthy models of interaction between economic agents from which to choose (Miller and Page, 2007), and the central bank may legitimately be uncertain about which models apply to the various sectors. We will demonstrate an info-gap policy analysis given uncertainty in the updating mechanisms and uncertainty in the economic model.

We consider a heterogenous population of economic sectors such as households, organized labor, small business, manufacturers, service industry, finance, government, etc. Each sector observes many things at the beginning of each period, including events which are idiosyncratic to the sector, as well as information which is common knowledge, such as previous values of inflation and output gap and the central bank's announced target bounds. Some sectors will also learn the beliefs of some other sectors about the credibility of the bank's announcement. With all this information, each sector updates its own beliefs about central bank credibility. These beliefs are aggregated and influence the inflation and output gap at the end of the period.

We will assume that the central bank knows the initial beliefs of the sectors but is uncertain about the updating mechanisms used by the various sectors. The bank is also uncertain about the model of the economy. The central bank must choose the interest rate and target bounds for inflation and output gap in light of these uncertainties. We use a modification of the Clarida-Galí-Gertler (1999) model, which is subject to random shocks.

3.4.1 Policy Preview

We observe the usual trade-off between robustness against uncertainty and probability of obeying a desired bound on inflation or output gap: greater robustness is obtained only at the cost of lower probability of success. The robustness is zero at the anticipated probability. Furthermore, policy can influence the cost of robustness: how much the probability of success must be reduced in exchange for an increase in robustness depends on choices which the central bank makes.

When the public believes that the bank's announced targets are credible, the bank can use this credibility to augment the reliability of achieving its goals. The bank can do this by influencing public expectations about inflation and output gap through its announced target values. This policy instrument can greatly increase the robustness to uncertainty, as manifested in large shifts in the robustness curve.

This policy instrument is not available when the bank has low credibility. One strategy which may enhance credibility is to slightly reduce expectations, thereby increasing success and building up the public's belief in the bank's ability to achieve its goals. Our analysis shows that in some situations very small reductions in target requirements can greatly enhance the robustness of attaining these targets.

However, even when the bank is credible, the impact of announced targets on outcomes and on robustness to uncertainty is not always intuitively obvious. On the one hand, announced targets will tend to focus public expectations in a direction which the bank desires. On the other hand, a countervailing impact can arise due to the mechanism by which these expectations are formed from historical data. Only a quantitative analysis of robustness can resolve this ambiguity and assist in the successful exploitation of the bank's credibility.

The interest rate very strongly influences both the anticipated probability of achieving the bank's targets and the robustness to uncertainty. However, the impact of the interest rate is complicated by the possible countervailing impacts of the bank's announced targets and the mechanism of expectation formation. We see this in the intersection between robustness curves corresponding to different interest rates. Once again, quantitative analysis assists in understanding the interactions between credibility, robustness, interest rates and target bounds.

3.4.2 Operational Preview

System model. The system model has two components: the economic dynamics in eqs.(3.32)–(3.34) on p.58, and the expectation-formation mechanism of the different sectors and their aggregation, eqs.(3.45)–(3.48).

Performance requirements. The central bank desires to keep inflation and output gap within specified bounds, eqs.(3.41) and (3.42), which it announces to the public. The bank quantifies the success of achieving these requirements in terms of the probability of obeying the target bounds, eqs.(3.43) and (3.44), since the economy is subject to random shocks.

Uncertainty models. In addition to the random shocks, the central bank is uncertain both about the coefficients of the economic model, represented by the info-gap model in eq.(3.28) on p.47, and about the mechanisms by which the sectors revise their beliefs in the bank's credibility, eq.(3.49).

Decision variables. The bank has two types of decision variables. The interest rate, as determined by the Taylor coefficients, has a direct impact on the economy. If the public believes that the bank's announced targets are credible, then the bank can use its announcements to influence the public's expectations about inflation and output gap, which in turn influence the economy.

Robustness functions. The lower- and upper-target bounds for the two state variables—inflation and output gap—generate four robustness functions. These robustness functions underlie the policy analysis because they depend on the decision variables.

3.4.3 Dynamics and Expectations

Dynamics. We continue with the Clarida, Galí and Gertler (1999) model used in section 3.3, eqs.(3.32) and (3.33), together with the Taylor rule, eq.(3.34), on p.58.

Likewise, as in section 3.3, the central bank requires satisfactory probability that inflation and output gap will fall within specified target bounds. The bank announces its intention to use the interest rate in attempting to maintain output gap and inflation within the following intervals:

$$\pi_{\mathrm{l}} \leq \pi_t \leq \pi_{\mathrm{u}} \tag{3.41}$$

$$y_{\mathrm{l}} \leq y_t \leq y_{\mathrm{u}} \tag{3.42}$$

The aspirations of the bank are that the probability of satisfying each of these four bounds be no less than a critical value, P_{c}. Let "x" denote either "π" or "y". The lower-target and upper-target probabilistic requirements for period t are:

$$\mathrm{Prob}(x_t \geq x_{\mathrm{l}}) \geq P_{\mathrm{c}} \tag{3.43}$$

$$\mathrm{Prob}(x_t \leq x_{\mathrm{u}}) \geq P_{\mathrm{c}} \tag{3.44}$$

Expectations. We consider a population of N distinct sectors. Each sector forms expectations about future inflation and output gap. These expectations are updated after observing economic outcomes, and depend on that sector's belief about central bank credibility. Furthermore, each sector's beliefs about credibility are also updated based on economic outcomes and on the beliefs of some of the other sectors, and perhaps also based on information known only to the sector.

At the start of period t the nth sector forms expectations about inflation and output gap by balancing between belief in the central bank's ability to achieve its goals, and adaptation to previous economic outcomes. Like eqs.(3.26) and (3.27) on p.47, the nth sector's expectations for period $t+1$ are:

$$\mathrm{E}_t^n \pi_{t+1} = \kappa_t^n[\pi_t - \psi_\pi(\pi_t - \pi_\mathrm{m})] + (1-\kappa_t^n)b'\pi_{t(K)} \quad (3.45)$$
$$\mathrm{E}_t^n y_{t+1} = \kappa_t^n[y_t - \psi_y(y_t - y_\mathrm{m})] + (1-\kappa_t^n)a'y_{t(J)} \quad (3.46)$$

κ_t^n is the nth sector's degree of belief in the central bank's credibility. Its value is between 0 and 1.

The expectations used in the economic model, eqs.(3.32) and (3.33), are population averages of the expectations of the N sectors:

$$\mathrm{E}_t\pi_{t+1} = \frac{1}{N}\sum_{n=1}^{N}\mathrm{E}_t^n\pi_{t+1} \quad (3.47)$$
$$\mathrm{E}_t y_{t+1} = \frac{1}{N}\sum_{n=1}^{N}\mathrm{E}_t^n y_{t+1} \quad (3.48)$$

The coefficients ψ_π and ψ_y in eqs.(3.45) and (3.46) are based on complete credibility, while the coefficient vectors b and a are based on complete lack of credibility. ψ_π, ψ_y, b and a are updated at the start of each period based on previous values of inflation and output gap, as described in appendix 3.7. All sectors observe the same economic outcomes and thus use the same values of these coefficients. The expectations differ between sectors because of their different beliefs about central bank credibility.

What distinguishes one sector from another is each sector's belief about the central bank's credibility. The nth sector updates its belief at the beginning of the period after observing the new outcomes, π_t and y_t together with knowing earlier outcomes, and learning the beliefs of some of the other sectors. The distribution of beliefs at the start of period t, κ_{t-1}^n for $n = 1, \ldots, N$, is known to the central bank. However, the bank is uncertain about how sectors update their beliefs to the values κ_t^n.

Summary of the sequence of events in a single period.

1. The central bank's target bounds, π_l, π_u, y_l and y_u, are known by all sectors.

2. At the start of period t:

   (a) Each sector has a belief, κ_{t-1}^n, for $n = 1, \ldots, N$, about central bank credibility. These beliefs are known to the central bank.

   (b) Each sector knows the values of $\pi_t, \pi_{t-1}, \ldots$ and $y_t, y_{t-1}, \ldots$.

   (c) Each sector observes the beliefs of some of the other sectors.

   (d) Each sector updates its beliefs to values κ_t^n. The central bank is uncertain about the updated values.

   (e) The expectation coefficients ψ_π, ψ_y, b and a are calculated by each sector based on the knowledge in steps 1 and 2b, as described in appendix 3.7. Each sector obtains the same expectation coefficients.

   (f) Each sector forms expectations for inflation and output gap at period $t+1$ according to eqs.(3.45) and (3.46).

   (g) The expectations are aggregated by eqs.(3.47) and (3.48).

   (h) The central bank implements the interest rate i_t with eq.(3.34).

   (i) Inflation and output shocks $\varepsilon_{\pi t}$ and ε_{yt} are zero-mean gaussian random variables with variances σ_π^2 and σ_y^2.

3. Inflation π_{t+1} and output gap y_{t+1} are calculated with eqs.(3.32) and (3.33) and are observed by all sectors.

3.4.4 Uncertainty and Robustness

Uncertainty. The central bank is uncertain about the coefficients of the macro-economic model, ϕ, λ and β, and about how the sectors update their beliefs concerning central bank credibility.

We use the fractional-error info-gap model of eq.(3.28) on p.47, $\mathcal{U}(h)$, to represent uncertainty in the macro-economic model coefficients.

The central bank knows the belief, κ_{t-1}^n, of each sector at the start of period t. The bank presumes that beliefs will not change substantially in a single period, but recognizes that this is not always true. However, the bank is uncertain about how the different sectors update their beliefs. Furthermore, the severity of this uncertainty differs between sectors. Specifically, the bank is more confident about the stability of the beliefs of sectors whose confidence in the bank is large. We use a fractional-error model to represent the bank's uncertainty about the updated credibilities, κ_t^n:

$$\mathcal{U}_\kappa(h) = \{ \kappa_t^n : \kappa_t^n \in [0,1], |\kappa_t^n - \kappa_{t-1}^n| \le v_n h, \quad n = 1, \ldots, N \}, \quad h \ge 0 \quad (3.49)$$

The "uncertainty weights" v_n reflect the relative stability of different sectors. In our example we calculate these uncertainty weights as follows:

$$v_n = \frac{1}{1 + \kappa_{t-1}^n} \quad (3.50)$$

Robustness. We define 4 different robustness functions, one for each variable, inflation or output gap, and for each of the two probabilistic performance requirements, eq.(3.43) and (3.44). The robustness for a specified variable at period t is the greatest horizon of uncertainty, h, up to which we are sure to satisfy the outcome requirement for that period, for all realizations of c in $\mathcal{U}(h)$ and all realizations of κ_t^n in $\mathcal{U}_\kappa(h)$. Let "x" denote either "π" or "y". We define the lower-target and upper-target robustness functions as:

$$\widehat{h}_{\mathrm{l}x}(t) = \max \left\{ h : \left(\min_{\substack{c \in \mathcal{U}(h) \\ \kappa_t^n \in \mathcal{U}_\kappa(h)}} \mathrm{Prob}(x_t \ge x_{\mathrm{l}}) \right) \ge P_{\mathrm{c}} \right\} \quad (3.51)$$

$$\widehat{h}_{\mathrm{u}x}(t) = \max \left\{ h : \left(\min_{\substack{c \in \mathcal{U}(h) \\ \kappa_t^n \in \mathcal{U}_\kappa(h)}} \mathrm{Prob}(x_t \le x_{\mathrm{u}}) \right) \ge P_{\mathrm{c}} \right\} \quad (3.52)$$

Let π_{t+1}^{e} and y_{t+1}^{e} denote the expected inflation and output gap at the end of period t based on the aggregated expectations of the sectors (step 2g) and the bank's interest rate (step 2h) and eqs.(3.32) and (3.33) on p.58 before the shocks are applied. Since the shocks are zero-mean random gaussian variables, the probabilities in eqs.(3.51) and (3.52) are:

$$\mathrm{Prob}(x_t \ge x_{\mathrm{l}}) = 1 - \Phi\left(\frac{x_{\mathrm{l}} - x_{t+1}^{\mathrm{e}}}{\sigma_x} \right) \quad (3.53)$$

$$\mathrm{Prob}(x_t \le x_{\mathrm{u}}) = \Phi\left(\frac{x_{\mathrm{u}} - x_{t+1}^{\mathrm{e}}}{\sigma_x} \right) \quad (3.54)$$

where $\Phi(\cdot)$ is the cumulative distribution function of the standard normal variable.

3.4.5 Policy Exploration

The central bank must choose the lower- and upper-targets for inflation and output gap, and the interest rate as determined by the Taylor coefficients. We now explore the policy implications of uncertainty in the economic model and in the updating of credibility. We consider a single period and 7 economic sectors whose initial credibility values are $\kappa_{t-1}^n = 0.5, 0.3, 0.3, 0.9, 0.9, 0.7$ and 0.9 for $n = 1, \ldots, 7$. The target values and Taylor coefficients, unless indicated otherwise, are $\pi_l = 1$, $\pi_u = 3$, $y_l = -2$ and $y_u = 2$ and $(g_\pi, g_y) = (1.5, 0.5)$. The estimated model coefficients and prior inflation and output data are given in footnote 10 on p.49. The standard deviations of the inflation and output-gap shocks are $\sigma_\pi = 0.5$ and $\sigma_y = 1$.

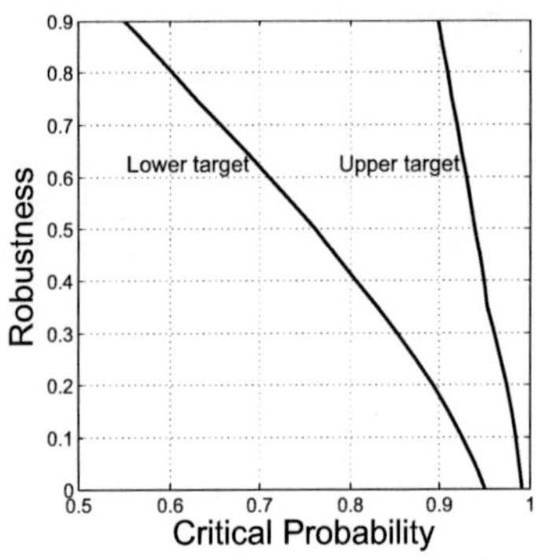

Figure 3.25: Lower- and upper target robustness for inflation.

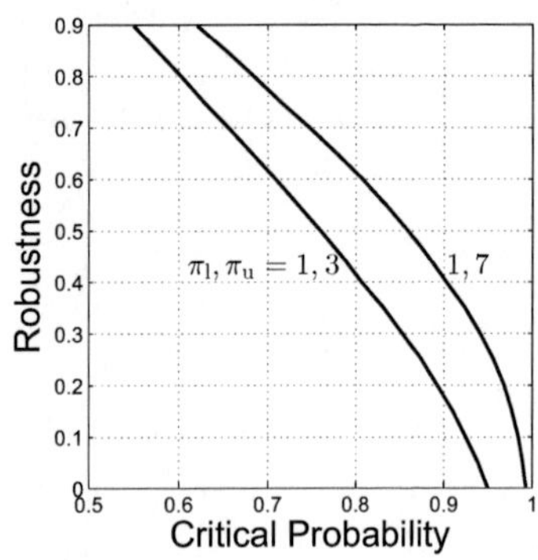

Figure 3.26: Lower-target robustness for inflation with two different values of π_u.

Zeroing and trade-off. Fig. 3.25 shows lower- and upper-target robustness curves for inflation. We observe the usual zeroing and trade-off properties. The robustness is zero for obtaining the estimated probability of obeying either target. Positive robustness is obtained only at lower probability of success. We also note that the cost of robustness is substantially higher for the lower-target robustness, as expressed by its more gradual slope. For instance, in fig. 3.25 we see that, for the lower-target bound, the robustness increases from 0 to 0.5 at the cost of reducing the probability of obeying this bound from 0.95 to 0.76. In contrast, for the upper-target bound, the robustness increases from 0 to 0.5 while the probability of success decreases from 0.99 to 0.94.

Credibility as a policy instrument. Suppose the central bank is worried about the prospect of a recession and is concerned primarily to keep the inflation above the lower target; the upper-target bound is less pressing. The lower-target robustness in fig. 3.25 is not large for high probabilities of success, and the central bank would like to shift the lower-target robustness curve to the right. In the present example most of the sectors believe in moderate or high credibility of the central bank.

It is widely recognized that central banks can use announcements to influence public expectations, though these announcements can do harm if they focus public expectations away from the true state of the economy (Morris and Shin, 2002; Demertzis and Viegi, 2008). It is thus important that the central bank can use its credibility to enhance its robustness against uncertainty, and thus enhance its confidence for attaining its lower-target goal for inflation despite the bank's uncertainty both about the state of the economy and about the mechanisms by which economic sectors revise their beliefs.

The bank can influence expectation formation by announcing a higher value for the upper-target bound, π_u. Since sectors form their inflation expectations in part by adapting to the mid-point of the bank's announced target range (π_m in eq.(3.45)), an augmented π_u will tend to pull expectations upward and enhance the robustness for achieving the lower-target bound.[22] We are interested specifically in how such announcements influence the robustness to uncertainty.

Fig. 3.26 illustrates this effect by showing lower-target robustness curves for two different choices of the upper-target inflation bound. (The lower curve is reproduced from fig. 3.25.) Raising π_m by 2 percentage points (which results from raising π_u by 4 points) causes the lower-target robustness curve to shift substantially to the right.

The gain in lower-target robustness by announcing a larger upper-target value works, as seen in fig. 3.26, because most sectors believe in moderate or high credibility of the central bank. This does not work if the credibility of the bank is low, because announcing a large π_u

[22]This argument is valid as far as it goes, but it ignores the fact that a shift in π_m or y_m also shifts the expectation coefficients ψ_π and ψ_y. We will see later that this can counter-balance the tendency mentioned here. Hence a quantitative analysis of robustness is necessary to determine the overall effect of announcing a larger π_u.

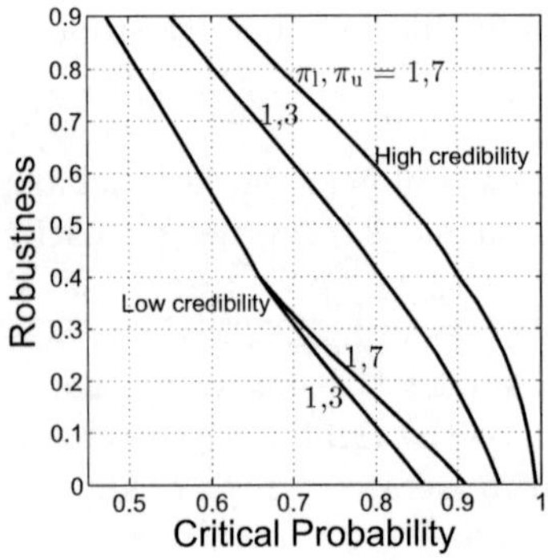

Figure 3.27: Lower-target robustness for inflation at two different levels of credibility and with two different values of π_u.

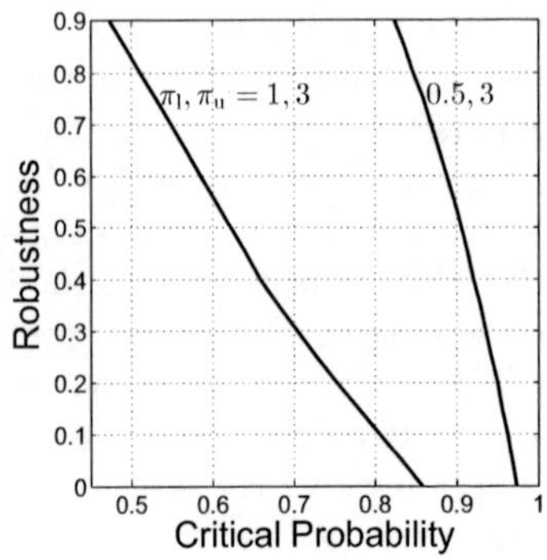

Figure 3.28: Lower-target robustness for inflation with two different values of π_l, and low credibility.

will not substantially alter the public's inflation expectations. This is illustrated in fig. 3.27. The upper two curves are reproduced from fig. 3.26. The lower curves are evaluated with substantially lower initial credibilities: $\kappa_{t-1}^n = 0.2$, 0.1, 0.1, 0.3, 0.3, 0.2 and 0.3 for $n = 1, \ldots, 7$. When the bank has such low credibility in the public's estimation, then the bank's announcements have very little impact on expectation formation, and hence little impact on the success of the bank in achieving its goals. The lower curves show substantially lower robustness, and almost negligible effect of announcing a larger value of π_u.

Building credibility. In a situation of low credibility the bank is not able to directly or immediately influence the public's expectations. This limits the bank's ability to reliably achieve its goals. The bank is therefore motivated to build its credibility over time, and one way to do this is to relax its goals so as to enhance its success, and thus enhance its credibility.

Fig. 3.28 shows two lower-target robustness curves at low credibility, using the same values of κ_{t-1}^n as in fig. 3.27. The lower curve is reproduced from fig. 3.27, and the upper curve has the same low values of credibility and a slightly lower value for the lower target bound π_l. We see that the robustness for satisfying this slightly more modest lower target is very substantially enhanced. The robustness curve is shifted strongly to the right, and the cost of robustness is greatly reduced: very large robustness is obtained with only minor reduction in the probability of violating the lower-target bound. This suggests that the bank may be able to strengthen its credibility over a relatively short period of time if it is willing (or able) to slightly relax its lower inflation target.

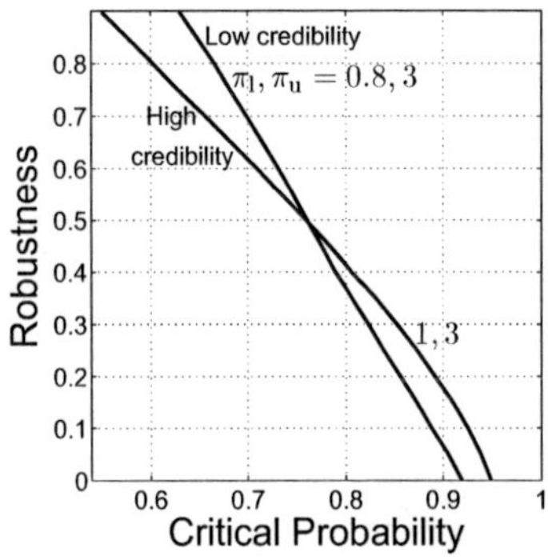

Figure 3.29: Lower-target robustness for inflation at two different levels of credibility and with two different values of π_l.

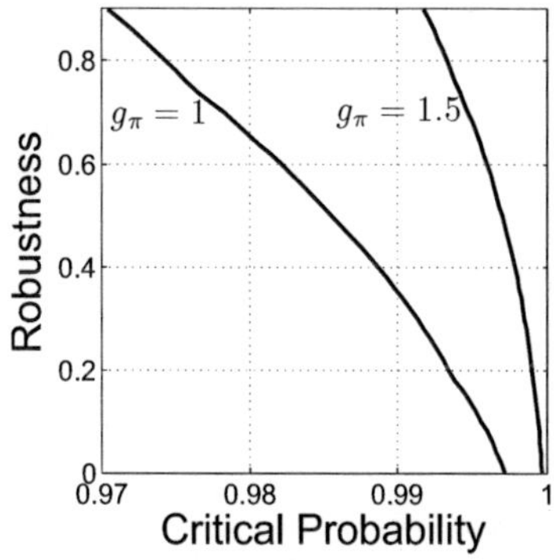

Figure 3.30: Upper-target robustness for output gap with two different values of g_π. $g_y = 0.5$, $y_l = -2$, $y_u = 2$.

Robustness, credibility and target bounds. Fig. 3.29 demonstrates another way to think about the relation between robustness, credibility and target bounds. The "high credibility" curve is reproduced from fig. 3.26, for which the initial sector-averaged credibility is about 0.6. The "low credibility" curve is evaluated with the low initial credibility values (with an average of about 0.2) used in figs. 3.27 and 3.28, but with a lower target for inflation of $\pi_l = 0.8$. These robustness curves are not very different, indicating that these two configurations are similar. In other words, one can roughly say that a decrease in credibility can be compensated for by a decrease in the lower-target bound without losing robustness. Specifically, the decrease in average credibility from 0.6 to 0.2, entails reduction of π_l from 1 to 0.8, while keeping the robustness approximately constant.

Taylor coefficients and interest rate. We now consider the effect of the interest rate—as specified by the Taylor coefficients—on the robustness of the output gap. The initial credibility values are the moderate- and high-confidence values introduced at the beginning of this section.

Fig. 3.30 shows robustness curves for the upper-target bound for two different choices of the Taylor coefficient g_π. A higher interest

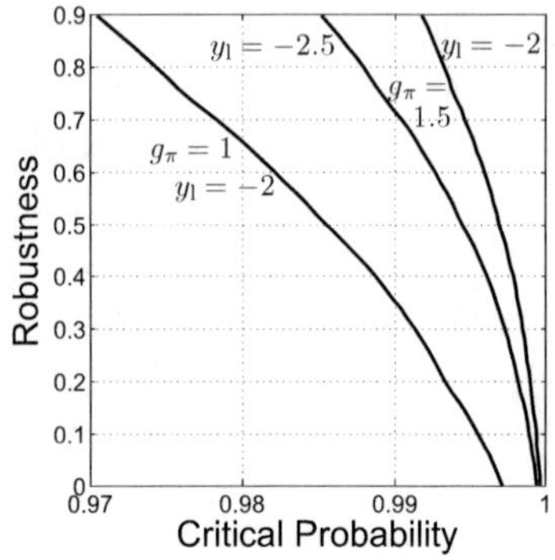

Figure 3.31: Upper-target robustness for output gap for different combinations of g_π and y_l. $g_y = 0.5$, $y_u = 2$.

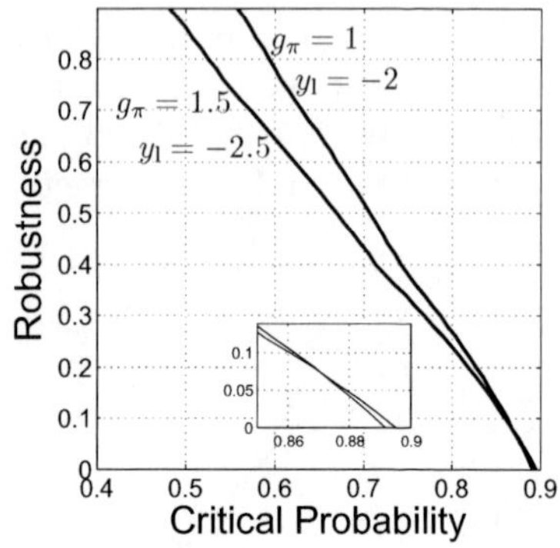

Figure 3.32: Lower-target robustness for output gap for different combinations of g_π and y_l. $g_y = 0.5$, $y_u = 2$.

rate, resulting from $g_\pi = 1.5$, results in lower output gap as seen in eq.(3.33) on p.58. As seen in the figure, this augments the upper-target robustness (the curve is shifted to the right) and reduces the cost of robustness (steeper slope).

However, things are not always so simple. Fig. 3.31 shows an initially counter-intuitive effect. The robustness curves from fig. 3.30 are reproduced here and appear as the upper and lower curves in fig. 3.31. The middle curve has high interest rate like the upper curve (resulting from $g_\pi = 1.5$) but a more negative value of the lower-target bound for the output gap ($y_l = -2.5$). This lower y_l reduces the center-point of the output gap, y_m, around which credible-bank expectations are formed. One would expect that this lower value of y_l would reduce expectations for the output gap, thus reducing the output gap itself and augmenting the upper-target robustness. We used this sort of argument on p.73 in explaining fig. 3.26. However, in fig. 3.31 we see the reverse effect: the robustness is lower with $y_l = -2.5$ than with $y_l = -2$ (while everything else is the same). The explanation, as suggested earlier in footnote 22 on p.73, is that the expectation coefficient ψ_y changes as y_m shifts. In the current case, with the specific output-gap data used, we find that ψ_y is in fact smaller with $y_l = -2.5$ than with $y_l = -2$, causing a *larger* expected output gap in the former case (see eq.(3.46)) and consequently a *lower* value for the upper-target robustness. In short, changing y_m can induce conflicting changes in expectations. Quantitative analysis can identify when such counter-intuitive effects occur and enable the policy maker to take them into account.

Crossing robustness curves. Up to now we have considered the upper-target robustness for output gap. In fig. 3.32 we consider the lower-target robustness for output gap, and use the Taylor coefficients and lower-target bound represented in the middle and lower curves of fig. 3.31.

The robustness curves in fig. 3.32 cross one another very close to the horizontal axis. This means that, at low robustness and high probability of success, the configuration with high interest and more negative lower-target bound, $g_\pi = 1.5$ and $y_l = -2.5$, is preferable over the configuration with lower interest and less negative lower-target bound. However, the intersection of the robustness curves shows that the reverse preference holds at higher robustness and lower probability of success. The intersection of these robustness curves occurs at $P_c = 0.87$ and $\widehat{h}_{ly} = 0.07$.

This crossing of the robustness curves, and the resulting reversal of preference between the two policy configurations, is a manifestation of the conflicting impact of raising the interest rate and reducing the lower-target bound. Greater interest rate reduces the output gap and will tend to reduce the lower-target robustness for output gap. On the other hand, making the lower-target bound, y_l, more negative, augments the lower-target robustness in the present case (though we know that this latter effect is sometimes reversed). These conflicting tendencies result in the reversal of the robustness preference between these two policy configurations. While one can intuitively understand the countervailing impact of these factors, only the quantitative analysis reveals which policy combination is preferred.

3.5 Extensions

Many extensions of the examples considered in this chapter are possible.

Larger macro-economic models. We have used low-dimensional lumped-parameter models of the economy. Larger and more refined macro-economic models can be used. An important question for exploration is whether or not the robustness to uncertainty is enhanced by using more sophisticated and information-intensive models. The extended model is based on additional knowledge and data, not all of which is correct. The added "weight" of the model may drag down the robustness rather than buoying it up.

Models of expectation formation. In section 3.4 we considered the central bank's uncertainty about the public's expectations about future economic variables. We did not consider any specific mechanism for the formation of those expectations. The example can be refined by considering uncertainty in a specific model of expectation formation.

Other monetary policy instruments. We have consider short-term interest rate, and central bank credibility, as instruments for monetary policy. Central banks have other policy instruments such as open market operations, regulatory actions, and control of other interest rates. These are all amenable to info-gap robustness analysis.

Opportuneness. We have only considered the pernicious side of uncertainty, and we have only used the robustness function as a method for protecting against failure. However, uncertainty can be propitious and outcomes can be better than anticipated. The opportuneness function can be used to explore the potential for windfall.

3.6 Appendix: Auto-Regressive Representation of the Rudebusch-Svensson Model

We will show that the Rudebusch-Svensson model, eqs.(3.1)–(3.5), can be represented in the generic form of eq.(3.7) with $J = 6$, and we will derive the matrices $C_0, \ldots, C_6$.

Define the following two matrices:

$$Z_{\mathrm{L}} = \begin{pmatrix} 0 & 0 \\ 1 & 0 \end{pmatrix}, \quad Z_{\mathrm{R}} = \begin{pmatrix} 0 & 0 \\ 0 & 1 \end{pmatrix} \tag{3.55}$$

Eqs.(3.1)–(3.5) can be written as:

$$\begin{aligned} x_{t+1} &= \begin{pmatrix} a_0 & b \\ 0 & c_0 \end{pmatrix} x_t + \begin{pmatrix} a_1 & 0 \\ 0 & c_1 \end{pmatrix} x_{t-1} \\ &\quad + \begin{pmatrix} a_2 & 0 \\ 0 & 0 \end{pmatrix} x_{t-2} + \begin{pmatrix} a_3 & 0 \\ 0 & 0 \end{pmatrix} x_{t-3} \\ &\quad \underbrace{-\frac{d}{4} Z_{\mathrm{L}}(x_t + x_{t-1} + x_{t-2} + x_{t-3})}_{-d\overline{\pi}} \end{aligned}$$

$$\underbrace{+\frac{d}{4}\left(\frac{g_\pi}{4}Z_\text{L}(x_t+x_{t-1}+x_{t-2}+x_{t-3})+g_yZ_\text{R}x_t\right)}_{di_t/4}$$
$$\underbrace{+\frac{d}{4}\left(\frac{g_\pi}{4}Z_\text{L}(x_{t-1}+x_{t-2}+x_{t-3}+x_{t-4})+g_yZ_\text{R}x_{t-1}\right)}_{di_{t-1}/4}$$
$$\underbrace{+\frac{d}{4}\left(\frac{g_\pi}{4}Z_\text{L}(x_{t-2}+x_{t-3}+x_{t-4}+x_{t-5})+g_yZ_\text{R}x_{t-2}\right)}_{di_{t-2}/4}$$
$$\underbrace{+\frac{d}{4}\left(\frac{g_\pi}{4}Z_\text{L}(x_{t-3}+x_{t-4}+x_{t-5}+x_{t-6})+g_yZ_\text{R}x_{t-3}\right)}_{di_{t-3}/4} \tag{3.56}$$

From these relations we can now define the 7 matrices $C_0, \ldots, C_6$:

$$C_0 = \begin{pmatrix} a_0 & b \\ 0 & c_0 \end{pmatrix} + \left(\frac{g_\pi d}{16} - \frac{d}{4}\right) Z_\text{L} + g_y Z_\text{R} \tag{3.57}$$
$$C_1 = \begin{pmatrix} a_1 & 0 \\ 0 & c_1 \end{pmatrix} + \left(2\frac{g_\pi d}{16} - \frac{d}{4}\right) Z_\text{L} + \frac{g_y d}{4} Z_\text{R} \tag{3.58}$$
$$C_2 = \begin{pmatrix} a_2 & 0 \\ 0 & 0 \end{pmatrix} + \left(3\frac{g_\pi d}{16} - \frac{d}{4}\right) Z_\text{L} + \frac{g_y d}{4} Z_\text{R} \tag{3.59}$$
$$C_3 = \begin{pmatrix} a_3 & 0 \\ 0 & 0 \end{pmatrix} + \left(4\frac{g_\pi d}{16} - \frac{d}{4}\right) Z_\text{L} + \frac{g_y d}{4} Z_\text{R} \tag{3.60}$$
$$C_4 = 3\frac{g_\pi d}{16} Z_\text{L} \tag{3.61}$$
$$C_5 = 2\frac{g_\pi d}{16} Z_\text{L} \tag{3.62}$$
$$C_6 = \frac{g_\pi d}{16} Z_\text{L} \tag{3.63}$$

3.7 Appendix: Derivation of Expectation Coefficients

Credible expectations, eqs.(3.22) and (3.23). The squared errors are:

$$S_\pi^2 = \sum_{i=0}^{t-1} \left(\pi_{i+1} - [\pi_i - \psi_\pi(\pi_i - \pi_\text{m})]\right)^2 \tag{3.64}$$

$$S_y^2 = \sum_{i=0}^{t-1} \left(y_{i+1} - [y_i - \psi_y(y_i - y_\mathrm{m})]\right)^2 \quad (3.65)$$

The least-squares estimates of the expectation coefficients are:

$$\psi_\pi = \frac{\sum_{i=0}^{t-1}(\pi_{i+1} - \pi_i)(\pi_\mathrm{m} - \pi_i)}{\sum_{i=0}^{t-1}(\pi_\mathrm{m} - \pi_i)^2} \quad (3.66)$$

$$\psi_y = \frac{\sum_{i=0}^{t-1}(y_{i+1} - y_i)(y_\mathrm{m} - y_i)}{\sum_{i=0}^{t-1}(y_\mathrm{m} - y_i)^2} \quad (3.67)$$

Not-credible expectations, eqs.(3.24) and (3.25). Define the data vectors $\pi_{t(K)} = (\pi_t, \ldots, \pi_{t-K})$ and $y_{t(J)} = (y_t, \ldots, y_{t-J})$. The squared errors of the estimates from the observations are:

$$S_\pi^2 = \sum_{i=0}^{t-1-K} \left(\pi_{t-i} - b'\pi_{t-i-1(K)}\right)^2 \quad (3.68)$$

$$S_y^2 = \sum_{i=0}^{t-1-J} \left(y_{t-i} - a'y_{t-i-1(J)}\right)^2 \quad (3.69)$$

The least squares estimates of the coefficients are:

$$b = \left[\sum_{i=0}^{t-K-1} \pi_{t-i-1(K)}\pi'_{t-i-1(K)}\right]^{-1} \sum_{i=0}^{t-K-1} \pi_{t-i}\pi_{t-i-1(K)} \quad (3.70)$$

$$a = \left[\sum_{i=0}^{t-J-1} y_{t-i-1(J)}y'_{t-i-1(J)}\right]^{-1} \sum_{i=0}^{t-J-1} y_{t-i}y_{t-i-1(J)} \quad (3.71)$$

3.8 Appendix: Derivation of Inverse 1-Step Robustnesses

In this section we derive explicit expressions for the inverse of each of the four robustness functions defined in eqs.(3.39) and (3.40), for 1 step in the future. That is, we will derive expressions for the inner minima in these equations. These inner minima provide the basis for numerical evaluation of the robustness, and for understanding some of the generic properties of the robustness functions.

Let $\mu_{\mathrm{l}x}(h, h_p)$ denote the inner minimum in the lower-target robustness for x (either π or y), eq.(3.39). The lower-target robustness for this variable, $\widehat{h}_{\rm lx}(P_{\rm c})$, is the greatest horizon of model uncertainty, h, at which $\mu_{\rm lx}(h, h_p) \ge P_{\rm c}$. Since $\mu_{\rm lx}(h, h_p)$ decreases monotonically as h increases, we see that the robustness is the greatest value of h satisfying $\mu_{\rm lx}(h, h_p) = P_{\rm c}$. Thus a plot of $\mu_{\rm lx}(h, h_p)$ vs. h is identical to a plot of $P_{\rm c}$ vs. $\widehat{h}_{\rm lx}(P_{\rm c})$. In other words, $\mu_{\rm lx}(h, h_p)$ is the inverse of $\widehat{h}_{\rm lx}(P_{\rm c})$:

$$\mu_{\rm lx}(h, h_p) = P_{\rm c} \quad \text{if and only if} \quad \widehat{h}_{\rm lx}(P_{\rm c}) = h \tag{3.72}$$

A similar relation exists between the upper-target robustness, $\widehat{h}_{\rm ux}(P_{\rm c})$ in eq.(3.40), and its inner minimum, $\mu_{\rm ux}(h, h_p)$.

We will now proceed to derive explicit expressions for $\mu_{\rm l\pi}(h, h_p)$, $\mu_{\rm u\pi}(h, h_p)$, $\mu_{\rm ly}(h, h_p)$ and $\mu_{\rm uy}(h, h_p)$. We derive these at period $t+1$ given observations for inflation and output gap for periods 0, 1, ..., t.

Lower-target probability for 1-step inflation, $\mu_{\rm l\pi}(h, h_p)$. The probability in eq.(3.39) can be written explicitly as:

$$\begin{aligned} \text{Prob}(\pi_{t+1} \ge \pi_{\rm l} | p, c) &= \text{Prob}(\underbrace{\lambda y_t + \beta \text{E}_t \pi_{t+1}}_{\pi^{\rm m}_{t+1}} + \varepsilon_{\pi t} \ge \pi_{\rm l} | p, c) \quad (3.73) \\ &= \text{Prob}(\varepsilon_{\pi t} \ge \underbrace{\pi_{\rm l} - \pi^{\rm m}_{t+1}}_{\delta} | p, c) \quad (3.74) \end{aligned}$$

$\pi^{\rm m}_{t+1}$, defined in eq.(3.73), is the model-based anticipated inflation at the next period, given model coefficients λ and β and the public's expectation of inflation. δ, defined in eq.(3.74), is the difference between the lower target and the model-based anticipation.

We will assume that $\delta \ge -\varepsilon_{\star\pi}$, which in practice is not a limitation since $\varepsilon_{\star\pi}$ will be large.

The pdf $p_\pi(\varepsilon_{\pi t})$ in $\mathcal{U}_p(h_p)$ which minimizes the probability in eq.(3.74), at horizon of uncertainty h_p, is the one whose lower tail is as thick as possible, causing the upper tail to vanish and the middle section to contract:[23]

$$p_\pi(\varepsilon_{\pi t}) = \begin{cases} 0, & \varepsilon > \varepsilon_{\star\pi} \\ \nu \widetilde{p}(\varepsilon_{\pi t}), & |\varepsilon_{\pi t}| \le \varepsilon_{\star\pi} \\ \dfrac{h_p}{\varepsilon_{\pi t}^2}, & \varepsilon_{\pi t} < -\varepsilon_{\star\pi} \end{cases} \tag{3.75}$$

[23] This solution is valid only for $h_p \le \varepsilon_{\star\pi}$, as we will see when we consider the normalization constant ν in eq.(3.76). For larger h_p's the solution is $\nu = 0$ with lower tail of $\varepsilon_{\star\pi}/\varepsilon_{\pi t}^2$.

where ν is determined by normalization of $p_\pi(\varepsilon_{\pi t})$ to be:[24]

$$\nu = \frac{1-(h_p/\varepsilon_{\star\pi})}{2\Phi(\varepsilon_{\star\pi}/\sigma_\pi)-1} \tag{3.76}$$

$\Phi(\cdot)$ is the cumulative distribution function for the standard normal variable (with zero mean and unit variance).

With the pdf in eq.(3.75) we see that the lowest probability, for any p_π in $\mathcal{U}_p(h_p)$, is:

$$\min_{p\in\mathcal{U}_p(h_p)} \text{Prob}(\varepsilon_{\pi t} \geq \delta|p,c) \tag{3.77}$$

$$= \begin{cases} \nu\Phi(\varepsilon_{\star\pi}/\sigma_\pi) - \nu\Phi(\delta/\sigma_\pi), & -\varepsilon_{\star\pi} \leq \delta \leq \varepsilon_{\star\pi} \\ 0, & \varepsilon_{\star\pi} < \delta \end{cases}$$

This probability depends on the model coefficients λ and β through the term $\delta = \pi_\text{l} - \pi^\text{m}_{t+1}$. Thus we can write:

$$\min_{\substack{p\in\mathcal{U}_p(h_p)\\ c\in\mathcal{U}(h)}} \text{Prob}(\varepsilon_{\pi t} \geq \delta|p,c) = \nu\Phi(\varepsilon_{\star\pi}/\sigma_\pi) - \nu\Phi\left[\frac{1}{\sigma_\pi}\left(\pi_\text{l} - \min_{c\in\mathcal{U}(h)} \pi^\text{m}_{t+1}\right)\right] \tag{3.78}$$

If this expression is negative then redefine it to be zero, which occurs if the minimum value of δ exceeds $\varepsilon_{\star\pi}$.

To complete our derivation of $\mu_{\text{l}\pi}(h, h_p)$, based on eq.(3.78), we need an expression for $\min \pi^\text{m}_{t+1}$, which we now derive.

We first define two helpful functions. $\text{sgn}(x)$ denotes the algebraic sign of x:

$$\text{sgn}(x) = \begin{cases} -1, & x < 0 \\ 0, & x = 0 \\ +1, & x > 0 \end{cases} \tag{3.79}$$

$r(x)$ is a truncated ramp function:

$$\overline{r}(x) = \begin{cases} 0, & x < 0 \\ x, & 0 \leq x \leq 1 \\ 1, & 1 < x \end{cases} \tag{3.80}$$

---

[24]We see from eq.(3.75) that the middle section of the pdf contracts if $\nu < 1$. This will result from the normalization if h_p is large enough so that the lower tail (whose area is $h_p/\varepsilon_{\star\pi}$) expands at least enough to compensate for the vanishing upper tail (whose area is $1-\Phi(\varepsilon_{\star\pi}/\sigma_\pi)$), namely if $h_p/\varepsilon_{\star\pi} > 2[1-\Phi(\varepsilon_{\star\pi}/\sigma_\pi)]$. This causes $\nu < 1$ in eq.(3.76).

From the macro-economic model in eq.(3.17), and the info-gap model in eq.(3.28), we can express the minimum of the model-based anticipation, at horizon of uncertainty h, as:

$$\min_{c\in\mathcal{U}(h)} \pi^{\mathrm{m}}_{t+1} = \overline{r}\Big(\widetilde{\lambda} - \mathrm{sgn}(y_t)s_\lambda h\Big)\, y_t + \overline{r}\Big(\widetilde{\beta} - \mathrm{sgn}(\mathrm{E}_t\pi_{t+1})s_\beta h\Big)\, \mathrm{E}_t\pi_{t+1} \tag{3.81}$$

If y_t is negative, then the first ramp function chooses the *largest* value of λ which is allowed by the info-gap model at horizon of uncertainty h. If y_t is positive, then the first ramp function chooses the *smallest* allowed value of λ. The second ramp function is explained similarly with respect to the sign of $\mathrm{E}_t\pi_{t+1}$.

Upper-target probability for 1-step inflation, $\mu_{\mathrm{u}\pi}(h, h_p)$. The probability in eq.(3.40) can be written explicitly as:

$$\mathrm{Prob}(\pi_{t+1} \le \pi_{\mathrm{u}}|p,c) = \mathrm{Prob}(\underbrace{\lambda y_t + \beta \mathrm{E}_t\pi_{t+1}}_{\pi^{\mathrm{m}}_{t+1}} + \varepsilon_{\pi t} \le \pi_{\mathrm{u}}|p,c) \tag{3.82}$$

$$= \mathrm{Prob}(\varepsilon_{\pi t} \le \underbrace{\pi_{\mathrm{u}} - \pi^{\mathrm{m}}_{t+1}}_{\delta}|p,c) \tag{3.83}$$

π^{m}_{t+1} is the model-based anticipated inflation at the next step, based on model parameters λ and β. δ is the difference between the upper target and this anticipation.

We will assume that $\delta \le \varepsilon_{\star\pi}$, which is very plausible.

The pdf $p_\pi(\varepsilon_{\pi t})$ which minimizes the probability in eq.(3.83), at horizon of uncertainty h_p, is the one whose upper tail is a thick as possible, causing the lower tail to vanish and the middle section to contract. This is the inversion of the pdf in eq.(3.75).

Arguing in a manner analogous to eqs.(3.75)–(3.77) we find:

$$\min_{p\in\mathcal{U}_p(h_p)} \mathrm{Prob}(\varepsilon_{\pi t} \le \delta|p,c) \tag{3.84}$$

$$= \begin{cases} \nu\Phi(\delta/\sigma_\pi) - \nu\Phi(-\varepsilon_{\star\pi}/\sigma_\pi), & -\varepsilon_{\star\pi} \le \delta \le \varepsilon_{\star\pi} \\ 0, & \delta \le -\varepsilon_{\star\pi} \end{cases}$$

where ν is defined in eq.(3.76).

This probability depends on the model coefficients, λ and β, through the term $\delta = \pi_{\mathrm{u}} - \pi^{\mathrm{m}}_{t+1}$. Thus, in analogy to eq.(3.78), we can write:

$$\min_{\substack{p\in\mathcal{U}_p(h_p)\\ c\in\mathcal{U}(h)}} \mathrm{Prob}(\varepsilon_{\pi t} \le \delta|p,c) \tag{3.85}$$

$$= \nu\Phi\left[\frac{1}{\sigma_\pi}\left(\pi_{\rm u} - \max_{c\in\mathcal{U}(h)} \pi^{\rm m}_{t+1}\right)\right] - \nu\Phi\left(\frac{-\varepsilon_{\star\pi}}{\sigma_\pi}\right)$$

If this expression is negative then redefine it to be zero, which occurs if the minimum value of δ is less than $-\varepsilon_{\star\pi}$.

Eq.(3.85) is the inverse of the upper-target robustness for inflation.

In analogy to eq.(3.81), we find:

$$\max_{c\in\mathcal{U}(h)} \pi^{\rm m}_{t+1} = \overline{r}\Big(\widetilde{\lambda} + {\rm sgn}(y_t)s_\lambda h\Big)\, y_t + \overline{r}\Big(\widetilde{\beta} + {\rm sgn}({\rm E}_t\pi_{t+1})s_\beta h\Big)\, {\rm E}_t\pi_{t+1} \quad (3.86)$$

Lower-target probability for 1-step output gap, $\mu_{\rm ly}(h, h_p)$. The inner probability can be written:

$$\begin{aligned} &{\rm Prob}(y_{t+1} \ge y_{\rm l}|p, c) &(3.87)\\ &= {\rm Prob}(\underbrace{-\phi(i_t - {\rm E}_t\pi_{t+1}) + {\rm E}_t y_{t+1}}_{y^{\rm m}_{t+1}(\phi)} + \varepsilon_{yt} \ge y_{\rm l}|p, c) \\ &= {\rm Prob}(\varepsilon_{yt} \ge \underbrace{y_{\rm l} - y^{\rm m}_{t+1}}_{\delta}|p, c) &(3.88)\end{aligned}$$

$y^{\rm m}_{t+1}(\phi)$ is the model-based anticipation of the output gap at the next step, and δ is the difference between the lower target and the model-based anticipation.

The pdf which minimizes the probability in eq.(3.88) is the same as eq.(3.75), with π replaced everywhere by y. The normalization constant, ν, is given in eq.(3.76), also with π replaced by y.

In analogy to eq.(3.77), the lowest probability in eq.(3.88), for any p_y in $\mathcal{U}_p(h_p)$, is:

$$\begin{aligned} &\min_{p\in\mathcal{U}_p(h_p)} {\rm Prob}(\varepsilon_{yt} \ge \delta|p, c) &(3.89)\\ &= \begin{cases} \nu\Phi(\varepsilon_{\star y}/\sigma_y) - \nu\Phi(\delta/\sigma_y), & -\varepsilon_{\star y} \le \delta \le \varepsilon_{\star y} \\ 0, & \varepsilon_{\star y} \le \delta \end{cases}\end{aligned}$$

This probability depends on the model coefficient ϕ through the term $\delta = y_{\rm l} - y^{\rm m}_{t+1}$. Thus we can write:

$$\begin{aligned} &\min_{\substack{p\in\mathcal{U}_p(h_p)\\ c\in\mathcal{U}(h)}} {\rm Prob}(\varepsilon_{yt} \ge \delta|p, c) &(3.90)\\ &= \nu\Phi(\varepsilon_{\star y}/\sigma_y) - \nu\Phi\left[\frac{1}{\sigma_y}\left(y_{\rm l} - \min_{c\in\mathcal{U}(h)} y^{\rm m}_{t+1}\right)\right]\end{aligned}$$

If this expression is negative then redefine it to be zero, which occurs if the minimum value of δ exceeds $\varepsilon_{\star y}$.

In analogy to eq.(3.81) we can write the inner minimum in eq.(3.90) as:

$$\min_{c\in\mathcal{U}(h)} y^{\mathrm{m}}_{t+1} = -\overline{r}\Big(\widetilde{\phi} + \mathrm{sgn}(i_t - \mathrm{E}_t\pi_{t+1})s_\phi h\Big)\,(i_t - \mathrm{E}_t\pi_{t+1}) + \mathrm{E}_t y_{t+1} \tag{3.91}$$

Upper-target probability for 1-step output gap, $\mu_{\mathrm{u}y}(h, h_p)$. The inner probability can be written:

$$\mathrm{Prob}(y_{t+1} \le y_{\mathrm{u}}|\nu, c) \tag{3.92}$$

$$= \mathrm{Prob}(\underbrace{-\phi(i_t - \mathrm{E}_t\pi_{t+1}) + \mathrm{E}_t y_{t+1}}_{y^{\mathrm{m}}_{t+1}(\phi)} + \varepsilon_{yt} \le y_{\mathrm{u}}|\nu, c)$$

$$= \mathrm{Prob}(\varepsilon_{yt} \le \underbrace{y_{\mathrm{u}} - y^{\mathrm{m}}_{t+1}}_{\delta}|p, c) \tag{3.93}$$

We will assume that $\delta \le \varepsilon_{\star y}$, which is very plausible.

The pdf $p_y(\varepsilon_{\pi t})$ which minimizes the probability in eq.(3.93), at horizon of uncertainty h_p, is the one whose upper tail is as thick as possible, causing the lower tail to vanish and the middle section to contract. This is the inversion of the pdf in eq.(3.75). Thus, in analogy to eq.(3.84), we find:

$$\min_{p\in\mathcal{U}_p(h_p)} \mathrm{Prob}(\varepsilon_{yt} \le \delta|p, c) \tag{3.94}$$

$$= \begin{cases} \nu\Phi(\delta/\sigma_y) - \nu\Phi(-\varepsilon_{\star\pi}/\sigma_y), & -\varepsilon_{\star y} \le \delta \le \varepsilon_{\star y} \\ 0, & \delta \le -\varepsilon_{\star y} \end{cases}$$

where ν is defined in eq.(3.76).

This probability depends on the model coefficient ϕ through the term $\delta = y_{\mathrm{u}} - y^{\mathrm{m}}_{t+1}$. Thus, in analogy to eq.(3.85), we can write:

$$\min_{\substack{p\in\mathcal{U}_p(h_p)\\ c\in\mathcal{U}(h)}} \mathrm{Prob}(\varepsilon_{yt} \le \delta|p, c) \tag{3.95}$$

$$= \nu\Phi\left[\frac{1}{\sigma_y}\left(y_{\mathrm{u}} - \max_{c\in\mathcal{U}(h)} y^{\mathrm{m}}_{t+1}\right)\right] - \nu\Phi(-\varepsilon_{\star y}/\sigma_y)$$

If this expression is negative then redefine it to be zero, which occurs if the minimum value of δ is less than $-\varepsilon_{\star y}$.

Eq.(3.95) is the inverse of the upper-target robustness for inflation.

In analogy to eq.(3.91) we can write the inner maximum in eq.(3.95) as:

$$\max_{c\in\mathcal{U}(h)} y^{\mathrm{m}}_{t+1} = -\overline{r}\left(\widetilde{\phi} - \mathrm{sgn}(i_t - \mathrm{E}_t\pi_{t+1})s_\phi h\right)(i_t - \mathrm{E}_t\pi_{t+1}) + \mathrm{E}_t y_{t+1} \tag{3.96}$$

Chapter 4

Financial Stability

We consider the analysis of decisions in four different aspects of financial stability. In section 4.1 we look at a simple example of structured securities as collateralized debt obligations. We explore the robustness to uncertain correlation between the underlying assets. In section 4.2 we study the robustness of the value at risk of a portfolio, when the probability distribution has uncertain fat tails. Stress testing is discussed conceptually in section 4.3 based on a suite of models. In section 4.4 we study the strategic allocation of assets using both the robustness and the opportuneness functions for exploring the risks and windfalls of uncertain payoffs.

~ ~ ~

4.1 Structured Securities: Simple Example

The aggregation of assets is a powerful approach to the management of risk. However, whether a particular diversification enhances or reduces risk depends in large measure on the extent and nature of the statistical correlation among the underlying assets. "Don't put all your eggs in one basket" is good advice, but putting them in baskets which are bound together does not solve the problem of risk management. The trouble is that it is often difficult to know how strongly correlated two seemingly unrelated assets are.

The 2008 financial crash of collateralized debt obligations and other structured-finance securities is a direct result of ignoring—or getting investors to ignore—the uncertain correlation among the underlying assets.

In this section we consider the info-gap analysis of a simple collateralized debt obligation (CDO), showing how one can evaluate the impact of uncertainty in probabilities of single and multiple defaults.

4.1.1 Policy Preview

We will construct a structured security with a senior and a junior tranche based on two underlying assets. We will find that the senior tranche is more robust to uncertainty than the junior tranche at any level of default probability. However, any reasonable level of robustness of the senior tranche is nonetheless accompanied by a large probability of default. In fact, this probability of default is large enough to entirely eliminate the advantage which was initially attributed to the senior tranche based on its estimated probability of default. While the estimated probability of default by the senior tranche improves geometrically (as the square of the underlying asset default probability), its robustness to uncertainty only increases linearly.

4.1.2 Operational Preview

System model. The system model is the probability of default of the junior and senior tranches, eqs.(4.3) and (4.4).

Performance requirements. The investor requires that these probabilities of default not exceed specified values, $P_{\rm cj}$ and $P_{\rm cs}$ for junior and senior tranches, as stated in eqs.(4.1) and (4.2).

Uncertainty model. The estimated probabilities of default of one or both of the underlying assets are uncertain. The info-gap model of eq.(4.7) represents the unknown error of these estimates, consistent with the non-negativity and normalization constraints on the underlying probability distribution.

Robustness functions. The robustness of each tranche, $\widehat{h}_{\rm j}(P_{\rm cj})$ and $\widehat{h}_{\rm s}(P_{\rm cs})$ for junior and senior, is the greatest horizon of uncertainty up to which that tranche defaults with probability no greater than the specified performance requirement, eqs.(4.14) and (4.16).

4.1.3 Formulation

We study a structured security with two underlying assets. We consider uncertainty in the individual and joint probabilities of default and derive robustness functions for a junior and a senior tranche. These robustness functions enable the evaluation of the impact of uncertainty in the initial estimates of single and multiple defaults. This example is based in part on Coval, Jurek and Stafford (2009).

Consider two assets, such as bonds or mortgages, each with face values of \$1. The probability of default of the first asset, regardless of what happens to the second asset, is thought to equal $\widetilde{p}_{\rm d}$, though the actual value is $p_{\rm d1}$ which is unknown. Likewise, probability of default of the second asset, regardless of what happens to the first, is also thought to equal $\widetilde{p}_{\rm d}$, though the actual value is $p_{\rm d2}$ which is unknown. Finally, the probability that both assets will default is thought to be $\widetilde{p}_{\rm dd}$, though the true value, $p_{\rm dd}$, is not known.

Define a junior tranche which returns \$1 if and only if neither asset defaults. Similarly, define a senior tranche which returns \$1 if and only if no more than 1 asset defaults.

Let P_0 denote the actual probability that neither asset will default. The probability that the junior tranche will default is $1 - P_0$. Let P_2 denote the actual probability that both assets default, which is the probability that the senior tranche will default. The values of P_0 and P_2 are uncertain.

The investor requires that the probabilities of default by these tranches not exceed specified critical values:

$$1 - P_0 \leq P_{\rm cj} \tag{4.1}$$

$$P_2 \leq P_{\rm cs} \tag{4.2}$$

These probabilities are:

$$1 - P_0 = p_{\rm d1} + p_{\rm d2} - p_{\rm dd} \tag{4.3}$$

$$P_2 = p_{\rm dd} \tag{4.4}$$

Eq.(4.3) is derived in eq.(4.62) in appendix 4.5.

For example, suppose $\widetilde{p}_{\rm d} = 0.01$ on a yearly basis and that the probabilities of default of the underlying assets are thought to be statistically independent, so $\widetilde{p}_{\rm dd} = 0.0001$. Thus P_0 is estimated to equal 0.0199. The underlying assets would be credit-rated as BB+ and the junior tranche as BB−, both of which are "speculative bonds" and not "investment grade". However, the senior tranche is estimated to be AAA investment grade.

4.1.4 Uncertainty Model

Our estimate of both p_{d1} and p_{d2} is $\widetilde{p}_d$, and our estimate of p_{dd} is $\widetilde{p}_{dd}$. We will now construct an info-gap model for uncertainty in p_{d1}, p_{d2} and p_{dd}.

The basic idea which the info-gap model must capture is that we do not know the magnitude of error of the estimates, $\widetilde{p}_d$ and $\widetilde{p}_{dd}$. Basically, the info-gap model must state the following:

$$|p_{di} - \widetilde{p}_d| \le h, \; i = 1, 2 \tag{4.5}$$

$$|p_{dd} - \widetilde{p}_{dd}| \le h \tag{4.6}$$

where the horizon of uncertainty, h, is unknown. Eq.(4.5) states that we do not know how much $\widetilde{p}_d$ errs as an estimate of either single-asset default, while eq.(4.6) states that we do not know how much $\widetilde{p}_{dd}$ errs as an estimate of default of both assets.

However, things are not quite so simple, since p_{d1}, p_{d2} and p_{dd} are inter-related by the non-negativity and normalization conditions which constrain any probability distribution. When we incorporate eqs.(4.5) and (4.6) into an info-gap model we must make sure that we respect these constraints on p_{d1}, p_{d2} and p_{dd}. In particular, we must consider the joint probability distribution for default of the two underlying assets. The following info-gap model is derived in appendix 4.5:

$$\begin{aligned}\mathcal{U}(h) = \Big\{ p_{d1}, p_{d2}, p_{dd} : \quad & p_{d1} \ge 0, \quad p_{d2} \ge 0, \quad p_{dd} \ge 0. \\ & p_{dd} \le \min[p_{d1}, \; p_{d2}]. \\ & p_{d1} + p_{d2} - p_{dd} \le 1. \\ & |p_{di} - \widetilde{p}_d| \le h, \; i = 1, 2. \\ & |p_{dd} - \widetilde{p}_{dd}| \le h \Big\}, \quad h \ge 0 \end{aligned} \tag{4.7}$$

$\mathcal{U}(h)$ is the set of all triplets, p_{d1}, p_{d2}, p_{dd}, which are consistent with the non-negativity and normalization conditions of the probability distribution to which they belong (first 3 lines), and which deviate from their estimated values by no more than h (last 2 lines). Since the horizon of uncertainty, h, is unknown, this is an unbounded family of nested sets of probability distributions.

4.1.5 Robustness Functions

We now are in a position to define and derive the robustness functions for the junior and senior tranches.

The robustness of the junior tranche is the greatest horizon of uncertainty at which the probability that the junior tranche defaults is no greater than $P_{\rm cj}$. Similarly, the robustness of the senior tranche is the greatest horizon of uncertainty at which the probability that the senior tranche defaults is no greater than $P_{\rm cs}$:

$$\widehat{h}_{\rm j}(P_{\rm cj}) = \max\left\{ h : \left(\max_{p_{{\rm d}i}, p_{\rm dd} \in \mathcal{U}(h)} (1 - P_0) \right) \le P_{\rm cj} \right\} \quad (4.8)$$

$$\widehat{h}_{\rm s}(P_{\rm cs}) = \max\left\{ h : \left(\max_{p_{{\rm d}i}, p_{\rm dd} \in \mathcal{U}(h)} P_2 \right) \le P_{\rm cs} \right\} \quad (4.9)$$

We now derive the robustness functions.

Junior tranche. Let $m_{\rm j}(h)$ denote the inner maximum in the definition of $\widehat{h}_{\rm j}$, eq.(4.8). This is a monotonically increasing function of h because the sets of the info-gap model, $\mathcal{U}(h)$, become more inclusive as h increases. The robustness, $\widehat{h}_{\rm j}$, is the greatest value of h for which $m_{\rm j}(h) \le P_{\rm cj}$. Because $m_{\rm j}(h)$ is monotonically increasing in h, we see that the robustness is the greatest h at which $m_{\rm j}(h) = P_{\rm cj}$. Hence a plot of $m_{\rm j}(h)$ vs. h is the same as a plot of $P_{\rm cj}$ vs. $\widehat{h}_{\rm j}(P_{\rm cj})$. In other words, $m_{\rm j}(h)$ is the inverse of $\widehat{h}_{\rm j}(P_{\rm cj})$.[1]

In order for the estimated values, $\widetilde{p}_{\rm d}$ and $\widetilde{p}_{\rm dd}$, to satisfy the non-negativity and normalization requirements, it is necessary that they satisfy eqs.(4.61) and (4.63) on p.133 in the appendix:

$$\widetilde{p}_{\rm dd} \le \widetilde{p}_{\rm d} \quad \text{and} \quad 2\widetilde{p}_{\rm d} - \widetilde{p}_{\rm dd} \le 1 \quad (4.10)$$

Let us introduce a truncated ramp function which will be useful shortly:

$$\overline{r}(x) = \begin{cases} 0 & \text{if } x < 0 \\ x & \text{if } 0 \le x \le 1 \\ 1 & \text{else} \end{cases} \quad (4.11)$$

[1] In this simple example we will derive an expression for $m_{\rm j}(h)$ and then algebraically invert it to obtain an explicit expression for $\widehat{h}_{\rm j}(P_{\rm cj})$. However, in some situations this inversion is difficult or even impossible. Because $m_{\rm j}(h)$ is the inverse of $\widehat{h}_{\rm j}(P_{\rm cj})$ it is not actually necessary to perform the inversion. We can evaluate and plot the robustness by evaluating and plotting its inverse.

Now, from eq.(4.62) and the info-gap model, and using the relations in eq.(4.10), we see that the maximum of $1 - P_0$ at horizon of uncertainty h is:

$$m_{\rm j}(h) = \overline{r}\left[2\overline{r}(\widetilde{p}_{\rm d} + h) - \overline{r}(\widetilde{p}_{\rm dd} - h)\right] \tag{4.12}$$

$$= \begin{cases} \overline{r}[2\widetilde{p}_{\rm d} - \widetilde{p}_{\rm dd} + 3h] & \text{if } h \le \widetilde{p}_{\rm dd} \\ \overline{r}[2(\widetilde{p}_{\rm d} + h)] & \text{else} \end{cases} \tag{4.13}$$

Equating eq.(4.13) to $P_{\rm cj}$ (which is no greater than one because it is a probability) and solving for h we obtain the robustness for the junior tranche:

$$\widehat{h}_{\rm j}(P_{\rm cj}) = \begin{cases} 0 & \text{if } P_{\rm cj} < 2\widetilde{p}_{\rm d} - \widetilde{p}_{\rm dd} \\ \dfrac{P_{\rm cj} - (2\widetilde{p}_{\rm d} - \widetilde{p}_{\rm dd})}{3} & \text{if } 2\widetilde{p}_{\rm d} - \widetilde{p}_{\rm dd} \le P_{\rm cj} \le 2(\widetilde{p}_{\rm d} + \widetilde{p}_{\rm dd}) \\ \dfrac{P_{\rm cj}}{2} - \widetilde{p}_{\rm d} & \text{else} \end{cases} \tag{4.14}$$

Senior tranche. Let $m_{\rm s}(h)$ denote the inner maximum in the definition of $\widehat{h}_{\rm s}$, eq.(4.9), which is the inverse of the robustness, $\widehat{h}_{\rm s}(P_{\rm cs})$. Examination of the info-gap model, and recalling that $\widetilde{p}_{\rm dd} \le \widetilde{p}_{\rm d}$, reveals that:

$$m_{\rm s}(h) = \overline{r}(\widetilde{p}_{\rm dd} + h) \tag{4.15}$$

Equating $m_{\rm s}(h)$ to $P_{\rm cs}$ (which is no greater than one) and solving for h we obtain the robustness of the senior tranche:

$$\widehat{h}_{\rm s}(P_{\rm cs}) = P_{\rm cs} - \widetilde{p}_{\rm dd} \tag{4.16}$$

or zero if this is negative which occurs only if $P_{\rm cs} < \widetilde{p}_{\rm dd}$.

4.1.6 Policy Exploration

We now consider a numerical example in which the estimated probability of default of each individual underlying asset is $\widetilde{p}_{\rm d} = 0.01$. Default of these assets is thought to be statistically independent, so the estimated probability of default of both assets is $\widetilde{p}_{\rm dd} = 0.0001$. We do not know by how much $\widetilde{p}_{\rm d}$ errs, though its error may be hundreds of percent. Similarly, the error of $\widetilde{p}_{\rm dd}$ is unknown but it also may be large. The question we ask is: does either tranche, and especially the senior, have substantial robustness to this uncertainty when requiring acceptable probability of default of the tranche?

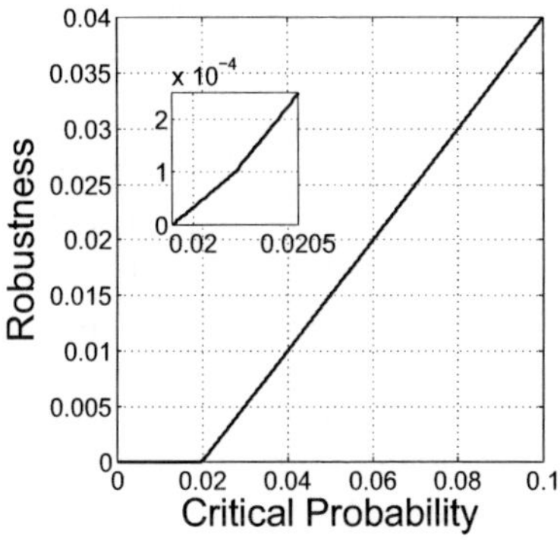

Figure 4.1: Robustness of junior tranche, $\widehat{h}_{\mathrm{j}}$, vs. default probability P_{cj}. $\widetilde{p}_{\mathrm{d}} = 0.01$, $\widetilde{p}_{\mathrm{dd}} = 0.0001$.

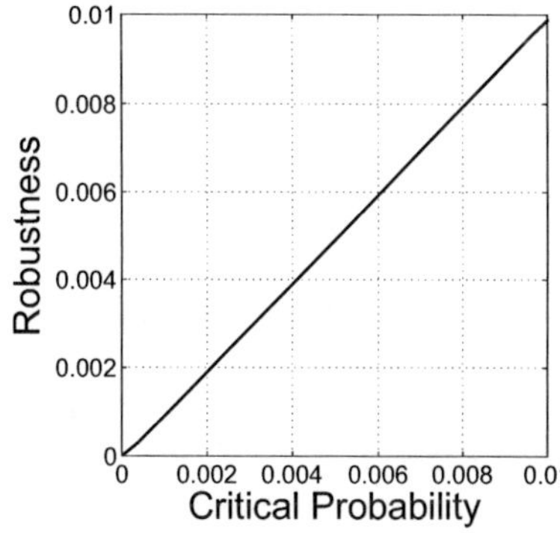

Figure 4.2: Robustness of senior tranche, $\widehat{h}_{\mathrm{s}}$, vs. default probability P_{cs}. $\widetilde{p}_{\mathrm{d}} = 0.01$, $\widetilde{p}_{\mathrm{dd}} = 0.0001$.

Trade-off and zeroing. Figs. 4.1 and 4.2 show robustness curves for the junior and senior tranches. The positive slopes of these curves express the trade-off between robustness and performance which is characteristic of all robustness curves, as explained in section 2.2.2. Greater robustness of either tranche is obtained only by accepting greater probability of default by that tranche.

These robustness curves reach the horizontal axis precisely at the estimated probability of default, $2\widetilde{p}_{\mathrm{d}} - \widetilde{p}_{\mathrm{dd}}$ for the junior tranche and $\widetilde{p}_{\mathrm{dd}}$ for the senior tranche. The estimated probabilities of default of the tranches have no robustness against uncertainty in the estimated probabilities for the underlying assets.

Junior tranche. The insert in fig. 4.1 shows the piece-wise linear form of the robustness of the junior tranche, as indicated in eq.(4.14). In the larger figure this is not evident due to the very small values of P_{cj} and $\widehat{h}_{\mathrm{j}}$ at which the kink occurs.

The slope of the junior-tranche robustness curve, $\widehat{h}_{\mathrm{j}}$ vs. P_{cj}, is 1/2 over most of its range, which entails a very large cost of robustness in units of probability of default. As we see in the figure, a robustness of 0.02 is obtained only by accepting a probability of 0.06 per annum for default of the junior tranche. A robustness of 0.02 means that the estimated single-asset default probabilities can err by as much as 0.02 without violating the performance requirement. While this is not very high robustness, the associated probability of junior-tranche default of 0.06 per annum, which would be rated as CCC+, makes this very unattractive.

Senior tranche. Fig. 4.2 shows the robustness curve for the senior tranche. We see that the slope of $\widehat{h}_{\mathrm{s}}$ vs. P_{cs} is twice that for the junior tranche, as expected from comparing eqs.(4.14) and (4.16). Consequently the cost of robustness for the senior tranche is half of the cost for the junior tranche. Nonetheless, robustness of 0.006—meaning that the estimated probability of two defaults can err by as much as 0.006—is obtained only by accepting a probability of senior-tranche default of 0.0061, which makes the senior tranche BBB rated and entirely unacceptable. Reducing the robustness to 0.002 improves the corresponding probability of default to 0.0021 which is still only A rated.

Conclusion. It is pretty clear from this simple analysis that ignoring the uncertainties in the underlying asset-default probabilities—including uncertain correlations—leads to unrealistic assessments of credit risk. Most importantly, the dazzlingly low estimated default probability of the senior tranche, $\widetilde{p}_{\mathrm{dd}}$, as compared to the junior tranche, $2\widetilde{p}_{\mathrm{d}} - \widetilde{p}_{\mathrm{dd}}$, is not reflected in increased robustness of the senior tranche. While the senior is more robust, and has lower cost of robustness, than the junior, the advantage is only a factor of 2, and not a geometric improvement as in the case of the estimated default probabilities.[2]

4.1.7 Extensions

Various extensions of this example are possible.

Multiple assets. The structured security can be built up from more than two underlying assets, which then allows for more than two tranches.

Higher-order structures. CDOs can be manufactured from the tranches of other CDOs, producing the so-called "CDO^2".

Term structure. The robustness analysis can be applied to more complex term structures and payoff conditions.

Uncertainty. One might have knowledge which would support more informative uncertainty models than eq.(4.7). First of all one might have information which differentiates between the uncertainties of the different default probabilities. Thus the term $|p_{\mathrm{d}i} - \widetilde{p}_{\mathrm{d}}| \leq h$ in the info-gap model would be replaced by $|p_{\mathrm{d}i} - \widetilde{p}_{\mathrm{d}}| \leq hs_i$ where the value of s_i comes from the additional information. One might be

[2]For statistically independent underlying assets, $\widetilde{p}_{\mathrm{dd}} = \widetilde{p}_{\mathrm{d}}^2$.

able to postulate a probability distribution for the values of correlation coefficients. Meaningful judgments such as "small correlation is highly likely" and "high correlation is implausible but not impossible" can be translated into quantitative form. This meta-probability distribution would itself be highly uncertain though still informative. It would therefore be necessary to model this uncertainty.

4.2 Value at Risk in Financial Economics

Hendricks (1996) finds extensive empirical evidence for

> two well-known characteristics of daily financial market data. First, extreme outcomes occur more often and are larger than predicted by the normal distribution (fat tails). Second, the size of market movements is not constant over time (conditional volatility).

More specifically, Hendricks (1996) writes:

> Virtually all of the approaches [to assessing value at risk] produce accurate 95th percentile risk measures. The 99th percentile risk measures, however, are somewhat less reliable and generally cover only between 98.2 percent and 98.5 percent of the outcomes.

The value at risk (VaR) in a financial portfolio is evaluated from an estimated probability density function (pdf) which is based on historical data. This dependence on the *past* tends to limit the accuracy of estimated VaRs as predictions of *future* risk for reasons which we will divide into two categories. The first category is the statistical error in the estimation of the pdf, while the second category is Knightian uncertainty, which is a non-statistical info-gap.

The evaluation and management of estimation error is in the field of statistical analysis. Numerous powerful methods are available for estimating quantiles and for evaluating the error of those estimates. Standard errors of quantile estimates can be evaluated (Kendall, Stuart and Ord, 1987, §10.9). Confidence intervals can be constructed for quantile values (DeGroot, 1986, p.563). Sign tests use order statistics for testing hypotheses on the value of an estimated quantile (Kendall, Stuart and Ord, 1979, §32.2–10). Kernel smoothing methods provide a rich array of methods for estimating a pdf (Härdle, 1990).

In this section we will assume that a pdf of returns has been competently estimated, and the reliability of this estimate, vis-à-vis the random variability of the historical data, has been established using appropriate statistical tools. We are not concerned with the statistical task of estimating a pdf or its moments and quantiles.

This section is concerned with the second class of factors which limit the accuracy of VaRs: Knightian uncertainty about the future. The systematic errors in VaRs mentioned earlier suggest that something more than random estimation error is involved. The most troublesome source of error in predicting *future* VaRs from *historical* data is that things can change. The true pdf in the future can differ substantially from the true realization in the past. Changes in a market or in its economic, social and political environment can cause significant changes in the actual shape of a pdf. Environmental change arising well outside the specific market in question is virtually impossible to predict, and experience has shown many examples of profound, surprising, and sometimes sudden alterations. This source of error can be neither assessed nor rectified by statistical methods since future surprises have no manifestation in historical data. Unpredictable changes are ones which cannot be modelled probabilistically, and against which one can in no way insure in any actuarial sense. This is what Frank Knight called a "true uncertainty" for which "there is no objective measure of the probability", as opposed to risk which is probabilistically measurable (Knight, 1921, pp.46, 120, 231–232). We focus on the unpredictable and non-stochastic Knightian info-gaps which accompany a VaR estimate.

There is at present no consensus about methods for management of financial risks, whose study is "still in its infancy" (González and Molitor, 2009, p.307). However, the value at risk concept is the basis of much work in this area. The info-gap analysis in this section focusses on the robustness of a VaR based on an empirically estimated pdf. The question of robustness is: how wrong, in the Knightian sense, can the estimated pdf be without jeopardizing the VaR estimate at a specified level of statistical confidence? A VaR which is highly robust to Knightian uncertainty in the pdf is a reliable assessment of risk, while a VaR whose robustness to Knightian error in the pdf is low is not a useful risk measure.

The assessment of value at risk is not only a matter of mathematics. Essential and difficult judgments must be made about the type and severity of the uncertainties involved. Even within the realm of Knightian info-gaps, these uncertainties can take different forms which the analyst must assess based on experience and personal judgment as much as on quantitative analysis. This judgment may sometimes draw on the organization's tolerance for risk and its philosophy for managing that risk as part of an integrated risk management strategy (Bindseil, 2009).

Judgments about the nature of the relevant uncertainty are expressed most directly in the choice of an info-gap model for uncertainty. The info-gap model developed in section 4.2.4 will be viewed by some analysts as reflecting extreme, even implausible, uncertainty. And indeed it is intended for situations subject to potentially disastrous surprise. The robustness function defined in section 4.2.5 and studied numerically in section 4.2.7 reflects quite considerable vulnerability to fat-tail uncertainty. In section 4.2.6 we consider an info-gap safety factor and incremental VaRs. We conclude with a discussion in section 4.2.8 of a more moderate info-gap model. This case, too, is not without its surprises.

4.2.1 Policy Preview

The VaR is the basis for choosing the reserve requirement which prevents financial insolvency at specified probability of failure. In addition, the VaR can be used to choose from among alternative portfolios. A VaR which is evaluated directly from an estimated pdf has no robustness against uncertainty in that pdf. Only more negative reserve requirements have positive robustness against Knightian uncertainty. This is the usual trade-off between performance and robustness.

The robustness is reduced as the estimated mean return is reduced. Likewise, the robustness is reduced as the estimated variance of the return increases. That is, we observe a mean-variance trade-off in the robustness plane.

The robustness curves of different portfolios can cross one another, indicating that the preference between them depends on the required robustness or on the acceptable reserve requirement.

The difference between the VaRs of two portfolios can be evaluated at different levels of robustness. The difference between the VaRs at zero robustness is the usual incremental VaR. The incremental VaRs at positive robustness can be much different from the zero-robustness incremental VaR, even different in sign if the robustness curves cross one another.

The safety factor is the ratio of the reserve requirement which has a specified value of robustness, to the reserve requirement at zero robustness. The safety factor is useful in comparing alternative portfolios.

The choice of the info-gap model of uncertainty can have a strong effect on the resulting robustness. If the Knightian uncertainty is deemed to be moderate then the robustness will be much larger than if the analyst assesses the impact of profound and potentially disastrous surprises.

4.2.2 Operational Preview

System model. The system model is the VaR, which is a quantile of the probability distribution of the returns, eq.(4.17). This quantile expresses the greatest loss per dollar at specified probability.

Decision variables and performance requirement. The portfolio manager chooses a reserve requirement, which is the greatest loss which would not result in financial insolvency. Since losses are random, the manager also chooses the value of the probability at which the loss would exceed the reserve requirement. The performance requirement is that the loss exceed the reserve requirement with likelihood no greater than the specified probability. This is expressed as a requirement on the VaR quantile, eq.(4.21).

Uncertainty model. The task of the portfolio manager is complicated by the combination of statistical error and info-gap uncertainty. Not only is loss a random phenomenon, but the tails of the pdf are highly uncertain. The uncertainty in the pdf is represented by an info-gap model of uncertainty, eq.(4.20). An info-gap model for much less severe Knightian uncertainty is defined in eq.(4.34).

Robustness function. The VaR expresses a statistical requirement, while the robustness function addresses the info-gap uncertainty about this statistical requirement. The robustness function thus provides a combined info-gap-and-statistical assessment of confidence. We derive an implicit expression for the numerical evaluation of the inverse of the robustness function, eq.(4.27), or eq.(4.28) if the estimated pdf is normal. An explicit expression for the robustness in the case of moderate info-gaps is also derived, eq.(4.39).

4.2.3 Value at Risk: Formulation

Let r denote the rate of return on a portfolio in a specified time interval, expressed in units of net dollars earned per dollar invested.

A negative value represents a loss; a positive value is a gain. Let $p(r)$ denote the probability density function (pdf)[3] of r, where $\widetilde{p}(r)$ is the estimated pdf. $\widetilde{p}(r)$ will typically be a normal distribution, or perhaps some other distribution, though usually the tails of the estimated distribution decay exponentially.

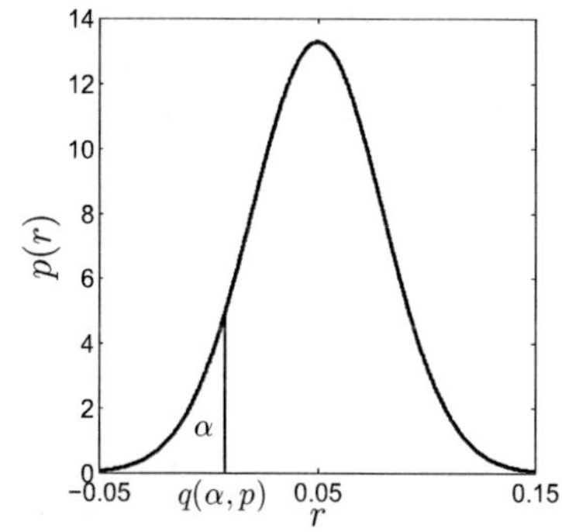

Figure 4.3: Illustration of the α quantile, $q(\alpha, p)$.

The α quantile of a distribution $p(r)$, denoted $q(\alpha, p)$, is the value of r for which the probability of losing r or more equals α. The quantile is illustrated in fig. 4.3 and defined in the following relation:

$$\alpha = \int_{-\infty}^{q(\alpha,p)} p(r)\,\mathrm{d}r \tag{4.17}$$

α is small, typically about 0.01, so $q(\alpha, p)$ will usually be a negative number, but we will often refer to its absolute value. $q(\alpha, p)$ is the fractional **value at risk** with confidence α based on the pdf $p(r)$ (Jorion, 2001). That is, if $p(r)$ is the correct pdf, then we have probability of α of losing $q(\alpha, p)$ or more dollars per dollar invested, in the specified time interval.

4.2.4 Uncertainty Model: Fat Tails

The pdf is highly uncertain, especially on its far tails. We consider an envelope-bound info-gap model in which the far tails may decay much more slowly than the estimated pdf.[4] The basic idea is that the

[3] We will assume, for simplicity, that $p(r)$ has no atoms, so that its cumulative distribution function is continuous.

[4] We will consider an info-gap model with less uncertainty in section 4.2.8.

actual pdf, $p(r)$, deviates fractionally from the estimated pdf, $\widetilde{p}(r)$, within an envelope of known shape but unknown size:

$$|p(r) - \widetilde{p}(r)| \le g(r)h \tag{4.18}$$

$g(r)$ is a known envelope function which is chosen primarily to reflect the possibility that the tails of the distribution may decay more slowly than anticipated. The horizon of uncertainty, h, is unknown.

We now specify the envelope function and then formulate the info-gap model.

Let μ denote the mean of the estimated pdf, $\widetilde{p}(r)$, and let $\mu \pm r_{\rm s}$ denote points on the lower and upper tails beyond which the estimated pdf is quite uncertain. For instance we might choose $r_{\rm s}$ to be 2 standard deviations from the mean.

Now define an envelope function whose tails decay as $1/r^2$, while the central part is proportional to the estimated pdf:

$$g(r) = \begin{cases} \dfrac{\widetilde{p}(\mu - r_{\rm s})(\mu - r_{\rm s})^2}{r^2} & \text{if } r < \mu - r_{\rm s} \\ \widetilde{p}(r) & \text{if } |r-\mu| \le r_{\rm s} \\ \dfrac{\widetilde{p}(\mu + r_{\rm s})(\mu + r_{\rm s})^2}{r^2} & \text{if } r > \mu + r_{\rm s} \end{cases} \tag{4.19}$$

$g(r)$ itself is not a pdf since it is not normalized. $g(r)$ defines the shape of the uncertainty envelopes within which the uncertain pdf's are contained at each horizon of uncertainty.

The function $1/r^2$ decays much more slowly than the exponential decay of the normal pdf which is proportional to $\exp[-(r-\mu)^2/2\sigma^2]$. Also, a pdf with a $1/r^2$ tail running out to infinity has infinite variance even though the distribution is normalized.

We can now define the info-gap model of mathematically legitimate (non-negative and normalized) pdf's whose fractional deviation from the estimated pdf is described by the envelope function $g(r)$:

$$\mathcal{U}(h) = \left\{ p(r) : \ p(r) \ge 0, \ \int_{-\infty}^{\infty} p(r)\,{\rm d}r = 1, \ |p(r) - \widetilde{p}(r)| \le g(r)h \right\}, \quad h \ge 0 \tag{4.20}$$

At horizon of uncertainty h, the set $\mathcal{U}(h)$ contains all pdf's, $p(r)$, whose deviation from the estimated pdf, $\widetilde{p}(r)$, is within the envelope $g(r)h$.

4.2.5 Performance and Robustness

Performance requirement. The portfolio manager must choose a reserve requirement, r_c, which is the greatest loss (most negative return) which will not lead to financial insolvency. However, the manager faces two foci of uncertainty. First, the returns are random, and second, the future pdf of this random variable is subject to unknown and substantial Knightian info-gaps. The performance requirement addresses the randomness, and the robustness function addresses the info-gap uncertainty. In addition, the manager may need to select from among a set of possible portfolios.

Since loss is a random phenomenon it is necessary to choose a value of r_c for which the probability of greater loss is acceptably small, for instance probability α. The value of α also must be chosen. If the manager knew the pdf of financial loss and gain, $p(r)$, then r_c could be chosen as the α quantile of that distribution, $q(\alpha, p)$. Since the pdf is estimated but uncertain, the performance requirement is:

$$q(\alpha, p) \geq r_c \tag{4.21}$$

This means that we require that the true VaR, based on the true but unknown pdf, must be no more negative than the reserve requirement r_c with probability α. Since $p(r)$ is uncertain, the requirement in eq.(4.21) will be incorporated in a robustness function. The robustness function will evaluate the confidence in satisfying this requirement for chosen values of α and r_c.

Robustness function. The robustness to uncertainty in the pdf is the greatest horizon of uncertainty up to which all pdf's result in a value of the α quantile which is no smaller (no more negative) than r_c:

$$\widehat{h}(\alpha, r_c) = \max \left\{ h : \left(\min_{p \in \mathcal{U}(h)} q(\alpha, p) \right) \geq r_c \right\} \tag{4.22}$$

The robustness of choices α and r_c is the greatest horizon of uncertainty up to which the performance requirement in eq.(4.21) is satisfied for all pdf's in the info-gap model.

Let $m(h)$ denote the inner minimum in eq.(4.22). $m(h)$ is the inverse of the robustness. That is, a plot of $m(h)$ vs. h is the same as a plot of r_c vs. $\widehat{h}(\alpha, r_c)$. We will derive an implicit expression from which to evaluate $m(h)$ based on two assumptions. First, we assume that r_s is large enough so that:

$$\mu - r_s < 0 \tag{4.23}$$

where μ is the mean of the estimated distribution, $\widetilde{p}(r)$. This means that the lower $1/r^2$ tail of the envelope is in the negative (loss) range of returns.

Second, we assume that α is small enough so that:

$$m(h) \le \mu - r_{\mathrm{s}} \tag{4.24}$$

This means that the greatest loss at horizon of uncertainty h is in the $1/r^2$ region of uncertainty of the lower tail of the pdf.

$m(h)$ is a quantile. In particular, it is the lowest (most negative) value of $q(\alpha, p)$ in eq.(4.17) for any pdf $p(r)$ in the set $\mathcal{U}(h)$. The quantile is minimized at horizon of uncertainty h by the pdf whose lower tail is as fat as possible at that value of h. Using the assumption in eq.(4.24), this fattest possible tail is the upper envelope for $r \le m(h)$:

$$p(r) = \widetilde{p}(r) + \frac{\widetilde{p}(\mu - r_{\mathrm{s}})(\mu - r_{\mathrm{s}})^2 h}{r^2}, \quad r \le m(h) \tag{4.25}$$

We must assure that the rest of this pdf, for $r > m(h)$, can be chosen from $\mathcal{U}(h)$ to be non-negative and normalized. We will consider this requirement shortly.

Eq.(4.25), together with eq.(4.17), imply that $m(h)$ must satisfy the following quantile relation:

$$\alpha = \int_{-\infty}^{m(h)} \left(\widetilde{p}(r) + \frac{\widetilde{p}(\mu - r_{\mathrm{s}})(\mu - r_{\mathrm{s}})^2 h}{r^2} \right) \mathrm{d}r \tag{4.26}$$

The assumptions in eqs.(4.23) and (4.24) guarantee that this integral is finite, so we can integrate the second term in eq.(4.26) and write the equation as:

$$\alpha = \int_{-\infty}^{m(h)} \widetilde{p}(r)\, \mathrm{d}r - \frac{\widetilde{p}(\mu - r_{\mathrm{s}})(\mu - r_{\mathrm{s}})^2 h}{m(h)} \tag{4.27}$$

This is an implicit expression for $m(h)$, the inverse of the robustness function. Eq.(4.27) can be solved numerically for $m(h)$.

It must be verified numerically that $m(h)$ in this relation satisfies eq.(4.24). Note that, from eqs.(4.23) and (4.24), $m(h)$ is negative so both terms in eq.(4.27) are positive. Note also that the right-hand side of eq.(4.27) increases strictly monotonically as $m(h)$ increases from $-\infty$, so any solution is unique.

If $\widetilde{p}$ is a normal distribution with mean μ and variance σ^2, then eq.(4.27) becomes:

$$\alpha = \Phi\left(\frac{m(h)-\mu}{\sigma}\right) - \frac{\widetilde{p}(\mu - r_{\rm s})(\mu - r_{\rm s})^2 h}{m(h)} \tag{4.28}$$

where $\Phi(\cdot)$ is the cumulative distribution function of the standard normal variate.

We must now check the issue of normalization: can the fat tail in eq.(4.25) belong to a non-negative normalized pdf in the info-gap model at horizon of uncertainty h? Can the excess probability on this fat tail be compensated by reduced probability over the rest of the pdf? The excess probability, over and above the probability of the estimated tail, is less than:

$$\int_{-\infty}^{m(h)} \frac{\widetilde{p}(\mu - r_{\rm s})(\mu - r_{\rm s})^2 h}{r^2}\, {\rm d}r = -\frac{\widetilde{p}(\mu - r_{\rm s})(\mu - r_{\rm s})^2 h}{m(h)} \tag{4.29}$$

This is positive since $m(h)$ is negative. The envelope of the info-gap model at horizon of uncertainty h allows the remainder of the pdf, for $r > m(h)$, to be reduced by at least as much as $\widetilde{p}(r)h$, whose integral is:

$$h \int_{m(h)}^{\infty} \widetilde{p}(r)\, {\rm d}r \tag{4.30}$$

A sufficient condition for the pdf to be normalizable is that the minimal potential *reduction* of probability, eq.(4.30), exceeds the maximal *excess* of probability, eq.(4.29). For the normal distribution this condition is:

$$-\frac{\widetilde{p}(\mu - r_{\rm s})(\mu - r_{\rm s})^2}{m(h)} \le 1 - \Phi\left(\frac{m(h)-\mu}{\sigma}\right) \tag{4.31}$$

Summary. Eq.(4.27) is an implicit expression for the inverse of the robustness function, and eq.(4.28) is the special case when the estimated pdf is normal. These relations are valid if eqs.(4.23), (4.24) and (4.31) hold. Numerical solution of eq.(4.27) or (4.28) to determine $m(h)$ enables the evaluation and plotting of the robustness function.

4.2.6 Safety Factor and Incremental VaR

Safety factor. The estimated value at risk, ignoring info-gap uncertainty in the pdf, is $q(\alpha, \widetilde{p})$. This is the greatest loss at probability

α, if $\widetilde{p}(r)$ is the correct pdf of the rate of return. The robustness for obtaining this value at risk is precisely zero.

The analyst recognizes that $\widetilde{p}$ is likely to err, and demands a positive robustness, $\widehat{h}_{\rm d}$. The value at risk corresponding to this demanded robustness is $m(\widehat{h}_{\rm d})$, the inverse of the robustness function.

We define a *safety factor* as the ratio of the robust value at risk $m(\widehat{h}_{\rm d})$, to the zero-robustness estimated value at risk:

$$S(\widehat{h}_{\rm d}, \alpha) = \frac{m(\widehat{h}_{\rm d})}{q(\alpha, \widetilde{p})} \tag{4.32}$$

This safety factor is the ratio between the reserve requirement $r_{\rm c}$ which has robustness $\widehat{h}_{\rm d}$, to the reserve requirement which has zero robustness.

Incremental VaR. The incremental VaR is a valuable tool for comparing portfolios, for instance in assessing the risk implications of including or removing a particular asset or set of assets (Dowd, 1998, p.48). A portfolio change which results in less negative VaR is desirable; a change which makes the VaR more negative is not.

However, VaRs are evaluated from estimated pdfs. A VaR calculated as the α quantile of an estimated pdf has no robustness against Knightian uncertainty in that pdf. Only a more negative VaR has positive robustness. The analyst faces an irrevocable trade-off between performance and robustness when estimating VaRs from distributions with Knightian uncertainty.

The info-gap robustness can be used to evaluate incremental VaRs. We will find that sometimes the robustness curves of different portfolios cross one another. This implies the possibility of a change in the sign of the incremental VaR and a consequent reversal of preference between these portfolios.

4.2.7 Policy Exploration

We now consider the policy implications of this analysis through a series of examples. The portfolio manager much choose the reserve requirement, which is the critical loss, $r_{\rm c}$, in the robustness function. In addition, the manager must choose the acceptable probability, α, of exceeding the reserve requirement. The robustness function, $\widehat{h}(\alpha, r_{\rm c})$, depends on both $r_{\rm c}$ and α, and is the basis for evaluating alternative choices of these quantities. Furthermore, the manager may need to choose between different portfolios.

The estimated pdf of the returns, $\widetilde{p}(r)$, is normal with mean μ and variance σ^2. We consider fat tails which may begin to appear at $r_s = 2\sigma$ on either side of the mean. Unless indicated otherwise, we consider a 1% risk, so $\alpha = 0.01$.

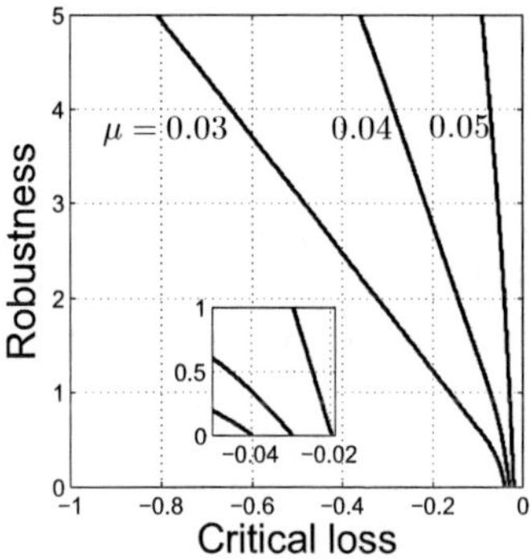

Figure 4.4: Robustness, $\widehat{h}$, vs. critical loss, r_c, for 3 values of μ. $\sigma = 0.03$.

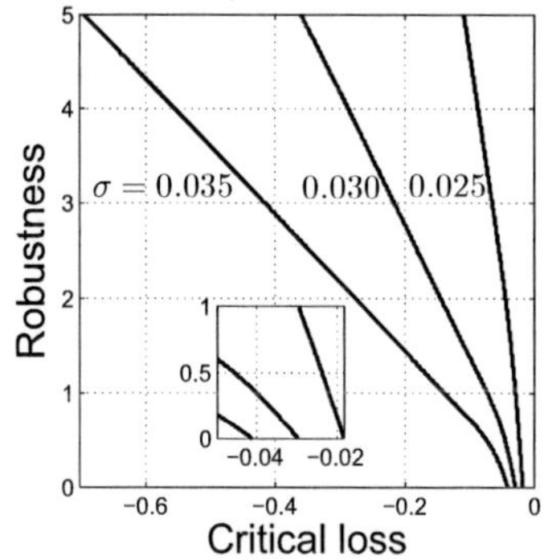

Figure 4.5: Robustness, $\widehat{h}$, vs. critical loss, r_c, for 3 values of σ. $\mu = 0.04$.

Trade-off and zeroing. Fig. 4.4 shows curves of robustness, $\widehat{h}(\alpha, r_c)$, vs the critical loss, r_c, for three different values of the mean of the estimated distribution of returns. These robustness curves can be thought of as representing 3 different portfolios. The negative slope of these curves expresses the trade-off between robustness to uncertainty and performance: high robustness is obtained in exchange for very negative critical loss. A large reserve requirement (very negative r_c) is needed in order to have confidence against both the statistical variability and the info-gap uncertainty.

These curves reach zero robustness at -0.02, -0.03 and -0.04 as seen in the insert of fig. 4.4. These are precisely the estimated VaRs of these three portfolios, based on the estimated pdf $\widetilde{p}(r)$. The estimated performance has zero robustness against Knightian uncertainty, as explained in section 2.2.2. If $\widetilde{p}(r)$ is the correct pdf, then reserve requirements at 2, 3 or 4% of the total portfolio value will protect against 99% of the random fluctuation for these three portfolios. However, we have every reason to believe that $\widetilde{p}(r)$ is *not* the correct pdf, and that we must protect against both statistical variability *and* Knightian info-gaps. Hence the VaRs on the horizontal axis—which have zero robustness—are not a good guide to policy. Only larger (more negative) critical loss has positive robustness against error in the tail of the pdf.

Effect of the mean. Fig. 4.4 shows that the robustness curve shifts to the right as the mean of the estimated distribution is reduced. Lower estimated returns entail lower robustness at any fixed critical loss.

We also note that the slopes of these curves become more moderate as the mean return decreases. The slope expresses the cost of robustness. Very steep slope, as in the case of the uppermost curve, indicates that the robustness can be increased without giving up too much performance. At $\mu = 0.05$ the robustness can be increased from zero to 5 by reducing the critical loss from -0.02 to -0.09. A 9% reserve requirement is not negligible, but the corresponding values for $\mu = 0.04$ and $\mu = 0.03$ are far greater: 36 and 81% respectively.

Calibrating the robustness. What does the numerical value of the robustness mean? Is robustness of 3 or 5 "large"? From the info-gap model, eq.(4.20) on p.100, we see that robustness of 3 means that the actual pdf of the returns, $p(r)$, can deviate from the estimated pdf, $\widetilde{p}(r)$, by as much as 3 times the envelope (subject to non-negativity and normalization). The envelope decays much more slowly than the estimated pdf on the tails, so this implies that the tails can be far heavier than expected.

To get a feel for what a unit of robustness implies, let's compare the standard normal distribution ($\mu = 0$, $\sigma = 1$) and the $1/r^2$ tails which sprout off at 2 standard deviations from the mean, as specified in eq.(4.19). The area of the tail of the standard normal distribution below -2σ is 0.0228, while the area of the fat tail of the envelope in eq.(4.19) below -2σ is 0.1080. Thus a single unit of robustness entails immunity against a lower tail which has nearly five times more cumulative probability than expected.

Effect of the standard deviation. Fig. 4.5 shows robustness curves for three values of the standard deviation of the estimated distribution, at fixed mean. The middle curve is the same as the middle curve in fig. 4.4. In fact, figs. 4.4 and 4.5 look quite similar, indicating that mean and variance have similar impact on the robustness to uncertainty. Comparing these figures, one can say that an increase of 0.005 in the standard deviation is roughly equivalent to a decrease of 0.01 in the mean, in this specific example. This is reminiscent of the well-known mean-variance trade-off, and suggests that there is an info-gap robustness analog.

Crossing robustness curves. One manifestation of the mean-variance trade-off is that there are combinations of μ and σ whose

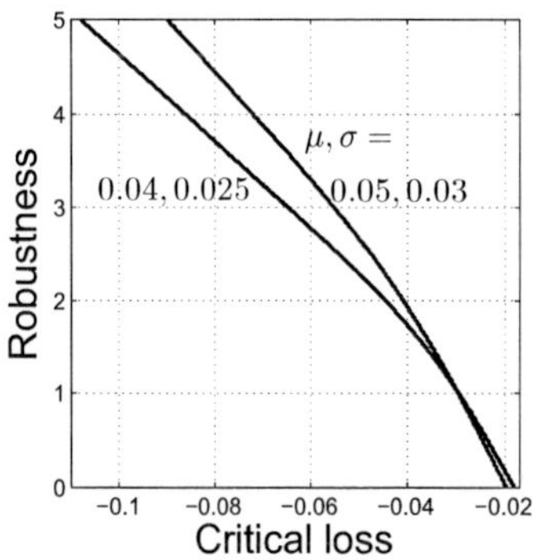

Figure 4.6: Robustness, $\widehat{h}$, vs. critical loss, r_c, for two different combinations of μ and σ.

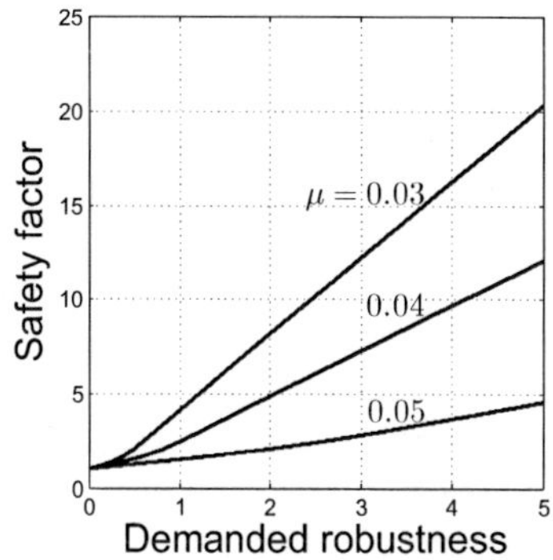

Figure 4.7: Safety factor, S, vs. demanded robustness, $\widehat{h}_d$, for 3 values of μ. $\sigma = 0.03$.

robustness curves cross one another, as seen in fig. 4.6.

The robustness curves in fig. 4.6 reach the horizontal axis at -0.018 and -0.020. These are the VaRs based on the estimated pdf's, showing that the smaller mean return with the smaller variance is weakly preferred over the larger mean return with the larger variance, *if* the estimated pdf's are correct. Since we have reason to believe that the estimated pdf is not correct, and since the robustnesses of these estimated VaRs are exactly zero, we suspect that this preference between these portfolios is not justified. Indeed, their robustness curves cross each other, and the portfolio with larger mean and larger variance has substantially greater robustness to uncertainty in the pdf over most of the range of critical loss shown in the figure. This suggests that one would prefer the larger-mean and larger-variance portfolio despite its more negative estimated VaR.

Safety factor. The safety factor, defined in eq.(4.32), does not contain new information since it is derived entirely from the robustness curve. It does, however, throw new light on the interpretation of the robustness. Fig. 4.7 shows three curves of the safety factor, $S(\widehat{h}_d, \alpha)$, vs. demanded robustness, $\widehat{h}_d$. These curves represent the same portfolios as in fig. 4.4.

The safety factor, $S(\widehat{h}_d, \alpha)$, is the ratio of the reserve requirement whose robustness equals $\widehat{h}_d$, to the reserve requirement based on the estimated pdf, whose robustness is zero. Consequently, all the curves in fig. 4.7 start at $S = 1$ for which $\widehat{h}_d = 0$. The subsequent separation between the curves shows the strong policy impact of the estimated mean.

Suppose the manager demands robustness to 300% error in the pdf, that is, $\widehat{h}_{\rm d} = 3$. The safety factors for the three curves, from bottom to top, are 2.8, 7.2 and 12, respectively. If the estimated mean is 0.05, then the estimated reserve requirement (based on the estimated pdf) must be multiplied by 2.8 in order to find the reserve requirement which has robustness of 3. A multiplier of 2.8 is quite substantial, but nonetheless far less than the amplified reserve requirement for the other portfolios. Naturally, lower demanded robustness entails lower safety factors. For instance, demanded robustness of one, which still entails considerable protection against uncertainty in the tail as discussed earlier, has safety factors of 1.5, 2.5 and 4.1 for the three cases shown in fig. 4.7.

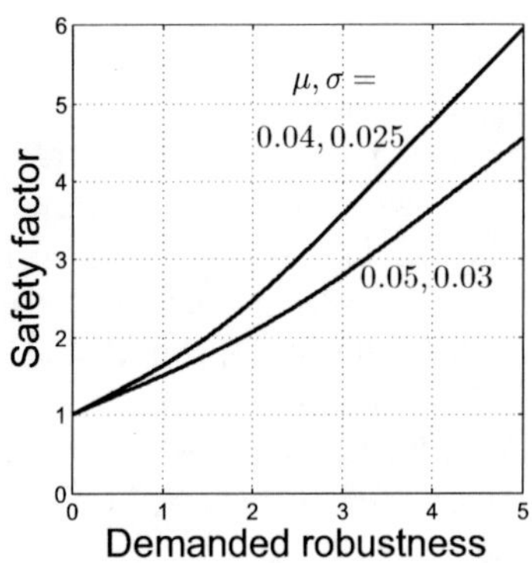

Figure 4.8: Safety factor, S, vs. demanded robustness, $\widehat{h}_{\rm d}$, for two different combinations of μ and σ.

Fig. 4.8 shows the safety-factor curves for the two portfolios in fig. 4.6. The robustness curves in fig. 4.6 cross each other at positive robustness, but the safety-factor curves do not. At first this is surprising since the safety factor is simply the inverse of the robustness divided by the estimated VaR, as seen in eq.(4.32). For these portfolios, the estimated VaRs are -0.0182 for the low-mean and low-variance case and -0.0198 for the high-mean and high-variance case. The higher estimated VaR of the latter portfolio is sufficient to reduce its safety factor below that of the other portfolio. The safety factor is the value by which the estimated VaR must be multiplied in order to find the VaR which has a specified robustness. The larger estimated

VaR results in a lower safety factor. The preference between the portfolios should be based primarily on consideration of the robustness curves, and supplemented by examination of the safety factor.

Incremental VaR. Let's return to fig. 4.4 and consider the three robustness curves as representing three different portfolios which are distinguished by their estimated mean returns. The estimated VaRs of these portfolios are -0.02, -0.03 and -0.04 as seen in the insert. This ranks our preferences among these portfolios in terms of their reserve requirements: the least negative VaR is most favored, etc. The incremental VaR—the difference between the VaRs—is an indication of the relative strength of these preferences.

These estimated VaRs are neither particularly large nor greatly different. A 3% reserve requirement is larger than a 2% requirement, but not overwhelmingly so, especially since even an intuitive analysis would recognize and wish to account for uncertainty, and thus perhaps not attribute great significance to the difference between these estimated VaRs.

However, we know that these estimated VaRs, which are read off the horizontal axis, have zero robustness against uncertainty in their pdf's. Consequently we are motivated to compare the VaRs of these portfolios at positive robustness. For example, the VaRs are quite substantial and distinct even at robustness equal to one: -0.03, -0.07 and -0.16. Comparing these VaRs at positive robustness with the corresponding values, -0.02, -0.03 and -0.04, at zero robustness, we see the very strong cost of robustness as the estimated mean decreases. The curve for $\mu = 0.03$ in fig. 4.4 is sharply tilted compared to the curve for $\mu = 0.04$, which itself is tilted compared to the curve for $\mu = 0.05$. The changed slope makes robustness most expensive for the portfolio with $\mu = 0.03$. Now the incremental VaRs are large and the differences in reserve requirements between the portfolios are quite substantial. The incremental VaRs at positive robustness establish much stronger preferences among these portfolios.

Effect of probability of failure. Fig. 4.9 shows robustness curves for three different values of the probability, α, of violating the reserve requirement. The uppermost curve is the same as the middle curve in figs. 4.4 and 4.5. We see the strong effect of reducing the acceptable probability of failure: the robustness is reduced as α is reduced.

In observing the similarity between figs. 4.4 and 4.5 we noted the trade-off between mean and variance when viewed on the robustness plane. We observe a similarity between these figures and fig. 4.9,

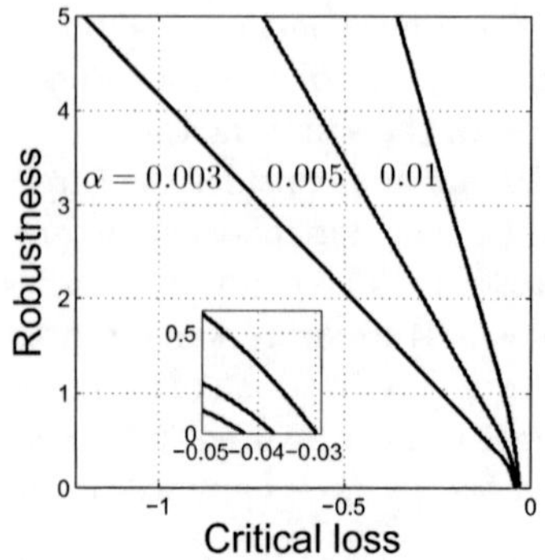

Figure 4.9: Robustness, $\widehat{h}$, vs. critical loss, r_c, for three different probabilities of failure, α. $\mu = 0.04$ and $\sigma = 0.03$.

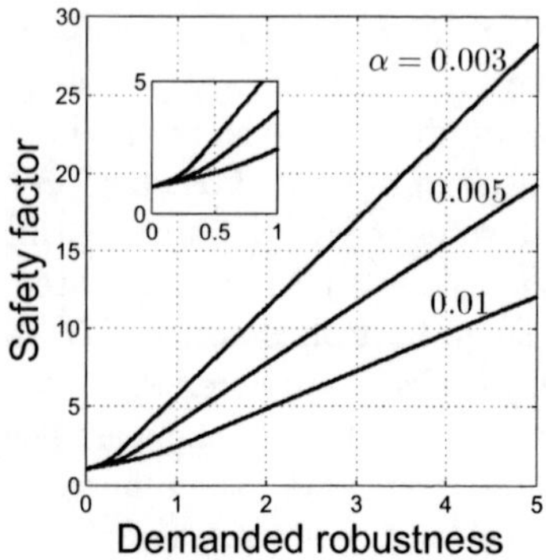

Figure 4.10: Safety factor, S, vs. demanded robustness, $\widehat{h}_d$, for three different probabilities of failure, α. $\mu = 0.04$ and $\sigma = 0.03$.

which shows that α, μ and σ all complement each other at any fixed robustness, $\widehat{h}$, and reserve requirement, r_c.

Fig. 4.10 shows the safety factors for the same three values of α. Accepting greater probability of failure allows lower reserve requirement at any fixed demanded robustness.[5]

4.2.8 Robustness with Uncertain Normal Distributions

In this section we perform a robustness analysis of much more moderate info-gap uncertainty about the probability distribution of the returns. We confidently believe that the pdf is normal, and we have estimates of the mean and variance. Our understanding is that the actual moments may differ from these estimates due to changes in the economy, but such changes would not alter the normality of the distribution.

Uncertainty model. The estimated mean and standard deviation, and the standard errors of those estimates, are $\widetilde{\mu}$, $\widetilde{\sigma}$, ε_μ and ε_σ. The basic idea is that the fractional deviations of the true mean and

[5] This is intuitively satisfying. However, the reverse can occur: the safety factor can *decrease* as the probability of failure decreases, unlike fig. 4.10. The safety factor is the ratio of two negative numbers, and its direction of change depends on how the slope of the robustness curve changes with r_c. We will encounter an example in fig. 4.12.

standard deviation, from these estimated values, are unknown:

$$\left| \frac{\mu - \widetilde{\mu}}{\varepsilon_\mu} \right| \le h, \quad \left| \frac{\sigma - \widetilde{\sigma}}{\varepsilon_\sigma} \right| \le h \tag{4.33}$$

where the standard deviation must also be non-negative and the horizon of uncertainty, h, is unknown. We state this as an info-gap model for uncertainty in the normal distribution of returns:

$$\mathcal{U}(h) = \left\{ p(r) \sim N(\mu, \sigma^2) : \left| \frac{\mu - \widetilde{\mu}}{\varepsilon_\mu} \right| \le h, \left| \frac{\sigma - \widetilde{\sigma}}{\varepsilon_\sigma} \right| \le h, \ \sigma \ge 0 \right\}, \quad h \ge 0 \tag{4.34}$$

Robustness function. The performance requirement is the same as eq.(4.21) on p.101, based on the quantile defined in eq.(4.17). The robustness function is defined the same as in eq.(4.22), though now we use the info-gap model in eq.(4.34). We will now derive an explicit expression for this robustness function.

Let $m(h)$ denote the inner minimum in the definition of the robustness, eq.(4.22). $m(h)$ is the inverse of the robustness. We will derive an explicit expression for $m(h)$, and then invert it to obtain an expression for the robustness.

Our derivation is based on one assumption. Let z_α denote the α quantile of the standard normal distribution, with zero mean and unit standard deviation. We assume that α is less than 1/2, so that z_α is negative. In practice this is an entirely unrestrictive assumption since we will be interested in values of α around 0.01.

Since we know that $p(r)$ is a normal distribution, the quantile relation, eq.(4.17), can be written:

$$\alpha = \Phi \left(\frac{q(\alpha, p) - \mu}{\sigma} \right) \tag{4.35}$$

where $\Phi(\cdot)$ is the cumulative distribution function of the standard normal variable. Inverting this relation one finds:

$$q(\alpha, p) = \sigma z_\alpha + \mu \tag{4.36}$$

From our assumption that z_α is negative, we see that the inner minimum in the definition of the robustness, eq.(4.22), occurs when the standard deviation is as large as possible, and the mean is as small as possible, at horizon of uncertainty h. Thus the inner minimum becomes:

$$m(h) = (\widetilde{\sigma} + \varepsilon_\sigma h) z_\alpha + \widetilde{\mu} - \varepsilon_\mu h \tag{4.37}$$

$$= \underbrace{\widetilde{\sigma} z_\alpha + \widetilde{\mu}}_{q(\alpha, \widetilde{p})} + (\varepsilon_\sigma z_\alpha - \varepsilon_\mu) h \tag{4.38}$$

where we note that the first two terms on the right-hand side of eq.(4.38) are the α quantile of the estimated normal distribution, $\widetilde{p}(r)$, whose moments are $\widetilde{\mu}$ and $\widetilde{\sigma}$.

The robustness is the greatest horizon of uncertainty, h, at which eq.(4.38) is no more negative than the critical loss, r_c. The robustness is zero if $q(\alpha, \widetilde{p})$ is more negative than r_c. If $q(\alpha, \widetilde{p})$ is not more negative than r_c, then the robustness is found by equating the right-hand side of eq.(4.38) to r_c and solving for h to obtain:

$$\widehat{h}(\alpha, r_c) = \frac{r_c - q(\alpha, \widetilde{p})}{\varepsilon_\sigma z_\alpha - \varepsilon_\mu} \tag{4.39}$$

The robustness is zero if this expression is negative, which occurs if the numerator is positive since the denominator is negative.

We will also consider the safety factor $S(\widehat{h}_d, \alpha)$, eq.(4.32), based on $m(h)$ in eq.(4.38). Recall that the safety factor is the ratio between the reserve requirement r_c which has robustness $\widehat{h}_d$, to the reserve requirement which has zero robustness. Combining eqs.(4.36) and (4.38) we find:

$$S(\widehat{h}_d, \alpha) = 1 + \frac{\varepsilon_\sigma z_\alpha - \varepsilon_\mu}{\widetilde{\sigma} z_\alpha + \widetilde{\mu}} \widehat{h}_d \tag{4.40}$$

Policy exploration. Fig. 4.11 shows robustness curves, eq.(4.39), for three different probabilities of failure, α. We observe the usual trade-off and zeroing properties. Also, the robustness increases as the probability of failure increases, as seen with the previous model in fig. 4.9.

Most importantly, we note that the robustness is now much greater at the same values of critical loss. This is a direct expression of the much more informative—less uncertain—info-gap model of eq.(4.34) than the info-gap model of eq.(4.20).

Fig. 4.12 shows the safety-factor curves for these three probabilities of failure. We note that the safety factor decreases as α decreases: requiring lower probability of failure entails lower reserve requirement at any fixed demanded robustness. This is the reverse of the situation displayed in fig. 4.10. As explained in footnote 5 on p.110, the

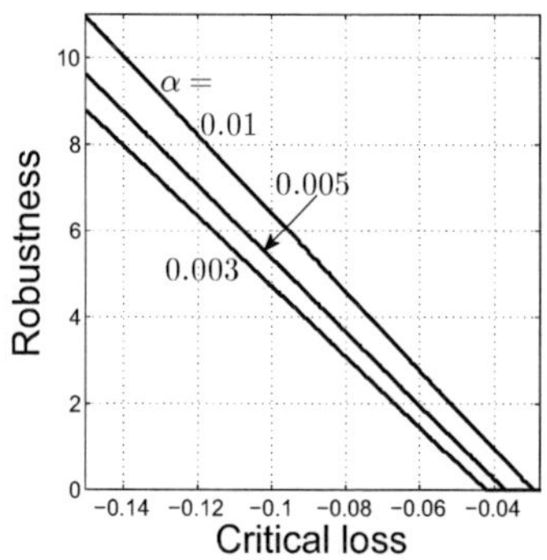

Figure 4.11: Robustness, $\widehat{h}$, vs. critical loss, r_c, for three different probabilities of failure, α. $\widetilde{\mu} = 0.04$, $\widetilde{\sigma} = 0.03$, $\varepsilon_\mu = 0.004$, $\varepsilon_\sigma = 0.003$.

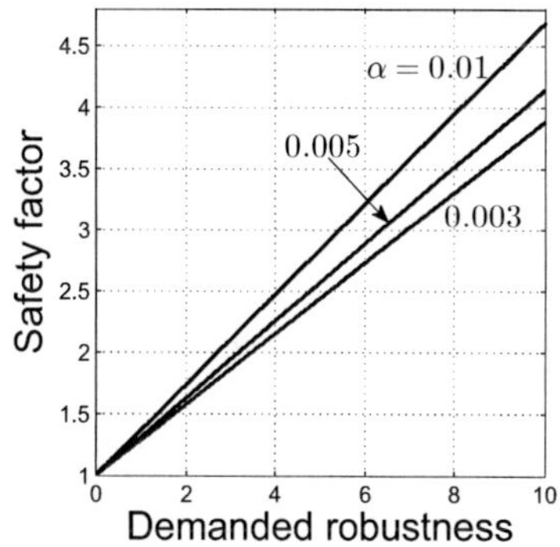

Figure 4.12: Safety factor, S, vs. demanded robustness, $\widehat{h}_d$, for three different probabilities of failure, α. $\widetilde{\mu}$, $\widetilde{\sigma}$, ε_μ and ε_σ as in fig. 4.11.

safety factor is the ratio of two negative numbers. In the present case, as α decreases, the denominator (which is the estimated VaR at each α) becomes more negative more rapidly than the numerator (which is $m(h)$, the inverse of the robustness). Hence the safety factor decreases with decreasing α.

Fig. 4.13 shows the robustness curves for two portfolios, one with higher mean and higher variance, and the other with lower mean and lower variance. The former has less negative—and hence preferable—estimated VaR equal to -0.030 rather than -0.038. However, at robustness of about 2.7 and VaR of -0.058, the curves cross one another. A need for greater robustness, or a willingness to accept a more negative VaR, would motivate a preference for the low-mean low-variance portfolio. This illustrates the possibility for reversal of preference, which is a characteristic consequence of crossing robustness curves.

Fig. 4.14 shows the safety-factor curves for these two portfolios. The low-mean low-variance portfolio has a lower safety factor since its estimated VaR is more negative.

4.2.9 Extensions

Numerous extensions of this analysis are possible.

Measures of value at risk. We have focussed entirely on the unconditional quantile assessment of VaR. Other measures of risk

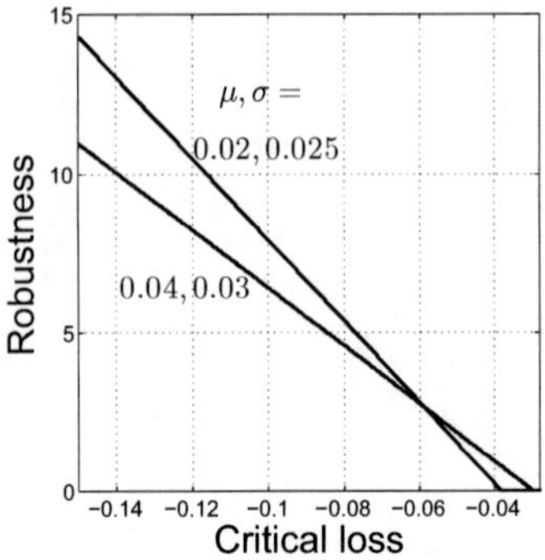

Figure 4.13: Robustness, $\widehat{h}$, vs. critical loss, r_c, for two different combinations of μ and σ. $\alpha = 0.01$.

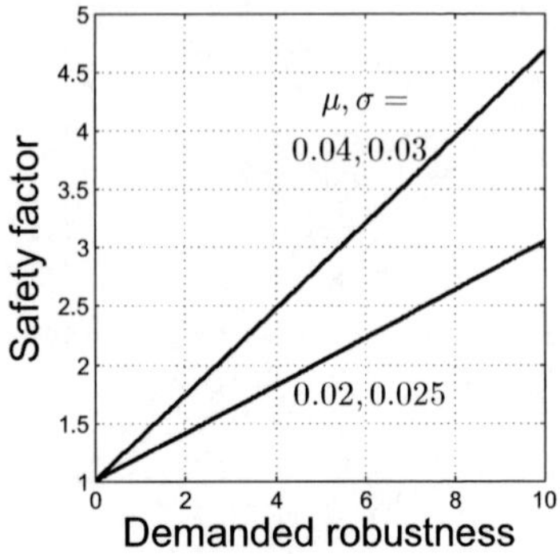

Figure 4.14: Safety factor, S, vs. demanded robustness, $\widehat{h}_d$, for two different combinations of μ and σ. $\alpha = 0.01$.

are available, such as the conditional VaR (Rockafellar and Uryasev, 2000, 2002) or extreme-value properties (Boudoukh *et al.* 1995; Longin, 1996; Dowd, 1998).

Non-normal estimated pdf's. Our numerical examples in sections 4.2.7 and 4.2.8 have assumed that the estimated pdf is normal. Other estimated pdf's are sometimes used.

Models of rare events and fat tails. Our info-gap model of fat-tail uncertainty in section 4.2.4 is rather extreme. More detailed information about extreme or rare events may be available, and this would enable a more informative—less uncertain—info-gap model. While a strictly probabilistic model is likely to require assumptions which are difficult to verify, a more informative info-gap model is possible in some situations.

Info-gap estimation. We have focussed on the Knightian uncertainty which remains unmodelled after the probability distribution is estimated by standard statistical tools. However, in some situations the assumptions which underlie these statistical tools—e.g. independence, large data set, normality, etc.—are violated. In this case, the estimation itself can be augmented by info-gap techniques. We discuss some problems of this sort in chapter 6.

Forecasting. We have cast the Knightian uncertainty as arising from the disparity between *historical* data upon which a probability distribution is based, and *future* returns which are risky. It is sometimes possible to augment the VaR assessment with forecasts of future returns. We discuss some aspects of info-gap forecasting in chapter 6.

4.3 Stress Testing: Suite of Models

Financial stability is an economy-wide phenomenon. The financial strengths and vulnerabilities of an economy reflect, at the very least, the evolving interactions between the major economic sectors. More realistically, vulnerabilities in times of crises reflect behavioral characteristics of the groups and societies involved as conditioned by historical and cultural context. The task of identifying and predicting vulnerabilities requires the integration of a suite of models representing these factors and phenomena. Different institutions—central banks, large financial institutions, or public research organizations—will do this in different ways. The analysis of small open economies will differ from the analysis of large (but nonetheless open) economies. Finally, judgments of what is uncertain, and how uncertain it is, will be made differently over time, place, and institutional affiliation.

This section is a conceptual discussion of the info-gap robustness analysis of system-wide financial stability. We will focus on how one incorporates the idea of stress testing in an analysis of robustness.

Stress testing is itself an assessment of robustness of the economy to untoward and unanticipated shocks. The added value of the info-gap robustness analysis is in incorporating two major classes of uncertainty.

First, the models are highly uncertain when applied to situations of stress. The Lucas critique—that behavior patterns (and hence models) change when new events occur—applies "with a vengeance" in testing crisis response with models calibrated in normal circumstances. The robustness question is: how wrong can these models be, and the conclusions or recommendations of the stress test will still be valid? The info-gap robustness function assists in formulating an answer.

Second, the shocks are highly uncertain. Stress testing as it is usually conceived entails examining specific severe scenarios. Judgment is used in order to identify relevant possibilities. By embedding a stress test in an info-gap robustness analysis we broaden the scope of scenarios. We do not diminish the need for careful informed judgment; we supplement it with the ability to consider a wider range of uncertainty. The robustness question once again is: how wrong can our choices of crises and shocks be, with the conclusions or recommendations of the stress test still being useful?

4.3.1 Suite of Models and their Uncertainties

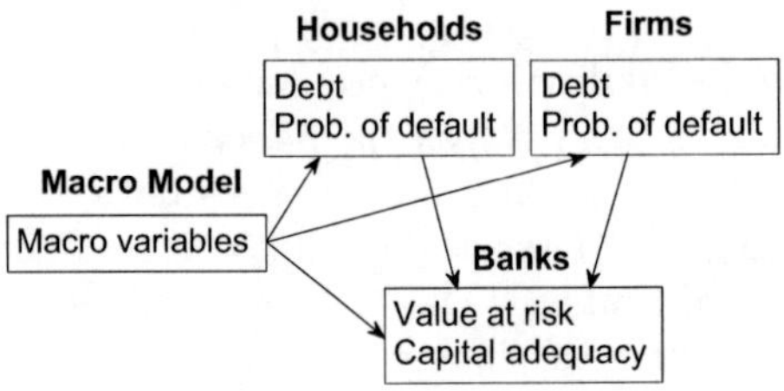

Figure 4.15: Suite of models for stress testing. Adapted from Andersen *et al.* (2008).

Stress testing the financial stability of an economy involves the use of a suite of models. Fig. 4.15 illustrates a simplified realization. A macro-economic model feeds into models of households and firms, which feed into banks and other financial institutions. Naturally, the interactions are bi-lateral on at least some of the connections. In addition, there may be many more modules, representing for instance exchange rates, security markets, commodities and natural resource markets, organized labor, and so on.

Two approaches to info-gap modelling. There are two approaches to formulating info-gap models for uncertainty in the modules of the suite of models: "grass roots" and "high level".

The **grass roots** approach looks at the equations and data sets in each model, and constructs info-gap models for their uncertainty. This can be done in different ways. For instance, in section 3.1.4 on p.33 we constructed an info-gap model for uncertainty in the coefficients of a macro-economic model.

In other situations we may consider uncertainty in functional relationships. For instance, the demand curve for a commodity may be estimated, and perhaps known to be monotonic, but its actual position and shape can deviate substantially in times of stress. Envelope-bound models such as those discussed in sections 7.2.1 and 7.2.2 (pp.221, 222) can be used.

Some models are themselves probabilistic, for instance the elements in fig. 4.15 for probability of default or value at risk. These models employ estimated probability distributions. We have considered info-gap models for uncertainty in the shape of fat or thin tails of a probability distribution in sections 3.3.4 (p.59) and 4.2.4 (p.99). In section 4.1.4 (p.90) we considered uncertainty in the probabilities of discrete events. In section 4.2.8 (p.110) we employed an info-gap model to represent uncertainty in the parameters of a normal distribution.

The **high level** approach to modelling the uncertainties in a suite of models ignores the details and equations of the individual modules, and focusses on the uncertainty in the end result of these models. For instance, a module representing the growth, equity, debt and investment of a firm or industry may be quite detailed and exploit extensive data. Nonetheless, the final output of the model may simply be a probability distribution of profit or loss, conditioned on macroeconomic variables. A high level approach would treat the model prediction of this probability distribution as a best estimate, and use an info-gap model to represent unknown deviation of the true distribution from this estimate.

We have essentially taken a high level approach in our study of value at risk in section 4.2. The info-gap model in eq.(4.20) on p.100 represents the net uncertainty in returns to a portfolio, without delving into the structure and composition of the portfolio.

In summary, the distinction between the grass roots and the high level approaches to modelling uncertainty is related to the distinction between strategic and tactical decision making discussed in the preface, p.xiii. Strategic decision makers will tend to prefer high level modelling of uncertainty. The broad contextual understanding which is incorporated in strategic thinking is more amenable to rough-cut high level models of uncertainty. In contrast, tactical decisions are specific directives and generally depend on detailed grass roots representations of data, models and their uncertainties.

Which approach to use? The grass roots and high level approaches may overlap to some extent, but they are still different. Which approach to adopt is a difficult and important judgment.

On the one hand, if one has information and insight into the uncertainties associated with specific models and data sets, then this information can be used in formulating a grass roots info-gap model. To ignore this information would be wasteful.

On the other hand, it is simply not true that the inclusion of information necessarily enhances the overall robustness to error. Every bushel of apples has a few worms, and the added unidentified error may outweigh the added information.

The choice between grass roots and high level modelling of uncertainty can be thought of in terms of the value of information (Ben-Haim, 2006, chap. 7). Information can be valuated in units of robustness. If the grass roots information-intensive representation of uncertainty is more robust to Knightian info-gaps than the high level approach, then the information is "valuable", and the grass roots approach should be preferred. If not, then the high level approach is preferable even though information about modules and data is ignored.

Of course, this method for selecting between the approaches requires that both be implemented and their robustness curves compared. This comparison raises delicate questions of the commensurability of robustnesses based on different info-gap models. There is also the practical question of whether it is feasible to implement both approaches and then use only one.

4.3.2 Shocks and their Uncertainties

Stress testing involves assessing the effects of severe shocks. While experience and judgment are invaluable in characterizing severe events, our experience of extreme circumstances is by definition limited. Stress testing hinges on the analysis of extreme scenarios, so the analysis depends on an inherently fragmentary part of our knowledge. Finally, the processes are inevitably more complex and inter-connected than our understanding would suggest. This means that causal connections and statistical correlations which in the past were latent and unnoticed, may become central in stressful situations. The crisis of sub-prime mortgages arose in part due to higher-than-anticipated correlation among default probabilities of different assets, as discussed in section 4.1. In short, severe shocks are info-gap entities.

Shocks are often modelled as random variables, and our prior discussion suggests that the underlying data generating processes are highly uncertain. The probability distributions describing the shocks are subject to uncertainties which are readily represented with info-gap models as mentioned earlier. The same is true of the means, variances, and correlation coefficients of these distributions.

Sometimes shocks are modelled as auto-regressive processes which reflect understanding about properties and limitations of the shocks. For instance, if a shock is certain to decay over time then a first-order auto-regressive relation can encode this knowledge. However, the value of the decay coefficient may be entirely unknown. An info-gap model of uncertain first-order auto-regressions is discussed in section 7.2.3 on p.225.

Shocks may be expressed as uni-modal disturbances. For example, oil prices may rise abruptly and then gradually return to more normal values. The slopes in the rise and fall, the peak value, and the duration may all be highly uncertain. An info-gap model of this sort is described in section 7.2.2 on p.224.

4.3.3 Embedding a Stress Test

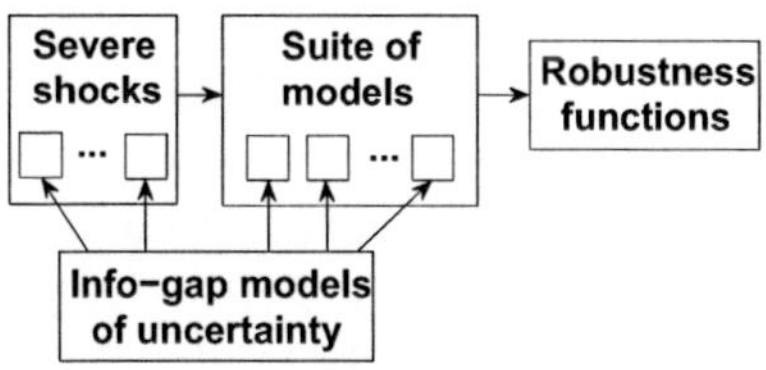

Figure 4.16: Embedding a stress test in an info-gap robustness analysis.

Fig. 4.16 schematically illustrates a stress test which is embedded in an info-gap robustness analysis. As always, a robustness analysis combines three components: system models, uncertainty models, and performance requirements.

System models. The suite of models, together with the severe shocks, make up this component.

Info-gap models. Info-gap models for uncertainties in the suite of models and for uncertainties in the shocks are formulated. Regarding the suite of models, it must first be decided whether to use grass roots or high level models, or a combination of both. Then the specific info-gap models are formulated as discussed in sections 4.3.1 and 4.3.2.

Performance requirements. The performance requirements are derived from the suite of models and the goals of the analyst. For instance, it may be required that the value at risk in major banks of the financial sector not be greater than a specified value. Additional requirements may, for example, relate to macro-economic variables such as inflation and unemployment.

We now evaluate, in the usual way, the robustness of these system models for satisfying the performance requirements, given the uncertainties. One can evaluate separate robustness functions for each performance requirement, or combine them.

The decisions which must be made, such as reserve requirements or resource allocations, are contained in the system models. Thus the robustness is a function of the decisions, and is used to establish preferences among the decision alternatives.

4.4 Strategic Asset Allocation

Central banks, investment banks, pension funds and other large financial institutions engage in long-range strategic allocation of assets. The strategic dimension involves consideration of both risks and returns. Market risk, credit risk, interest rate risk, exchange rate risk and other factors are all relevant in various circumstances and for various types of investments. The level of return, and the parameters which measure performance, also depend on the organization and type of investment. Investment yield, value at risk, capital reserve and other parameters may be used to assess the performance of the allocation.

The strategic allocation of resources depends on the risk-return preferences of the organization, its definition of acceptable risk, its perception of the nature of the relevant uncertainties, its long-range goals or mandate, and the time horizon for achieving these goals. These issues must be resolved at the executive level of the organization.

Given the organization's "philosophy" of investment, a quantitative model-based strategy for the allocation of assets can be developed (Koivu *et al.* 2009). This can be realized in different ways, ranging from a comprehensive suite of models to a more limited and pragmatic quantification. In any case, the model for strategic allocation of assets represents a benchmark in two respects. It is a quantitative reflection of the institution's attitude to risk and return, and it provides a guideline for the day-by-day tactical decisions made by investment personnel.

In this section we will consider a simple model for strategic allocation of assets. The theoretical development is generic and the numerical example focusses on choosing the allocation between a risk-free and a risky asset, where the resulting capital reserve is the measure of performance. We consider an investment philosophy which stresses the need for confidence in capital reserves, and which perceives moderate uncertainty in the tails of the probability distribution of returns.

4.4.1 Policy Preview

Estimated quantiles of the capital reserve have zero robustness to uncertainty in the probability distribution of the payoff. Only lower—possibly negative—quantiles of the capital reserve have positive robustness. This trade-off between robustness and capital reserve is unavoidable, and means that allocations must be evaluated not only in terms of the outcomes which are estimated to occur, but also in terms of the less desirable outcomes which have substantial robustness to uncertainty.

Susceptibility to uncertainty also means that better-than-anticipated capital reserves may occur, and this is possible precisely because there is uncertainty in the payoffs. The opportuneness function quantifies the feasibility of windfall outcomes, augmenting the robustness analysis of the allocation.

A classical dilemma facing investors is the choice between an allocation which has both higher estimated outcomes and higher uncertainty, vs. an allocation with lower estimated outcomes which are nonetheless more confidently predicted. This dilemma is manifested graphically in the intersection between the corresponding robustness curves. The values of robustness and capital reserve at which the intersection occurs assist the investor in deciding between these allocations.

The temporal sequence of allocations can have a profound impact both on the estimated outcomes and on the robustness to uncertainty. We consider allocation between a risk-free and a risky asset over two time steps. A modest increase in the fraction allocated to the risk-free asset is far more promising than the reverse sequence of allocations. While this conclusion may vary with the characteristics of the assets, the method reveals sequence effects, whatever they may be.

4.4.2 Operational Preview

System model. The example focusses on reliably achieving acceptably large capital reserves as a result of the allocation. The budget constraint, eq.(4.41), relates the capital reserve to the asset prices, the allocations at the previous and current time step, and the payoffs. The payoff is a random variable, so the investor requires that the probability be small that the capital reserve is too low. Thus the system model is a quantile of the probability distribution of the capital reserve, eq.(4.46).

Performance requirement and windfall aspiration. The investor requires that the quantile of the capital reserve exceed a critical value, eq.(4.47). The allocation is chosen to assure large robustness for achieving this *critical requirement.* A *windfall aspiration* is that the quantile of the capital reserve exceed a substantially greater value, eq.(4.50). The opportuneness function is used to evaluate the feasibility of this aspiration.

Uncertainty model. The probability distribution of the risky-asset payoff is uncertain. The judgment is made that this is moderate uncertainty which is manifested in unknown variability of the mean and variance of the distribution. The distribution itself is confidently assumed to be normal. The info-gap model is defined in eq.(4.45).

Robustness and opportuneness functions. The robustness of a particular allocation is the greatest horizon of uncertainty in the moments of the payoff distribution up to which the critical requirement is guaranteed to be satisfied, eqs.(4.48) and (4.49). The opportuneness of an allocation is the lowest horizon of uncertainty at which it is possible—though not necessarily guaranteed—that the windfall aspiration will be realized, eqs.(4.51) and (4.53).

4.4.3 Budget Constraint

The investment decisions are constrained by the requirement that the capital reserve must remain adequate. This requirement depends on a budget constraint relating investments, asset prices, payoffs and capital reserve. We must first define these basic variables.

x_{it} is the quantity of the ith asset which is purchased at time t. x_{it} can be either positive or negative. The allocation vector is $x_t = (x_{1t}, \ldots, x_{Nt})'$ where the prime denotes matrix transposition. This is chosen by the investor at time t.

p_{it} is the ex-dividend price of the ith asset for purchase at time t. The vector of prices is $p_t = (p_{1t}, \ldots, p_{Nt})'$. This is known by the investor at time t.

d_{it} is the dividend, per unit of the ith asset purchased at time t, which is paid at time $t+1$. The vector of dividends is $d_t = (d_{1t}, \ldots, d_{Nt})'$. This is *not* known by the investor at time t.

$y_{it} = p_{it} + d_{it}$ is the payoff of the ith asset at time $t+1$. The vector of payoffs is $y_t = (y_{1t}, \ldots, y_{Nt})'$. This is *not* known by the investor at time t.

c_t is the capital reserve of the financial institution[6] at time $t+1$. This is *not* known by the investor at time t.

The budget constraint relates capital reserve c_t, prices p_t, allocations at times $t-1$ and t, x_{t-1} and x_t, and payoffs y_t:

$$c_t + p_t' x_t = y_t' x_{t-1} \tag{4.41}$$

The investor requires that the values of c_{it} be adequately large (e.g. not negative or at least not too negative).

4.4.4 Uncertainty

We will consider a situation of moderate uncertainty, in which the payoff vector, y_t, is random and known to be normally distributed, but the moments of the distribution are uncertain. The development in this section is thus similar to section 4.2.8. We will not consider extremely uncertain fat tails as studied in section 4.2.4.

The estimated mean of the payoff vector is μ_{yt} and the estimated covariance matrix of the payoff is Σ_{yt}. Thus, from the budget constraint in eq.(4.41), the capital reserve is a normal random variable with estimated mean and variance:

$$\widetilde{\mu}_{ct} = -p_t' x_t + \mu_{yt}' x_{t-1} \tag{4.42}$$

$$\widetilde{\sigma}_{ct}^2 = x_{t-1}' \Sigma_{yt} x_{t-1} \tag{4.43}$$

Associated with the estimated mean and standard deviation, $\widetilde{\mu}_{ct}$ and $\widetilde{\sigma}_{ct}$, are error values, ε_μ and ε_σ. These may be standard errors which are evaluated from the standard errors of the moments of y_t. Alternatively, ε_μ and ε_σ may be estimated by numerical simulation or simply chosen by judgment.

The basic idea of the info-gap model for uncertainty in the distribution of the capital reserve, c_t, is that the fractional deviations of the true mean and standard deviation, μ_{ct} and σ_{ct}, from their estimated values, $\widetilde{\mu}_{ct}$ and $\widetilde{\sigma}_{ct}$, are unknown:

$$\left| \frac{\mu_{ct} - \widetilde{\mu}_{ct}}{\varepsilon_\mu} \right| \le h, \quad \left| \frac{\sigma_{ct} - \widetilde{\sigma}_{ct}}{\varepsilon_\sigma} \right| \le h \tag{4.44}$$

The standard deviation must also be non-negative and the horizon of uncertainty, h, is unknown. We state this as an info-gap model for

[6] For an individual investor c_t could be thought of as consumption.

uncertainty in the normal distribution of the capital reserve:

$$\mathcal{U}(h) = \left\{ f(c_t) \sim N(\mu_{ct}, \sigma^2_{ct}) : \left| \frac{\mu_{ct} - \widetilde{\mu}_{ct}}{\varepsilon_\mu} \right| \le h, \right. \tag{4.45}$$

$$\left. \left| \frac{\sigma_{ct} - \widetilde{\sigma}_{ct}}{\varepsilon_\sigma} \right| \le h,\ \sigma_{ct} \ge 0 \right\}, \quad h \ge 0$$

4.4.5 Performance and Robustness

Performance requirement. The investor must choose the portfolio (defined in terms of its estimated mean and covariance, μ_{yt} and Σ_{yt}), and the allocation x_t at time t among the assets. These choices must be made so that the capital reserve c_t will be adequately large when the payoffs y_t become known at time $t+1$. Since c_t is a random variable, the investor requires low probability that c_t is too small. The performance requirement is stated in terms of a quantile of the distribution of c_t. This is therefore a value-at-risk analysis as in section 4.2.3.

The α quantile of the distribution $f(c_t)$, denoted $q(\alpha, f)$, is the value of c_t for which the probability of being less than this value equals α. This quantile is defined in:

$$\alpha = \int_{-\infty}^{q(\alpha,f)} f(c_t)\,\mathrm{d}c_t \tag{4.46}$$

α is typically small so $q(\alpha, f)$ may be a negative number. If $f(c_t)$ is the correct pdf, then we have probability of α that the capital reserve will fall below $q(\alpha, f)$. However, though $f(c_t)$ is known to be normal, its moments are uncertain.

A capital reserve requirement, r_c, is the lowest acceptable value of c_t. The investor either chooses r_c or it is imposed exogenously. Since c_t is a random variable it is necessary to choose the investment x_t so that the probability of capital reserve less than r_c is acceptably small, for instance probability α. The value of α must also be chosen or be imposed exogenously.

If the investor knew the pdf of the capital reserve, $f(c_t)$, then r_c could be chosen as the α quantile of that distribution, $q(\alpha, f)$. Since the pdf is estimated but uncertain, the performance requirement is:

$$q(\alpha, f) \ge r_c \tag{4.47}$$

We will use the robustness function to evaluate the confidence in satisfying this requirement for chosen investment, x_t.

Robustness function. Consider an allocation x_t for a specified portfolio. Its robustness to uncertainty in the pdf of the capital reserve is the greatest horizon of uncertainty up to which all pdf's result in a value of the α quantile which is no smaller than $r_{\rm c}$:

$$\widehat{h}(x_t, r_{\rm c}) = \max\left\{h: \left(\min_{f\in\mathcal{U}(h)} q(\alpha, f)\right) \geq r_{\rm c}\right\} \tag{4.48}$$

The robustness is the greatest horizon of uncertainty up to which the performance requirement in eq.(4.47) is satisfied for all pdf's in the info-gap model of eq.(4.45). The robustness depends on the allocation, x_t, which appears in the info-gap model in the moments $\widetilde{\mu}_{ct}$ and $\widetilde{\sigma}_{ct}$ and perhaps also in the error terms ε_μ and ε_σ.

The derivation of the robustness function is the same as in section 4.2.8 and will not be repeated. Let z_α denote the α quantile of the standard normal distribution, with zero mean and unit standard deviation. As before, we assume that α is less than 1/2, so that z_α is negative. In practice this is an entirely unrestrictive assumption, since we will typically choose α around 0.01.

The estimated distribution of the capital reserve, $\widetilde{f}(c_t)$, is normal with moments $\widetilde{\mu}_{ct}$ and $\widetilde{\sigma}_{ct}$ in eqs.(4.42) and (4.43). The robustness is zero if the estimated reserve, $q(\alpha, \widetilde{f})$, is less than $r_{\rm c}$. Otherwise, the robustness is:

$$\widehat{h}(x_t, r_{\rm c}) = \frac{r_{\rm c} - q(\alpha, \widetilde{f})}{\varepsilon_\sigma z_\alpha - \varepsilon_\mu} \tag{4.49}$$

The numerator and denominator are both negative, so the robustness decreases as $r_{\rm c}$ increases towards $q(\alpha, \widetilde{f})$.

The robustness function depends on the contemplated allocation, x_t, the previous allocation, x_{t-1}, and the mean and standard deviation of the capital reserve as determined by the moments of the payoff vector. We will use the robustness to formulate preferences between alternative allocations and portfolios.

4.4.6 Opportuneness Function

It is necessary to satisfy the reserve requirement in eq.(4.47). However, surprises can be favorable and capital reserves may turn out to be substantially larger than anticipated. Consider a level of reserve, $r_{\rm w}$, which is not only much larger than the critical value $r_{\rm c}$, but which also exceeds the anticipated reserve, $q(\alpha, \widetilde{f})$. It would be a windfall if the reserve was this large, though this is not a requirement. The investor's windfall aspiration is:

$$q(\alpha, f) \geq r_{\mathrm{w}} \tag{4.50}$$

A reserve as large as r_{w} can occur only as a result of favorable deviation from the anticipated payoffs. An allocation, x_t, for which a reserve as large as r_{w} is possible—though not necessarily guaranteed—is opportune to uncertainty.

For allocation x_t, its opportuneness from uncertainty in the pdf is assessed as the lowest horizon of uncertainty at which at least one pdf results in a value of the α quantile which is no smaller than r_{w}, where r_{w} is a large and desirable reserve requirement:

$$\widehat{\beta}(x_t, r_{\mathrm{w}}) = \min \left\{ h : \left(\max_{f \in \mathcal{U}(h)} q(\alpha, f) \right) \geq r_{\mathrm{w}} \right\} \tag{4.51}$$

The opportuneness is the lowest horizon of uncertainty at which the windfall aspiration in eq.(4.50) is satisfied for at least one pdf in the info-gap model. Note that the investment decision, x_t, appears in the definition of the opportuneness only in the info-gap model.

Let $M(h)$ denote the inner maximum in eq.(4.51). $M(h)$ is the inverse of the opportuneness. That is, a plot of $M(h)$ vs. h is the same as a plot of r_{w} vs. $\widehat{\beta}(x_t, r_{\mathrm{w}})$. We will derive an explicit expression from which to evaluate $M(h)$.

Define $r(x) = 0$ if $x < 0$ and $r(x) = x$ if $x \geq 0$.

Our derivation is based on one assumption, as before. Let z_α denote the α quantile of the standard normal distribution, with zero mean and unit standard deviation. We assume that α is less than 1/2, so that z_α is negative. In practice this is an entirely unrestrictive assumption, since we will choose α around 0.01.

As explained in connection with eq.(4.36) on p.111, the α quantile of the normal distribution $f(c_t)$ is:

$$q(\alpha, f) = \sigma_{ct} z_\alpha + \mu_{ct} \tag{4.52}$$

From our assumption that z_α is negative, we see that the inner maximum in eq.(4.51) occurs when the standard deviation is as small as possible, and the mean is as large as possible, at horizon of uncertainty h. Thus the inner maximum in eq.(4.51) becomes:

$$M(h) = r(\widetilde{\sigma}_{ct} - \varepsilon_\sigma h) z_\alpha + \widetilde{\mu}_{ct} + \varepsilon_\mu h \tag{4.53}$$

As noted earlier, this is all we need in order to calculate and plot the opportuneness function. We could invert this relation to obtain an explicit expression for the opportuneness, but that is not necessary and we will not do it.

We can understand from eq.(4.53) that the opportuneness function entails a trade-off between aspiration and uncertainty. From eq.(4.53) we see that $M(h)$ is a piece-wise linear increasing function of the horizon of uncertainty, h. Recall that a plot of $M(h)$ vs. h is the same as a plot of $r_{\rm w}$ vs. $\widehat{\beta}(x_t, r_{\rm w})$. Thus the opportuneness function, $\widehat{\beta}(x_t, r_{\rm w})$, is also a piece-wise linear increasing function of the windfall aspiration, $r_{\rm w}$. The trade-off is that high aspirations (large $r_{\rm w}$) are possible only in the presence of high ambient uncertainty (large $\widehat{\beta}$).

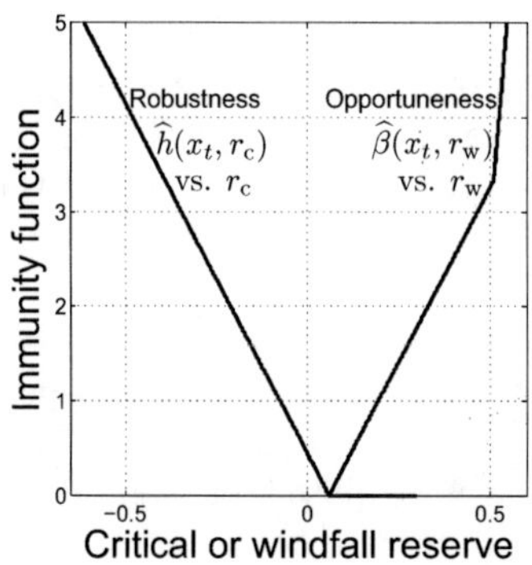

Figure 4.17: Robustness and opportuneness curves. $x_{t-1} = x_t = (0.7, 0.3)'$. $\mu_{yt} = (1.04p_{1t}, 1.08p_{2t})'$. $\varepsilon_\mu = 0.05\widetilde{\mu}_{ct}$. $\varepsilon_\sigma = 0.3\widetilde{\mu}_{ct}$.

4.4.7 Policy Exploration

We consider the allocation of resources between a single risk-free asset, labeled $i = 1$, and a single uncorrelated risky asset, $i = 2$. We will explore the use of the robustness and opportuneness functions to select the allocation. We will consider various properties of the two underlying assets.[7]

[7]Throughout the example the price vector is $p_t = (7, 10)$. The level of confidence of the quantile is $\alpha = 0.01$. The standard deviation of the payoff of the risky asset is 5% of its estimated mean unless indicated otherwise. Thus

Trade-off and zeroing. Fig. 4.17 shows the immunity functions, robustness and opportuneness, for a particular allocation between the risk-free and risky asset. The negative slope of the robustness curve demonstrates the trade-off between critical reserve, $r_{\rm c}$, and robustness, $\widehat{h}(x_t, r_{\rm c})$. The positive slope of the opportuneness curve shows that windfall reserve, $r_{\rm w}$, trades off against opportuneness, $\widehat{\beta}(x_t, r_{\rm w})$: large uncertainty is needed in order to facilitate large windfall.

The standard deviation of the payoff of the risky asset is 30% of its estimated mean: $(\Sigma_{yt})_{22} = (0.3\mu_{yt,2})^2$. The estimated mean capital reserve is $\widetilde{\mu}_{ct} = 0.44$ and its estimated standard deviation is 0.16, based on eqs.(4.42) and (4.43). However, the estimated α quantile of the capital reserve, for $\alpha = 0.01$, is $q(\alpha, \widetilde{f}) = 0.059$. This is the point on the horizontal axis at which the immunity curves meet. While the estimated 1% quantile is positive, its robustness against uncertainty in the moments is zero. Only smaller critical reserve values have positive robustness. For instance, we see that $\widehat{h} = 3$ at $r_{\rm c} = -0.35$. This means that the moments of the estimated distribution can err, fractionally, by as much as a factor of 3 and the α quantile of the critical reserve will be no more negative than -0.35 with probability 0.01.

If the fractional error in the moments is as large 3, then we see from the opportuneness curve that there is a pdf for which the $\alpha = 0.01$ quantile of the reserve is as large as 0.46. That is, with large error it is possible to achieve quite large capital reserves, though these windfalls are not guaranteed to occur.

We also see in fig. 4.17 that the opportuneness curve displays a kink, which results from the fact that the variance must be positive. This is manifested in eq.(4.53) with the $r(\cdot)$ function. The increased steepness at large values of $\widehat{\beta}$ means that larger windfalls are available only at rapidly increasing horizons of uncertainty.

Table 4.1: Parameters of two portfolios. Robustness curves in fig. 4.18.

Portfolio	$\mu_{yt,1}/p_{1t}$	$\mu_{yt,2}/p_{2t}$	$\widetilde{\mu}_{ct}$	$\widetilde{\sigma}_{ct}$	$\varepsilon_\mu/\widetilde{\mu}_{ct}$	$\varepsilon_\sigma/\widetilde{\sigma}_{ct}$
1	0.04	0.08	0.436	0.162	0.05	0.1
2	0.036	0.076	0.404	0.161	0.035	0.075

$(\Sigma_{yt})_{22} = (0.05\mu_{yt,2})^2$. The other elements of the 2×2 covariance matrix Σ_{yt} are zero.

Two portfolios. We now consider the choice between two portfolios whose differences are specified in table 4.1. From the table we see that portfolio 1 has higher mean payoffs, μ_{yt}, than portfolio 2. Consequently, the estimated capital reserve, $\widetilde{\mu}_{ct}$, and the estimated standard deviation, $\widetilde{\sigma}_{ct}$, are greater for the first portfolio. Furthermore, estimated errors of these moments, ε_{μ} and ε_{σ}, are greater for the first portfolio

The investor faces the classical dilemma in choosing between these portfolios: portfolio 1 is better on average, but more uncertain.

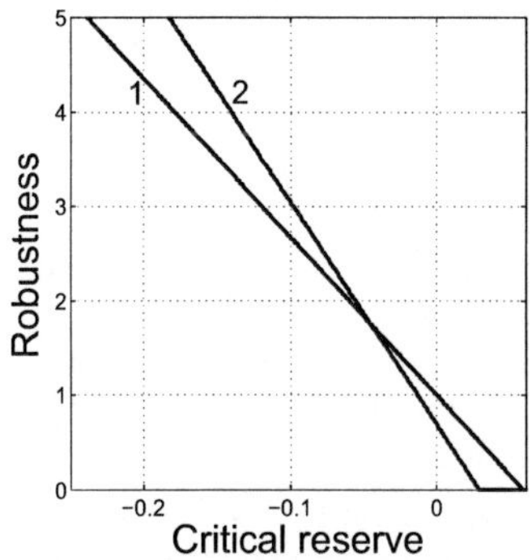

Figure 4.18: Robustness curves. $x_{t-1} = x_t = (0.7, 0.3)'$. See table 4.1.

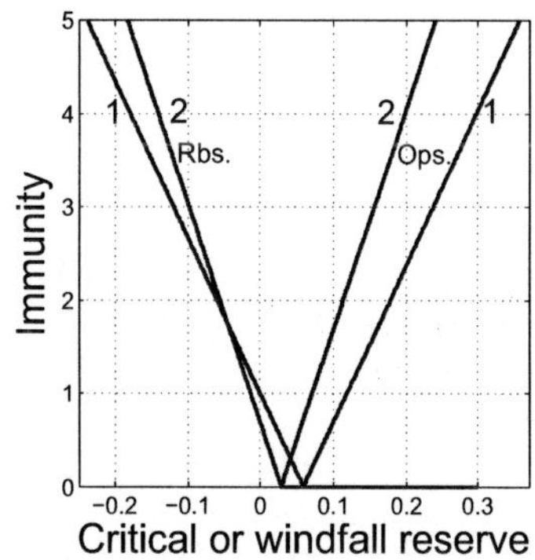

Figure 4.19: Robustness and opportuneness curves for portfolios in fig. 4.18.

The robustness curves for these portfolios are shown in fig. 4.18, which express the dilemma graphically. The estimated quantiles (for $\alpha = 0.01$) are 0.059 and 0.029 for portfolios 1 and 2, which are the points at which their robustness curves hit the $r_{\rm c}$-axis. Thus portfolio 1 is preferable at low robustness. However, the robustness curves cross one another at moderate robustness, so that portfolio 2 is more robust at lower critical reserve and higher robustness. The choice between these portfolios depends on a judgment of how much robustness is needed, and how low an α quantile of the critical reserve is acceptable.

Fig. 4.19 shows opportuneness curves for these two portfolios, together with their robustness curves which are reproduced from fig. 4.18. The opportuneness curves introduce a new dimension to the decision. Portfolio 1 is more opportune than portfolio 2: greater windfall is possible with the first portfolio at any horizon of uncertainty. To what extent the investor weighs the opportuneness against the robustness is a delicate judgment depending in large measure on the context of the investment and the risk sensitivity of the investor.

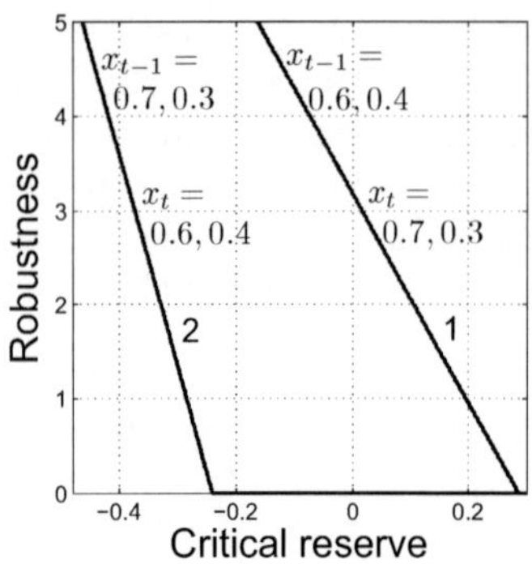

Figure 4.20: Robustness curves for two sequences of investments.

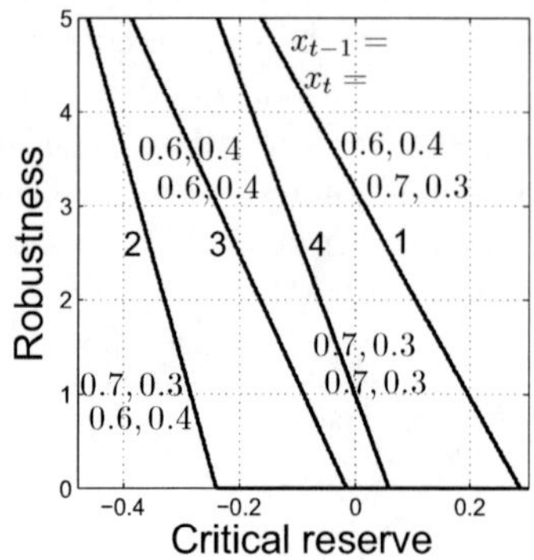

Figure 4.21: Robustness curves for 4 sequences of investments. Curves 1 and 2 reproduced from fig. 4.20.

Sequence matters. Fig. 4.20 shows robustness curves for two different sequences of allocations. In portfolio 1 the previous allocation was $x_{t-1} = (0.6, 0.4)$, and the current allocation, $x_t = (0.7, 0.3)$, has a higher fraction devoted to the risk-free asset. In portfolio 2 the order is reversed: the risk-free fraction decreases from $t-1$ to t.

The robustness curves reveal two differences between these sequences of allocations. The estimated α quantile of portfolio 1 (the value at which the curve hits the axis) is positive, and far greater than the estimated α quantile of portfolio 2 which is negative. This results primarily from the much larger estimated capital reserve for portfolio 1, $\widetilde{\mu}_{ct}$, which equals 0.79 as opposed to 0.14 for portfolio 2. We can understand this from eq.(4.42). The expenditure term, $-p_t' x_t$, is less negative with a higher proportion of low-price risk-free asset, while the estimated income term, $\mu_{yt}' x_{t-1}$, is more positive with a larger proportion of high-return risky asset.

The second difference between these two sequences of allocations is in the slopes of their robustness curves. Portfolio 1 has a more gradual slope than portfolio 2. This means that the *cost of robustness*, in units of critical reserve, is greater with portfolio 1 than with portfolio 2. In order to increase the robustness of the first portfolio from 0 to 3, it is necessary to reduce the critical reserve from 0.29 to 0.017, a reduction of 0.27. The same increase in robustness for portfolio 2 is achieved by reducing the critical reserve from -0.24 to

−0.37, a reduction of 0.13. The cost of robustness is twice as great in portfolio 1 than in portfolio 2. This does not imply that one would prefer portfolio 2; portfolio 1 is far more robust. But it does indicate a sense in which portfolio 1 is more vulnerable to uncertainty.

Fig. 4.21 shows again that sequence matters by displaying the robustness curves of portfolios 1 and 2 from fig. 4.20 together with curves for two new portfolios. Portfolio 3 has a lower allocation to the risk-free asset in both steps, while portfolio 4 has a higher risk-free proportion in both steps. In this particular constellation, these two new combinations produce similar results. While portfolio 4 is better than portfolio 3, both in its estimated quantile of the capital reserve (at zero robustness) and in the cost of robustness (slope of the curve), the difference is not as great as between portfolios 1 and 2.

4.4.8 Extensions

This simple example can be extended in many ways.

Multiple assets. The numerical example considered only two assets, one risk-free and the other risky, though the theoretical development was generic. The consideration of multiple assets opens new directions. The allocation decision is multi-dimensional, but the robustness curve is still a single curve on the plane, thus providing a concise comparison of different allocations in terms of estimated outcomes and costs of robustness. The correlations between the assets are likely to be more uncertain than the asset payoffs themselves, which can have significant influence on the robustness.

Multiple risks. We have only considered uncertainty in the payoffs. Many other risks may be relevant, such as credit risk, interest rate risk, exchange rate risk, and others. Also, we have assumed that the distribution of payoffs is known to be normal and that only the moments of the distribution are uncertain. Fat-tail uncertainty, such as considered in section 4.2.4 on p.99, may be relevant to some of these risks.

Suite of models. The prediction of future returns can be formulated with a suite of models dealing with macro-economic fundamentals, asset price dynamics, credit risks, financing costs, etc. (Koivu *et al.* 2009). This will inevitably introduce multiple risks as well. An important question will be whether the added realism of a multi-faceted model adds more information or more uncertainty. It is not a foregone conclusion that adding models and data will necessarily increase the decision's robustness to uncertainty.

Robust-satisficing asset pricing. We have compared specified allocations in terms of their robustness against uncertainty. The logical extension is to seek the robust-satisficing allocation. This is the allocation which maximizes the robustness while satisficing the capital reserve requirement (or satisficing whatever other performance measure the analyst employs). The robust-satisficing allocation is specified by the info-gap asset pricing equations (Ben-Haim, 2006, section 11.5.3). A necessary condition for the robust-satisficing investment is that the robustness is stationary:

$$\frac{\partial \widehat{h}(x_t, r_c)}{\partial x_t} = 0 \tag{4.54}$$

These equations are different from ordinary asset pricing equations for two reason. First, the performance requirement is a value-at-risk rather than a consumer utility. Second, the performance is not optimized but rather satisficed.

4.5 Appendix: Derivation of an Info-Gap Model

We derive eq.(4.7), which is the info-gap model used in section 4.1.

Let $p(0,0)$ denote the probability that neither asset defaults, which is P_0. Let $p(1,0)$ be the probability that only the first asset defaults, and $p(0,1)$ be the probability that only the second asset defaults. $p(1,1)$ is the probability of default of both assets, which equals $p_{\rm dd}$. These four probabilities, $p(i,j)$, must all be non-negative and they must sum to unity.

For non-negativity it is necessary (though not sufficient) that:

$$p_{\rm d1} \geq 0, \quad p_{\rm d2} \geq 0, \quad p_{\rm dd} \geq 0 \tag{4.55}$$

We will impose an additional condition later.

The definition of normalization is:

$$1 = P_0 + p(0,1) + p(1,0) + p_{\rm dd} \tag{4.56}$$

We can write the marginal probabilities of default, $p_{\rm d1}$ and $p_{\rm d2}$, as follows:

$$p_{\rm d1} = p(1,0) + p(1,1) \tag{4.57}$$

$$p_{\rm d2} = p(0,1) + p(1,1) \tag{4.58}$$

Recalling that $p(1,1) = p_{\rm dd}$, we see from eqs.(4.57) and (4.58) that:

$$p(1,0) = p_{\rm d1} - p_{\rm dd} \tag{4.59}$$
$$p(0,1) = p_{\rm d2} - p_{\rm dd} \tag{4.60}$$

Thus non-negativity of $p(0,1)$ and $p(1,0)$ requires:

$$p_{\rm dd} \le \min[p_{\rm d1},\ p_{\rm d2}] \tag{4.61}$$

This relation also says that the probability that both underlying assets default cannot exceed the probability of default of either single asset.

Eqs.(4.55) and (4.61) are necessary and sufficient to assure that $p(0,1)$, $p(1,0)$ and $p(1,1)$ are non-negative.

Using eqs.(4.59) and (4.60) we can write the normalization condition, eq.(4.56), as:

$$1 = P_0 + p_{\rm d1} + p_{\rm d2} - p_{\rm dd} \tag{4.62}$$

Hence, for normalization to be possible for some $P_0 \in [0,1]$, it is necessary and sufficient that:

$$p_{\rm d1} + p_{\rm d2} - p_{\rm dd} \le 1 \tag{4.63}$$

Now we can combine these results to obtain the uniform-bound info-gap model in eq.(4.7).

Chapter 5

Topics in Public Policy

We consider three different examples of public policy selection. Section 5.1 develops an info-gap robustness analysis of welfare considerations in the choice between imposing a limit on pollution emission or imposing a tax on emissions. The marginal costs and benefits are uncertain to the regulatory agency, and emissions quotas are traded in a competitive market. In section 5.2 we study the policy choices of a regulator responsible for enforcement of pollution limits. The regulator chooses the number of emission permits traded in a competitive market, the audit frequencies of the firms, and the allocation of enforcement resources. Firms are distinguished according to their costs of abatement, which are uncertain to the regulator. Non-proportional "profiling" audit and allocation strategies are examined. Section 5.3 studies policy choices regarding long-range economic impacts of climate change which may result from industrial emission of greenhouse gases. The potential for drastic economic impact of global warming motivates strong abatement measurements, while the great uncertainties in the processes motivates extensive research. We study the robustness implications of the policy maker's choices between abatement and research.

~ ~ ~

5.1 Emissions Compliance

In this section we consider a welfare analysis of regulatory policy for abatement of the emission of a pollutant. Two policy options are available. In the first policy option the regulator specifies an *abatement quantity* which is the total amount by which pollutant emission must be reduced. The regulator then allows competitive trading of emissions quotas between polluters whereby the price of pollution is set by market forces. In the second policy option the regulator imposes a direct *tax* on polluters. The tax sets the price of pollution and the market then determines the quantity. We consider a welfare analysis of this problem in which aggregate social benefits and costs are uncertain. This section draws on previous work by Stranlund and Ben-Haim (2008) which in turn is motivated by Weitzman's early seminal work (1974). Metcalf (2009) provides a concise overview of many aspects of this topic.

5.1.1 Policy Preview

A policy suggestion—tax level or abatement quantity—should not be evaluated only in terms of its estimated outcome. The estimated outcome is very vulnerable to error in the underlying data and models: there is no robustness to uncertainty for achieving the estimated outcome. Only less ambitious outcomes have positive robustness. A policy whose estimated outcome is very good may nonetheless have very low robustness for acceptable outcomes, and thus be undesirable.

It is nonetheless true in this specific example that, for any specified outcome which the policy maker deems acceptable, the tax level based on the estimated outcome is more robust to uncertainty than any other tax level. Similarly, the abatement quantity based on the estimated outcome is more robust than any other abatement level. Whether the tax or quantity policy is more robust depends on the parameter values.

The most robust policy—whether tax or quantity—may be impractical for exogenous reasons. Perhaps policy constraints require a lower tax, or technological constraints mitigate for a lower quantity. In this case one compares a sub-optimal tax, for instance, against the optimal quantity policy. The robustness curves for these policies may cross one another, implying the possibility for reversal of preferences between them. That is, the preferred policy will depend on the policy maker's outcome requirements.

The welfare analysis is based on highly uncertain benefit and cost functions. The analysis of robustness indicates how policy choices would change as new information becomes available resulting in reduced uncertainty. Conversely, the analysis shows how much reduction in uncertainty is needed to cause a policy shift.

5.1.2 Operational Preview

System model. The system model is the loss of welfare between the proposed policy and the full-information realization of that policy. The system model is eq.(5.9) for the case of abatement quantity and eq.(5.14) for the tax-based policy.

Decision variables and performance requirement. The policy maker must choose between the tax-based policy and the abatement quantity policy. The specific value of tax or quantity must also be chosen. The performance requirement is that the loss of welfare be acceptably small, eq.(5.17).

Uncertainty model. The welfare analysis is based on estimated benefit and cost as a function of the amount of reduction in pollutant emission, eqs.(5.1) and (5.2). The uncertainty in the coefficients of these functions is represented by the info-gap model of eq.(5.16).

Robustness function. The robustness of any policy is the greatest horizon of uncertainty in the benefit and cost functions up to which the welfare loss is guaranteed to be acceptable. This is formulated in eq.(5.18). Important special cases appear in eqs.(5.19), (5.21), (5.22) and (5.24).

5.1.3 Welfare Loss: Formulation

We first formulate the welfare loss due to uncertainty. After specifying the basic variables, we consider the policy based on abatement quantity and then the tax-based policy.

Basic variables. An abatement policy is specified by q which is the aggregate reduction in the quantity of emitted pollutant. q is non-negative.

The aggregate benefit of reducing pollution by an amount q is:

$$B(q) = b_1 q - \frac{b_2 q^2}{2} \tag{5.1}$$

The aggregate cost of reducing pollution by an amount q is:

$$C(q) = c_1 q + \frac{c_2 q^2}{2} \tag{5.2}$$

The vectors of coefficients are $b = (b_1, b_2)$ and $c = (c_1, c_2)$. We will subsequently consider uncertainty in these coefficients.

Under ordinary conditions the coefficients b and c are all positive and $b_1 > c_1$.

The social welfare resulting from reducing emissions by q is:

$$W(q, b, c) = B(q) - C(q) \tag{5.3}$$

A tax policy is specified by t which is the tax imposed on the firms of the industry. Assuming that each firm chooses its abatement level to minimize its cost,[1] each firm will choose its abatement level so that the tax t equals the marginal cost. The aggregate effect is that tax and quantity are related as:

$$t = \frac{\mathrm{d}C(q)}{\mathrm{d}q} \tag{5.4}$$

$$= c_1 + c_2 q \tag{5.5}$$

We denote the policy generically with p which is either a tax, t, or an abatement quantity q.

Abatement quantity. If we knew the actual coefficients of the welfare function, b and c, we could choose the abatement quantity q to maximize the social welfare, $W(q, b, c)$ in eq.(5.3). This welfare-maximizing quantity is:

$$q^\star = \frac{b_1 - c_1}{b_2 + c_2} \tag{5.6}$$

The resulting welfare is $W(q^\star, b, c)$.

For any other quantity, q, the resulting welfare is $W(q, b, c)$. For instance, we might choose q based on the best estimates of b and c, which we denote $\widetilde{b}$ and $\widetilde{c}$. The quantity which maximizes welfare if $\widetilde{b}$ and $\widetilde{c}$ are correct is:

$$\widetilde{q} = \frac{\widetilde{b}_1 - \widetilde{c}_1}{\widetilde{b}_2 + \widetilde{c}_2} \tag{5.7}$$

The resulting actual welfare, if $\widetilde{b}$ and $\widetilde{c}$ err, is $W(\widetilde{q}, b, c)$.

Our **system model** when choosing the **abatement quantity** q is the loss of welfare between q and the full-information case, $q^\star$:

$$L(q, b, c) = W(q^\star, b, c) - W(q, b, c) \tag{5.8}$$

[1]One might suppose that firms are aware of many uncertainties, and that they consequently robustly satisfice their costs rather than try to minimize them. We will not pursue this model.

Using eqs.(5.1)–(5.3) and (5.6) one finds the welfare loss function for abatement quantity q to be:

$$L(q, b, c) = \frac{[b_1 - c_1 - (b_2 + c_2)q]^2}{2(b_2 + c_2)} \tag{5.9}$$

Emission tax. The social welfare of tax t is:

$$W(t, b, c) = B[q(t)] - C[q(t)] \tag{5.10}$$

where $q(t)$ is evaluated from eq.(5.5).

If we knew the values of b and c we could choose the tax to maximize the welfare. The welfare-maximizing tax is:

$$t^\star = \frac{b_1 c_2 + b_2 c_1}{b_2 + c_2} \tag{5.11}$$

It is readily shown that $t^\star$ and $q^\star$ are related by eq.(5.5).

The regulator who only knows estimates $\widetilde{b}$ and $\widetilde{c}$ might choose the tax to maximize the estimated welfare, for which the tax is:

$$\widetilde{t} = \frac{\widetilde{b}_1 \widetilde{c}_2 + \widetilde{b}_2 \widetilde{c}_1}{\widetilde{b}_2 + \widetilde{c}_2} \tag{5.12}$$

$\widetilde{t}$ and $\widetilde{q}$ are related by eq.(5.5) in which one uses $\widetilde{c}_1$ and $\widetilde{c}_2$.

Our **system model** when choosing the **tax** t is the loss of welfare between t and the full-knowledge case, $t^\star$:

$$L(t, b, c) = W(t^\star, b, c) - W(t, b, c) \tag{5.13}$$

Combining eqs.(5.5), (5.10), (5.11) and (5.13) one finds:

$$L(t, b, c) = \frac{[(b_1 - c_1)c_2 - (b_2 + c_2)(t - c_1)]^2}{2(b_2 + c_2)c_2^2} \tag{5.14}$$

5.1.4 Uncertainty

We know estimated values of the coefficients b_i and c_i, which we denote $\widetilde{b}_i$ and $\widetilde{c}_i$. We assume that these estimates are positive numbers with $\widetilde{b}_1 > \widetilde{c}_1$. Also, we have estimated errors of these values denoted s_{b_i} and s_{c_i}, which are non-negative. These error values do not constitute worst cases, but only roughly indicate the confidence we have in the estimates. The actual errors of b_i and c_i are unknown.

The basic idea of the info-gap model for uncertainty in the coefficients b_i and c_i is that we don't know the fractional deviations of the true values, b_i and c_i, from their estimated values, $\widetilde{b}_i$ and $\widetilde{c}_i$, in units of the errors, s_{b_i} and s_{c_i}:

$$\left| \frac{b_i - \widetilde{b}_i}{s_{b_i}} \right| \le h, \quad \left| \frac{c_i - \widetilde{c}_i}{s_{c_i}} \right| \le h \tag{5.15}$$

The value of h is unknown. We state this as an info-gap model for uncertainty in the coefficients:

$$\mathcal{U}(h) = \left\{ b, c : \left| \frac{b_i - \widetilde{b}_i}{s_{b_i}} \right| \le h, \quad \left| \frac{c_i - \widetilde{c}_i}{s_{c_i}} \right| \le h, \quad i = 1, 2 \right\}, \quad h \ge 0 \tag{5.16}$$

$\mathcal{U}(h)$ is an unbounded family of nested sets of possible welfare coefficients b and c.

5.1.5 Robustness

We now formulate the robustness function and consider several special cases.

The performance requirement for policy p, either emission tax or abatement quantity, is that the welfare loss not exceed a critical value, L_c:

$$L(p, b, c) \le L_c \tag{5.17}$$

Consider policy p, where p equals either quantity q or tax t. The loss function is $L(p, b, c)$, eq.(5.9) or eq.(5.14). The policy's robustness to uncertainty in the coefficients b and c is the greatest horizon of uncertainty, h, up to which all coefficients result in a loss which is no greater than L_c:

$$\widehat{h}(p, L_c) = \max \left\{ h : \left(\max_{b,c \in \mathcal{U}(h)} L(p, b, c) \right) \le L_c \right\} \tag{5.18}$$

The robustness is the greatest horizon of uncertainty up to which the performance requirement in eq.(5.17) is satisfied for all coefficients in the info-gap model.

Abatement quantity: Special cases. Consider a special case of the robustness of an abatement quantity when there is no uncertainty in the slope coefficients, so $b_2 = \widetilde{b}_2$ and $c_2 = \widetilde{c}_2$ and

$s_{b_2} = s_{c_2} = 0$. As shown in appendix 5.4, the robustness of abatement quantity q is:

$$\widehat{h}(q, L_c) = \frac{\sqrt{2(\widetilde{b}_2 + \widetilde{c}_2)L_c} - \left|\widetilde{b}_1 - \widetilde{c}_1 - (\widetilde{b}_2 + \widetilde{c}_2)q\right|}{s_{b_1} + s_{c_1}} \tag{5.19}$$

or zero if this is negative. Referring to eq.(5.9), we note that the right-hand side of eq.(5.19) is zero or negative if:

$$L_c \le L(q, \widetilde{b}, \widetilde{c}) \tag{5.20}$$

$L(q, \widetilde{b}, \widetilde{c})$ is the estimated welfare loss. Thus the robustness is zero for any critical welfare loss L_c which is equal to or less than the estimated welfare loss. This is the "zeroing" phenomenon discussed in section 2.2.2.

As an extension of this special case, let q be the best-estimated abatement quantity, $\widetilde{q}$ in eq.(5.7). The absolute-value term in eq.(5.19) vanishes and the robustness becomes:

$$\widehat{h}(\widetilde{q}, L_c) = \frac{\sqrt{2(\widetilde{b}_2 + \widetilde{c}_2)L_c}}{s_{b_1} + s_{c_1}} \tag{5.21}$$

This is the result obtained by Stranlund and Ben-Haim (2008) for $s_{b_1} = \widetilde{b}_1$ and $s_{c_1} = \widetilde{c}_1$.

Comparing the robustness functions in eqs.(5.19) and (5.21) we see that, in the special case that the slopes of the benefit and cost functions are known with certainty, the best-estimated abatement quantity $\widetilde{q}$ is more robust than any other quantity q.

Emission tax: Special cases. Consider a special case of the robustness of tax t when there is no uncertainty in the slope coefficients, so $b_2 = \widetilde{b}_2$ and $c_2 = \widetilde{c}_2$ and $s_{b_2} = s_{c_2} = 0$. As shown in appendix 5.5, the robustness of tax t is:

$$\widehat{h}(t, L_c) = \frac{\widetilde{c}_2\sqrt{2(\widetilde{b}_2 + \widetilde{c}_2)L_c} - |\widetilde{b}_1\widetilde{c}_2 + \widetilde{b}_2\widetilde{c}_1 - (\widetilde{b}_2 + \widetilde{c}_2)t|}{s_{b_1}\widetilde{c}_2 + s_{c_1}\widetilde{b}_2} \tag{5.22}$$

or zero if L_c is less than the estimated welfare loss:

$$L_c \le L(t, \widetilde{b}, \widetilde{c}) \tag{5.23}$$

As an extension of this special case let the tax equal the best-estimated tax $\widetilde{t}$ in eq.(5.12). The absolute-value term in eq.(5.22) vanishes and the robustness becomes:

$$\widehat{h}(\widetilde{t}, L_c) = \frac{\widetilde{c}_2\sqrt{2(\widetilde{b}_2 + \widetilde{c}_2)L_c}}{s_{b_1}\widetilde{c}_2 + s_{c_1}\widetilde{b}_2} \tag{5.24}$$

This is the result obtained by Stranlund and Ben-Haim (2008) for $s_{b_1} = \widetilde{b}_1$ and $s_{c_1} = \widetilde{c}_1$.

5.1.6 Policy Exploration

In this section we will explore some policy implications of the previous development. We will begin by considering the special case of uncertainty only in the intercepts, b_1 and c_1, of the marginal benefit and cost functions, eqs.(5.1) and (5.2). The robustness functions are presented in eqs.(5.19) and (5.22) for the abatement and tax policies, respectively.[2]

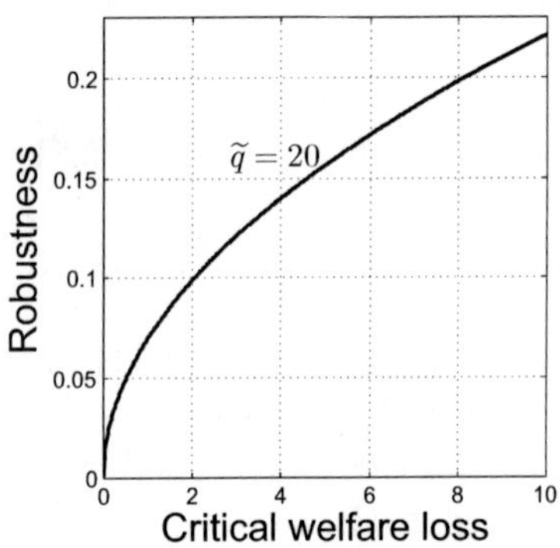

Figure 5.1: Robustness curve $\widehat{h}(\widetilde{q}, L_c)$ for abatement quantity with uncertain intercept, eq.(5.21).

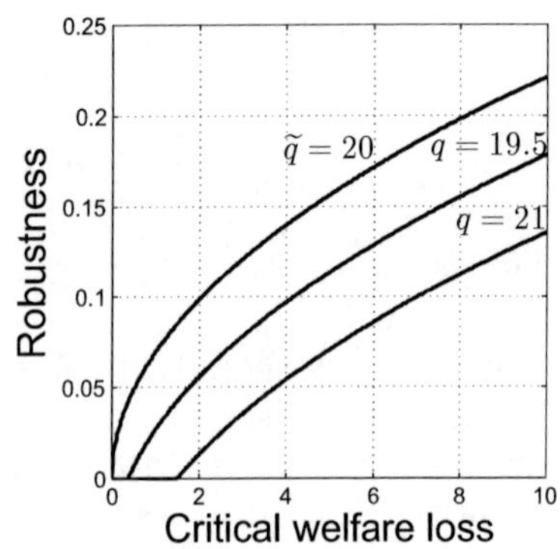

Figure 5.2: Robustness curves $\widehat{h}(q, L_c)$ for abatement quantities with uncertain intercept, eq.(5.19).

Trade-off and zeroing. Fig. 5.1 shows robustness, $\widehat{h}(\widetilde{q}, L_c)$, vs. critical welfare loss, L_c, for abatement level $\widetilde{q}$ based on the estimated coefficients, eq.(5.7). The positive slope of the robustness curve expresses the trade-off between robustness and welfare loss. As explained in section 2.2.2, better performance (smaller welfare loss

[2] Unless otherwise indicated, throughout this section we use the following parameter values: $\widetilde{b}_1 = 100$, $s_{b_1} = 25$, $\widetilde{b}_2 = 1$, $s_{b_2} = 0$, $\widetilde{c}_1 = 40$, $s_{c_1} = 10$, $\widetilde{c}_2 = 2$, $s_{c_2} = 0$.

L_c) entails lower immunity against uncertainty (smaller robustness, $\widehat{h}$).

Fig. 5.2 shows three robustness curves. The upper curve is reproduced from fig. 5.1 and the other curves are for different values of abatement level q.

As explained in connection with eq.(5.20), each robustness curve in fig. 5.2 reaches the horizontal axis—and the robustness becomes zero—when L_c is equal to the estimated value of the welfare loss, $L(q, \widetilde{b}, \widetilde{c})$. Since $\widetilde{q}$ is the abatement level which minimizes the welfare loss based on the estimated coefficients, its robustness curve reaches the axis to the left of the robustness curve for any other value of q. As noted following eq.(5.21), $\widetilde{q}$ is strictly more robust than any other choice of the abatement level, as illustrated in fig. 5.2.

Fig. 5.3 shows similar results for three values of the tax policy. The robustness curves in this figure have steeper slope than in fig. 5.2, a point to which we will return later.

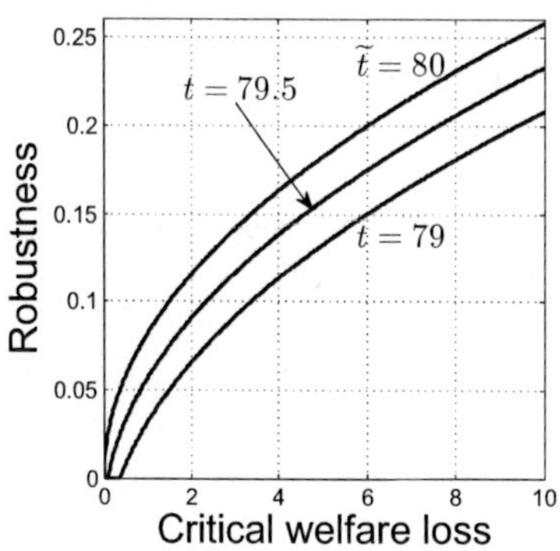

Figure 5.3: Robustness curves $\widehat{h}(t, L_c)$ for tax policies with uncertain intercept, eq.(5.22).

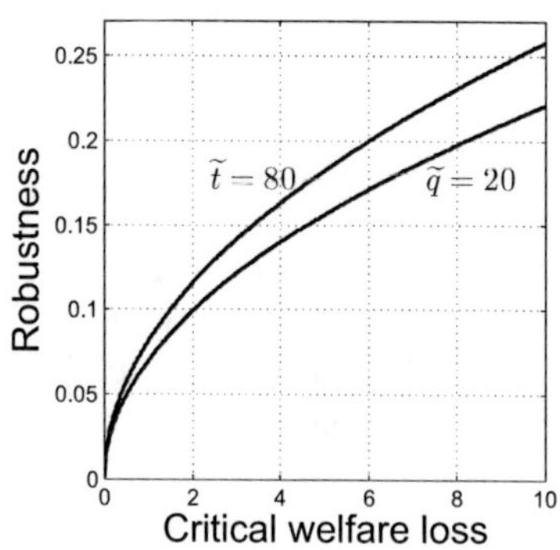

Figure 5.4: Robustness curves $\widehat{h}(\widetilde{t}, L_c)$ and $\widehat{h}(\widetilde{q}, L_c)$ with uncertain intercept, eqs.(5.21) and (5.24).

Policy preference. Now consider the choice between the tax $\widetilde{t}$ and the abatement quantity $\widetilde{q}$, based on the estimated coefficients. We continue to consider the case in which only the intercepts are uncertain. The robust-satisficing policy preference is for the policy with greater robustness at any specified loss. The difference between the robustnesses, eqs.(5.21) and (5.24), is:

$$\widehat{h}(\widetilde{t}, L_{\rm c}) - \widehat{h}(\widetilde{q}, L_{\rm c}) = \frac{(\widetilde{c}_2 - \widetilde{b}_2)s_{c_1}\sqrt{2(\widetilde{b}_2 + \widetilde{c}_2)L_{\rm c}}}{(s_{b_1} + s_{c_1})(s_{b_1}\widetilde{c}_2 + s_{c_1}\widetilde{b}_2)} \tag{5.25}$$

Thus, in this special case, the tax $\widetilde{t}$ is preferred over the abatement quantity $\widetilde{q}$ if and only if:

$$\widetilde{c}_2 > \widetilde{b}_2 \tag{5.26}$$

When this condition holds then the tax policy $\widetilde{t}$ is preferred over the quantity policy $\widetilde{q}$ at *all* values of the critical welfare loss, $L_{\rm c}$. The reverse inequality implies that the quantity policy is preferred at all $L_{\rm c}$ values.

This is the same as the result in Stranlund and Ben-Haim (2008). This also corresponds to the original conclusion by Weitzman (1974). Fig. 5.4 illustrates the robust dominance of the tax policy for the coefficients in footnote 2, which satisfy the inequality in eq.(5.26). Both curves start at the origin, but the tax policy $\widetilde{t}$ is strictly more robust than the abatement quantity $\widetilde{q}$ at all positive values of $L_{\rm c}$.

Preference reversal. Now consider the slopes of the robustness curves, which express the cost of robustness in units of lost welfare. A steep slope means that the robustness can be increased substantially by increasing the welfare loss by only a small amount: low cost of robustness. A small slope implies high cost of robustness. We still consider the special case of full knowledge of the slopes, $\widetilde{b}_2$ and $\widetilde{c}_2$, of the benefit and cost functions in eqs.(5.1) and (5.2).

From eqs.(5.19) and (5.22):

$$\frac{\partial \widehat{h}(q, L_{\rm c})}{\partial L_{\rm c}} = \frac{\sqrt{\widetilde{b}_2 + \widetilde{c}_2}}{(s_{b_1} + s_{c_1})\sqrt{2L_{\rm c}}} \tag{5.27}$$

$$\frac{\partial \widehat{h}(t, L_{\rm c})}{\partial L_{\rm c}} = \frac{\widetilde{c}_2\sqrt{\widetilde{b}_2 + \widetilde{c}_2}}{(s_{b_1}\widetilde{c}_2 + s_{c_1}\widetilde{b}_2)\sqrt{2L_{\rm c}}} \tag{5.28}$$

Note that the cost of robustness—as determined by the slope—does not depend on the value of t or q, but differs between these two classes of policy options.

The difference between the slopes is:

$$\frac{\partial \widehat{h}(t, L_{\rm c})}{\partial L_{\rm c}} - \frac{\partial \widehat{h}(q, L_{\rm c})}{\partial L_{\rm c}} = \sqrt{\frac{\widetilde{b}_2 + \widetilde{c}_2}{2L_{\rm c}}}\,\frac{(\widetilde{c}_2 - \widetilde{b}_2)s_{c_1}}{(s_{b_1} + s_{c_1})(s_{b_1}\widetilde{c}_2 + s_{c_1}\widetilde{b}_2)} \tag{5.29}$$

From this relation we see that $\widehat{h}(t, L_c)$ vs. L_c is steeper than $\widehat{h}(q, L_c)$ vs. L_c if and only if $\widetilde{c}_2 > \widetilde{b}_2$. This means that the cost of robustness—in units of welfare loss—is lower for any tax policy t than for any quantity policy q if and only if condition (5.26) holds. Thus the same condition, eq.(5.26), causes $\widetilde{t}$ to be more robust than $\widetilde{q}$, and any t to trade off more favorably against lost welfare than any q.

This has an implication for policy choice.

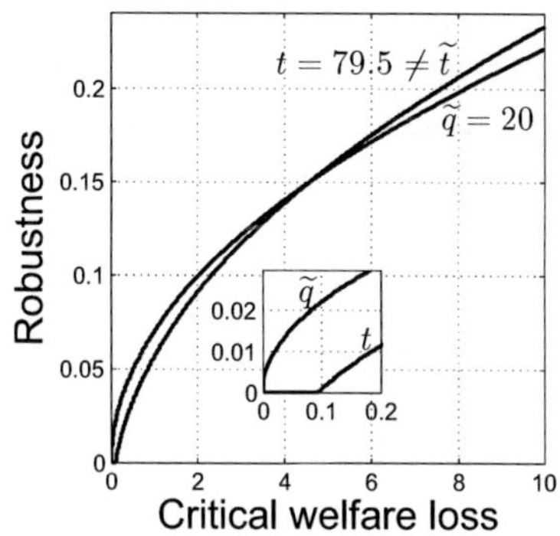

Figure 5.5: Robustness curves $\widehat{h}(\widetilde{q}, L_c)$ and $\widehat{h}(t, L_c)$ for tax and quantity policies with uncertain intercept, eqs.(5.21) and (5.22).

Suppose that $\widetilde{c}_2 > \widetilde{b}_2$, which means that $\widetilde{t}$ is more robust than $\widetilde{q}$, and that $\widehat{h}(t, L_c)$ is steeper than $\widehat{h}(q, L_c)$ for any t and q, as in the examples we have considered previously. However, suppose we wish to impose a tax t which is different from $\widetilde{t}$, for instance $t < \widetilde{t}$ which may result from practical exogenous constraints on implementation of the policy. Eq.(5.29) implies that the robustness curve for any $t \neq \widetilde{t}$ will cross the robustness curve for $\widetilde{q}$ at some positive robustness.

This is illustrated in fig. 5.5. In this example $\widetilde{c}_2 > \widetilde{b}_2$, so $\widetilde{t}$ is more robust than $\widetilde{q}$. However, suppose we cannot impose the tax $\widetilde{t} = 80$, but only a slightly smaller value, $t = 79.5$. The quantity policy $\widetilde{q} = 20$ is more robust than this tax policy at low robustness and small welfare loss as we see from the insert in the figure. However, the robustness curves cross one another at a welfare loss of $L_c = 4.6$ and a robustness of $\widehat{h} = 0.15$. The tax $t = 79.5$ is more robust than the quantity $\widetilde{q} = 20$ at larger loss and larger robustness. The robustness difference between these policies is small; later we will see more substantial differences.

This example shows that the sub-optimal tax $t = 79.5$ may be preferred over the optimal quantity $\widetilde{q} = 20$. This results from recognizing that very low welfare loss is not robustly achieved by either policy, and that t is more robust than $\widetilde{q}$ at slightly larger welfare loss.

The reverse situation also holds. If $\widetilde{c}_2 < \widetilde{b}_2$, so that $\widetilde{q}$ is more robust than $\widetilde{t}$, the robustness curve for $q \neq \widetilde{q}$ will cross the robustness curve for $\widetilde{t}$.

Slope and intercept uncertainty. Up to now we have only considered uncertainty in the intercepts of the marginal benefit and cost functions, b_1 and c_1 in eqs.(5.1) and (5.2). We now abandon the assumption that the estimated slopes, $\widetilde{b}_2$ and $\widetilde{c}_2$, are correct. We consider the full uncertainty represented by the info-gap model of eq.(5.16).[3] The robustness is defined in eq.(5.18).

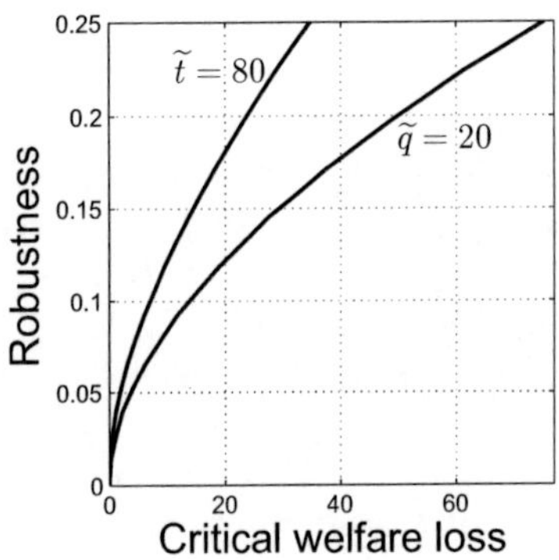

Figure 5.6: Robustness curves $\widehat{h}(\widetilde{t}, L_c)$ and $\widehat{h}(\widetilde{q}, L_c)$, eq.(5.18).

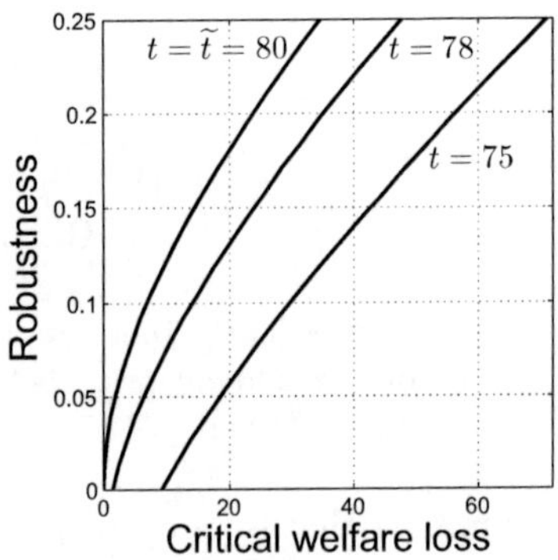

Figure 5.7: Robustness curves $\widehat{h}(t, L_c)$, eq.(5.18).

Fig. 5.6 shows robustness curves for the quantity policy $\widetilde{q}$ and the tax policy $\widetilde{t}$, based on the estimated coefficients, eqs.(5.7) and (5.12). For the particular values of the estimated coefficients used in these examples, the tax policy is more robust than the quantity policy. Furthermore, $\widehat{h}(\widetilde{t}, L_c)$ is steeper than $\widehat{h}(\widetilde{q}, L_c)$, so the cost of robustness is lower with the tax policy. This is similar to the situation in fig. 5.4 (with intercept uncertainty only), except that now the policy maker must accept far greater welfare loss in order to achieve comparable levels of robustness. This is not surprising since the uncertainty in the slopes of the benefit and cost functions is quite

[3] Unless indicated otherwise, we use the parameter values in footnote 2 on p.142, except that now $s_{b_2} = 1$ and $s_{b_2} = 2$.

significant in the loss functions, eqs.(5.9) and (5.14).

Fig. 5.7 shows robustness curves for three different choices of the tax. The uppermost curve is reproduced from fig. 5.6. The robustness is reduced as the tax is made increasingly different from the estimated tax $\widetilde{t}$. This is similar to fig. 5.3. We note, however, that now a larger range of tax levels is relevant since the robustness is less sensitive to the value of t.

Fig. 5.8 shows the intersection of robustness curves for two different policy choices, like fig. 5.5. We know from fig. 5.6 that $\widetilde{t}$ is robust-preferred over $\widetilde{q}$. But suppose that exogenous considerations require a slightly smaller tax, $t = 78$. The robustness curve for this lower tax is shifted to the right with respect to the curve for $\widetilde{t}$, as seen in fig. 5.7. However, since the cost of robustness is lower with the tax policy than with the quantity policy, the robustness curves for $t = 78$ and $\widetilde{q}$ cross each other as we see in fig. 5.8. The sub-optimal tax policy $t = 78$ is preferred over $\widetilde{q}$ for robustness above about 11%, with substantial robustness advantage for the tax policy.

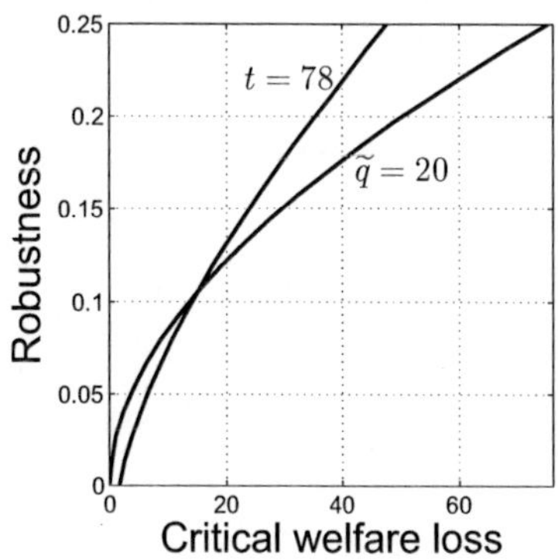

Figure 5.8: Robustness curves $\widehat{h}(\widetilde{q}, L_c)$ and $\widehat{h}(t, L_c)$, eq.(5.18).

Value of information. We noted in connection with fig. 5.6 that the added uncertainty causes a substantial reduction in robustness. In some situations it might be possible to gather information about the benefit and cost functions, and thereby reduce the uncertainty. Additional information is readily represented by reducing the error coefficients s in the info-gap model, eq.(5.16). We now explore the value of reducing the uncertainty on the slopes of the marginal benefit and cost.

Fig. 5.9 compares two different realizations of the tax policy $\widetilde{t}$.

The lower curve is reproduced from fig. 5.6. The upper curve uses substantially smaller error coefficients s_{b_2} and s_{c_2} in the info-gap model of eq.(5.16). These error terms may be obtained as standard errors of historical estimates of the corresponding coefficients, b_2 and c_2. Alternatively, they may reflect the analyst's judgment of relative error between the past and the future. In either case, the robustness is substantially increased by reducing the relative error. This reduction in uncertainty may make the tax policy $\widetilde{t}$ much more attractive. Conversely, this analysis indicates how much reduction of uncertainty is needed in order to substantially change the confidence—as expressed by the robustness—in the tax policy.

Fig. 5.10 compares two different tax policies based on different values of the error coefficients for b_2 and c_2. The policy $\widetilde{t} = 80$ is analyzed with larger errors than the other tax policy, $t = 78$. The intersection of these two robustness curves shows that enhanced information (reduced s_{b_2} and s_{c_2}) compensates for deviating from $\widetilde{t}$. Specifically, reducing the error causes the cost of robustness to be reduced, as manifested in a steeper robustness curve. Thus, while $\widehat{h}(t, L_c)$ is shifted to the right of $\widehat{h}(\widetilde{t}, L_c)$, the former curve is steeper which causes the curves to intersect one another. Thus a lower tax level becomes feasible—and even preferable—if cost and benefit uncertainties are reduced.

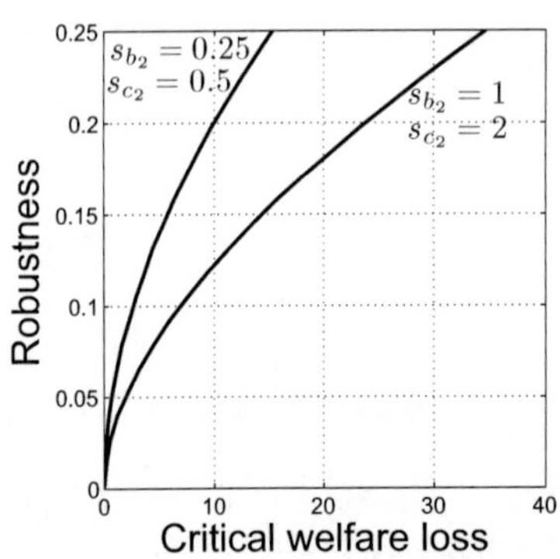

Figure 5.9: Robustness curves $\widehat{h}(\widetilde{t}, L_c)$, eq.(5.18), showing value of information.

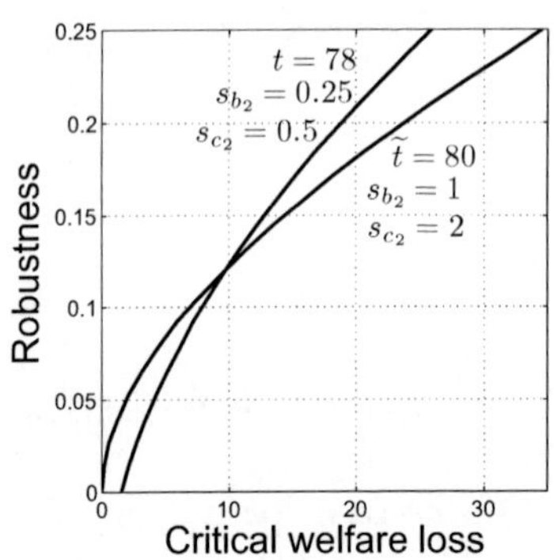

Figure 5.10: Robustness curves $\widehat{h}(t, L_c)$, eq.(5.18), showing value of information.

5.1.7 Extensions

This simple analysis can be extended in various ways.

Subsidies for technology. Many emissions can be reduced by developing and deploying technological devices. Public subsidy for research and development, as well as for acquisition of these technologies by private industry, may be justified by consideration of social welfare. However, the costs and benefits become more difficult to assess because of the uncertainties of developing and deploying new technology.

Multi-generational analysis. Our analysis has ignored the dimension of time. However, benefits and costs of reducing the emission of pollutants are not instantaneous, and may accrue over an extended duration. It is then important to consider the uncertainty of future costs and benefits, as well as the uncertainty in discounting over time.

Surveillance strategy. Compliance depends on surveillance. The costs of surveillance are uncertain and may depend on the compliance policy which is implemented. Furthermore, the design of a surveillance program depends on the probability of detecting violations which may be poorly known.

Refined policy options. We have considered simple implementations of tax and abatement-quantity policies. More refined policies can be considered, such as imposing upper or lower limits on trading prices for emission permits, or deciding to either distribute emission permits for free or to auction them, or adjusting the tax structure to account for distributional and sectorial effects. Metcalf (2009) discusses various alternatives.

Non-linear marginal cost and benefit. We have considered uncertainty in the parameters of the cost and benefit functions, without considering that the functional forms may be different from eqs.(5.1) and (5.2). In particular, the marginal cost and benefit functions may be non-linear in some unknown way. An info-gap analysis can study the robustness to this functional uncertainty.

Satisficing behavior. Our analysis of social welfare depended on assuming that firms seek to minimize their costs. We noted in footnote 1 on p.138 that firms may face many uncertainties and therefore may satisfice rather than minimize their costs. The regulator may be unsure what strategy firms use, and this uncertainty should then be incorporated in the analysis. Alternatively, it may be known that firms satisfice rather than optimize, in which case the welfare analysis should be adapted to account for this.

5.2 Enforcing Pollution Limits

In this section we study the policy choices made by a regulatory agency empowered to enforce the legal limits on the emission of pollutants. The regulatory agency has the authority to audit emissions and to take legal action against firms which are discovered to pollute in excess of legal limits. The regulatory agency issues a fixed number of tradable licenses for pollution emission, which are traded in a competitive market. The equilibrium market price of an emission permit is uncertain due to uncertainty in the abatement costs of the firms. We explore how many emission permits the enforcement agency should issue, and how it should allocate its resources for auditing and for enforcement. Our study is based on an economic analysis by Stranlund and Dhanda (1999), which we extend by performing an info-gap robustness analysis. See also Murphy and Stranlund (2006).

5.2.1 Policy Preview

The industry is composed of a large number of firms of different types, which are distinguished by the firms' costs for abatement of pollution. The regulator desires to keep either the aggregate level of violations, or the aggregate level of emissions, below a specified value. We will find some robustness differences between these two closely related policy goals. The regulator has three policy instruments: the number of pollution permits which are initially issued—free of charge—to the industry, the probability of auditing each type of firm, and the amount of enforcement resources which are allocated to each type of firm.

The regulator has estimates of the cost-of-abatement functions for each type of firm. These cost functions can be used to evaluate the aggregate level of emission or violation for any choice of policy. However, these cost functions are highly uncertain. Consequently, the estimated outcome of any policy is uncertain. Furthermore, the robustness is zero for achieving the estimated outcome of any policy; only worse outcome (greater aggregate violation or emission) has positive robustness to uncertainty in the abatement cost functions. That is, robustness trades off against quality of outcome.

If the regulator desires to keep the aggregate level of *violations* below a specified level, then the robustness to uncertainty increases as the number of emission permits increases. Thus, when limiting aggregate violations, the regulator will prefer issuing more permits rather than fewer permits, when all else is the same. However, if it is aggregate *emissions* which must be limited, then robustness increases as the number of permits decreases. In this case the preferences on the number of permits are reversed: one prefers fewer total permits.

A uniform auditing policy is one in which each firm is audited with equal probability. Likewise, a uniform policy for enforcement resources is one which allocates enforcement resources equally to audited firms of all types. In the context of a specific example, it is shown that more uniform policies are more robust than less uniform policies. For this specific example, this is an info-gap robustness extension of a general theorem by Stranlund and Dhanda (1999).

With the same example we find that the slope of the robustness curve is steeper with a more uniform policy. Steep slope means low cost of robustness in units of performance. That is, a steep robustness curve means that robustness can be increased by increasing the critical value of aggregate violation by only a small amount. In short, the cost of robustness decreases as we move toward uniformity.

Using the same example, it is shown that essentially the same robustness to uncertainty can be obtained with different specific combinations of number of permits, auditing probabilities, and enforcement resource allocations. The regulator is thus indifferent between these policy mixes, in terms of confidence in achieving specified outcomes. Stated differently, the regulator can use an exogenous criterion, such as political feasibility, to choose between these robustness-equivalent policies.

Finally, we show policy mixes whose robustness curves cross one another, indicating that the choice between these policies depends on the regulator's requirements: one policy will be more robust for more demanding requirements, while the other policy will be more robust for less demanding requirements.

5.2.2 Operational Preview

System models. There are two different, though closely related, system models, depending on the regulator's policy goal. The system model for limiting the aggregate equilibrium number of violations is $R_{\rm v}$ in eq.(5.36). The system model for limiting the aggregate equilibrium level of pollution emission is $R_{\rm e}$ in eq.(5.37). These aggregate quantities result from an economic model described in section 5.2.3.

Performance requirements. For either policy goal—limit on aggregate violations or emissions—the regulator requires that the corresponding system model not exceed a critical value, R_c.

Decision variables. The industry is made up of K different types of firms which are distinguished according to their costs of pollution abatement. The regulator has three policy instruments: the number of permits for pollution emission which are initially issued to the industry free of charge, L, the probability of auditing a type k firm, π_k, and the amount of resources which are allocated for enforcing the pollution limits on type k firms, ϕ_k, for $k = 1, \ldots, K$. The audit probabilities and resource allocations are denoted vectorially as π and ϕ.

Uncertainty model. The regulator knows an estimate of the cost function for pollution abatement for each type of firm. However, these cost functions are highly uncertain, as expressed by the info-gap model of eq.(5.45).

Robustness functions. The regulator may consider either of two policy goals: limitation of either violations or emissions. For any policy, $q = (L, \pi, \phi)$, the robustness of the violation-limitation goal is the greatest horizon of uncertainty in the abatement-cost functions up to which the violation limitation is satisfied, $\widehat{h}_v(q, R_c)$ in eq.(5.46). Likewise, the robustness of the emission-limitation goal is the greatest horizon of uncertainty up to which the emission limitation is satisfied, $\widehat{h}_e(q, R_c)$ in eq.(5.47). A procedure for evaluating the inverses of these robustness functions is outlined on p.157. Knowledge of the inverses of the robustness functions is sufficient for plotting the robustness functions themselves and for evaluating alternative policies.

5.2.3 Economic Model

In this section we formulate the economic model, presenting results derived by Stranlund and Dhanda (1999).

Basic definitions. There are K different types of firms in this industry, with n_k identical firms of type k. The value of n_k is large enough so that each firm is a price taker, and its permit purchases do not alter the market price. The different types of firms are distinguished by a vector, α, of parameters, where the value of this vector for firms of type k is α_k. The amount of pollution emitted by a type k firm is e_k, and the cost of abatement for this firm is $c(e_k, \alpha_k)$. All type k firms *produce* the same amount of pollutant, so a firm which *emits* more *remediates* less and thus has lower abatement costs. Hence $c(e_k, \alpha_k)$ is a decreasing function: $\partial c(e_k, \alpha_k)/\partial e_k < 0$. The cost function is also convex: $\partial^2 c(e_k, \alpha_k)/\partial e_k^2 > 0$.

The enforcement agency issues a total of L permits for pollution emission to the firms of the industry, free of charge, where each type k firm is issued ℓ_{0k} emission permits. Firms then trade permits in a competitive market, resulting in ℓ_k permits held by each type k firm. The price of a single permit is p. A firm is compliant with the emission regulations if it owns a number of permits equal to (or greater than) its emissions: $\ell_k \geq e_k$. The magnitude of violation of the emissions regulations by a type k firm is $v_k = e_k - \ell_k$, or zero if this is negative.

The enforcement agency must choose the probability, π_k, with which a type k firm will be audited. We use the definition by Stranlund and Dhanda (1999), with minor notational change:

> Suppose that each k-type firm is audited with constant probability π_k. We have in mind here that the enforcement authority commits to auditing $\overline{n}_k < n_k$ firms of type k at random so that $\pi_k = \overline{n}_k / n_k$. (p.270)

A uniform auditing policy has $\pi_j = \pi_k$ for all j and k. π_k is a conditional probability: given that a type k firm will (now) be audited, the probability that a specific type k firm is audited is π_k. These probabilities, $\pi_1, \ldots, \pi_K$, need not add up to unity. In practice they will add up to much less than unity: only a very small fraction of all firms of any type are audited. (In principle $\pi_1 + \cdots + \pi_K$ could exceed unity, e.g. if all firms are audited.)

The agency also chooses the level of resources, ϕ_k, it will bring to bear in enforcing legal sanctions on a type k firm. ϕ_k is the amount of enforcement resource allocated to each audited type k firm. The definition by Strandlund and Dhanda (1999), with minor notational change, is:

> Since the authority audits $\overline{n}_k$ k-type firms, the cost of establishing its enforcement commitment for all of these firms is $\phi_k \overline{n}_k$ .... (p.275)

A uniform allocation of enforcement resources has $\phi_j = \phi_k$ for all j and k.

π_k and ϕ_k are known to all firms.

Finally, the agency must choose (or recommend to the legislature) the schedule of fines, $f(v_k, \phi_k)$, which will be imposed through legal proceedings on a type k firm which is found to be in violation of the emissions regulation. We assume that there is no fine for no violation, $f(0, \phi_k) = 0$, that the fine increases monotonically with the size of the violation, $\partial f(v_k, \phi_k)/\partial v_k > 0$, and that the marginal rate of increase is positive, $\partial^2 f(v_k, \phi_k)/\partial v_k^2 > 0$. We also assume that the penalty and the marginal penalty both increase as the commitment of resources increases: $\partial f(v_k, \phi_k)/\partial \phi_k > 0$ and $\partial^2 f(v_k, \phi_k)/\partial \phi_k^2 > 0$.

The cost of auditing a firm of any type is w. The enforcement agency's budget B is exhausted if:

$$B = \sum_{k=1}^{K} (w + \phi_k) n_k \pi_k \tag{5.30}$$

Optimization by firms. A type k firm chooses its emission level e_k and its permit holdings ℓ_k to minimize its expected costs, which are made up of abatement costs, purchase of emission permits, and expected fines. The optimization decision facing a type k firm is:

$$\min \left[c(e_k, \alpha_k) + (\ell_k - \ell_{0k})p + \pi_k f(e_k - \ell_l, \phi_k) \right] \tag{5.31}$$

subject to the requirement that the firm has no unutilized emission permits: $e_k - \ell_k \geq 0$.

This optimization results in the firm choosing its emissions, e_k, so that the marginal abatement cost equals the permit price:

$$p = -\frac{\partial c(e_k, \alpha_k)}{\partial e_k} \tag{5.32}$$

The firm's demand for permits, ℓ_k, depends on whether it is compliant or not. A compliant firm equates its demand for permits to its emissions:

$$\ell_k = e_k \tag{5.33}$$

A non-compliant firm chooses its demand for permits so that the price of a permit equals the marginal expected fine:

$$p = \pi_k \frac{\partial f(e_k - \ell_k, \phi_k)}{\partial v_k} \tag{5.34}$$

Note that, for a non-compliant firm, the permit price determines a firm's level of violation, $v_k = e_k - \ell_k$.

We will henceforth assume that all firms are non-compliant.

Aggregate equilibrium outcomes. Given the permit price, p, the emissions of a type k firm, e_k, is determined from eq.(5.32). The firm's demand for permits, ℓ_k, is then determined from eq.(5.33) or eq.(5.34) (compliant or non-compliant, respectively). This then determines the firm's level of violation, $v_k = e_k - \ell_k$.

These equations depend on the permit price, which is the value which clears the market for permits. A type k firm's demand for permits depends on its characteristics, α_k, the probability of audit π_k, the enforcement resources ϕ_k and the permit price p. The equilibrium permit price, $\overline{p}$, is the price which clears the market:

$$L = \sum_{k=1}^{K} n_k \ell_k(\alpha_k, \pi_k, \phi_k, \overline{p}) \tag{5.35}$$

We now have a set of equations—(5.32), (5.33) or (5.34), and (5.35)—which entirely determine e_k, ℓ_k (and hence $v_k = e_k - \ell_k$) and p, depending on the abatement cost functions $c_k(\cdot)$, the fine schedule $f(\cdot)$ and the policy choices L, π_k and ϕ_k for $k = 1, \ldots, K$.

We will consider two closely related performance functions which the enforcement agency may use. The aggregate equilibrium number of violations is:

$$R_{\text{v}} = \sum_{k=1}^{K} n_k v_k(\pi_k, \phi_k, \overline{p}) \tag{5.36}$$

The aggregate equilibrium level of emission is:

$$R_{\text{e}} = \sum_{k=1}^{K} n_k e_k(\pi_k, \phi_k, \overline{p}) \tag{5.37}$$

Recall that $e_k = v_k + \ell_k$. This, together with eqs.(5.35)–(5.37), shows that:

$$R_{\text{e}} = R_{\text{v}} + L \tag{5.38}$$

Thus the aggregate equilibrium level of emission is simply the aggregate equilibrium number of violations plus the number of permits which are issued. However, aggregate violations can be reduced by issuing many permits, but aggregate emissions may increase. Thus when the number of permits, L, is a decision variable it is useful to keep both R_{e} and R_{v} in mind.

Example. Suppose the abatement cost function for type k firms is:

$$c(e_k, \alpha_k) = \frac{\alpha_{k1}}{e_k + \alpha_{k2}} \tag{5.39}$$

where α_{k1} and α_{k2} are positive. The marginal cost is $\partial c / \partial e_k = -\alpha_{k1}/(e_k + \alpha_{k2})^2$. From eq.(5.32) the firm's emissions level is:

$$e_k = \sqrt{\frac{\alpha_{k1}}{p}} - \alpha_{k2} \tag{5.40}$$

or zero if the permit price, p, is so large that this is negative. Firms cannot have negative emissions, and they will reduce their emissions as the permit price rises until they can reduce emissions no more.

Let the fine schedule be a quadratic function of the level of violation v_k, and of the enforcement resource ϕ_k:

$$f(v_k, \phi_k) = \gamma v_k^2 \phi_k^2 \tag{5.41}$$

where γ is a positive constant. The non-compliant firm's level of violation is determined from eq.(5.34) as:

$$v_k = \frac{p}{2\gamma\pi_k\phi_k^2} \tag{5.42}$$

or equal to e_k in eq.(5.40) if e_k is less than eq.(5.42). That is, the level of violation cannot exceed the level of emission.

The firm's demand for permits is determined from $\ell_k = e_k - v_k$:

$$\ell_k = \sqrt{\frac{\alpha_{k1}}{p}} - \alpha_{k2} - \frac{p}{2\gamma\pi_k\phi_k^2} \tag{5.43}$$

or zero if this is negative, in accord with the conditions on eqs.(5.40) and (5.42).

We now introduce a convenient notation. Let $(x)^+$ equal x unless $x < 0$, in which case it equals zero.

Eqs.(5.40), (5.42) and (5.43) all depend on the price of a permit, whose equilibrium value is determined by the market clearing condition, eq.(5.35), which becomes:

$$L = \sum_{k=1}^{K} n_k \left(\sqrt{\frac{\alpha_{k1}}{p}} - \alpha_{k2} - \frac{p}{2\gamma\pi_k\phi_k^2} \right)^+ \tag{5.44}$$

Note that this function decreases continuously from $+\infty$ to zero as p increases from zero, so it has a unique solution for the market-clearing price.

5.2.4 Uncertainty and Robustness

Let us consider uncertainty in each firm's cost function and evaluate the robustness of the regulatory agency's policy for each of the two performance functions. The policy maker can specify the number L of emission permits which are issued, the vector π of auditing probabilities π_k, and the vector ϕ of resource allocations ϕ_k. Let $q = (L, \pi, \phi)$ denote a policy choice.

Let $\widetilde{c}_k(e_k)$ denote the estimated cost function for type k firms, eq.(5.39), whose coefficients are denoted $\widetilde{\alpha}_{k1}$ and $\widetilde{\alpha}_{k2}$. We assume that the actual cost functions, $c_k(e_k)$, are of the same form but that the values of the coefficients, though non-negative, are uncertain. We use the following info-gap model:

$$\mathcal{U}(h) = \left\{ c_k(e_k) = \frac{\alpha_{k1}}{e_k + \alpha_{k2}}, \forall\, k: \ \alpha_{ki} \geq 0, \quad \left| \frac{\alpha_{ki} - \widetilde{\alpha}_{ki}}{\widetilde{\alpha}_{ki}} \right| \leq h,\ i = 1, 2 \right\}, \quad h \geq 0 \tag{5.45}$$

Let $c = (c_1, \ldots, c_K)$ denote the vector of cost functions of the K types of firms. The robustness for aggregate violation, eq.(5.36), is the greatest horizon of uncertainty up to which the aggregate equilibrium number of violations does not exceed the critical value R_c:

$$\widehat{h}_v(q, R_c) = \max \left\{ h: \ \left(\max_{c \in \mathcal{U}(h)} R_v(c) \right) \leq R_c \right\} \tag{5.46}$$

The robustness function for aggregate emissions, eq.(5.37), is defined by replacing $R_v(p)$ in eq.(5.46) by $R_e(p)$:

$$\widehat{h}_e(q, R_c) = \max \left\{ h: \ \left(\max_{c \in \mathcal{U}(h)} R_e(c) \right) \leq R_c \right\} \tag{5.47}$$

We now demonstrate how to evaluate these robustness functions. Our approach will be to evaluate the inverse of the robustness, namely, the inner maxima in eqs.(5.46) and (5.47), as a function of the horizon of uncertainty, h. Let $\mu_v(h)$ denote the inner maximum in eq.(5.46) and let $\mu_e(h)$ denote the inner maximum in eq.(5.47). $\mu_v(h)$ is the inverse of $\widehat{h}_v(q, R_c)$: a plot of $\mu_v(h)$ vs. h is the same as a plot of R_c vs. $\widehat{h}_v(q, R_c)$. Similarly, $\mu_e(h)$ is the inverse of $\widehat{h}_e(q, R_c)$.

The evaluation of $\mu_v(h)$ and $\mu_e(h)$ proceeds as follows. At each value of $h \geq 0$:

1. Choose a vector of cost functions c in the info-gap model $\mathcal{U}(h)$, as specified by the coefficients α_{k1} and α_{k2}, for $k = 1, \ldots, K$. With these cost functions:

   (a) Calculate the equilibrium permit price $\overline{p}(c)$ from eq.(5.44) based on the coefficients of the chosen cost functions.

(b) Calculate the equilibrium emissions levels $e_k[\overline{p}(c)]$ with eq.(5.40), and then the equilibrium aggregate emission level $R_{\rm e}(c)$ with eq.(5.37).

(c) Calculate the equilibrium violations $v_k[\overline{p}(c)]$ with eq.(5.42), and then the aggregate equilibrium violation level, $R_{\rm v}(c)$, from eq.(5.36).

2. Return to step 1 and vary $c \in \mathcal{U}(h)$ to maximize:

   (a) $R_{\rm v}(c)$, yielding $\mu_{\rm v}(h)$.

   (b) $R_{\rm e}(c)$, yielding $\mu_{\rm e}(h)$.

5.2.5 Policy Exploration

We now explore the policy implications of a robustness analysis of the example introduced on p.155. We will examine the choice of the number of licenses L, the audit probabilities π, and the allocation of enforcement resources ϕ.

The performance functions, eqs.(5.36) and (5.37), are homogeneous in the numbers of firms of the various types. This means that we can do all our calculations on a per-firm basis. Denote the total number of firms by N, and define $L' = L/N$ which is the average number of licenses issued per firm. Similarly, let $n'_k = n_k/N$ denote the fraction of type k firms.[4]

Number of permits, L. Fig. 5.11 shows robustness curves for aggregate violations, $\widehat{h}_{\rm v}$ vs. $R_{\rm c}/N$, for three values of the average number of licenses per firm, L'. The audit probabilities and enforcement resources which are directed to each type of firm are uniform across the industry, so every firm is equally likely to be audited and every audited firm has equal enforcement resources directed towards it.

The positive slopes of the robustness curves in fig. 5.11 reflect the trade-off between performance and robustness to uncertainty as explained in section 2.2.2: requiring lower aggregate violations entails lower robustness to uncertainty. The robustness curves each reach the horizontal axis at the estimated value of aggregate violation for the

[4] We will consider two types of firms, so $K = 2$. The estimated values of the coefficients of the abatement-cost functions, eq.(5.39), for these two types of firms are $(\widetilde{\alpha}_{11}, \widetilde{\alpha}_{12}) = (1, 1)$ and $(\widetilde{\alpha}_{21}, \widetilde{\alpha}_{22}) = (1.5, 0.7)$. Thus the 2nd type of firm has higher estimated abatement costs. The number fractions of the two types of firms are $n = (0.9, 0.1)$, so the low-cost firms are in the majority. The coefficient in the penalty function, eq.(5.41), is $\gamma = 1$.

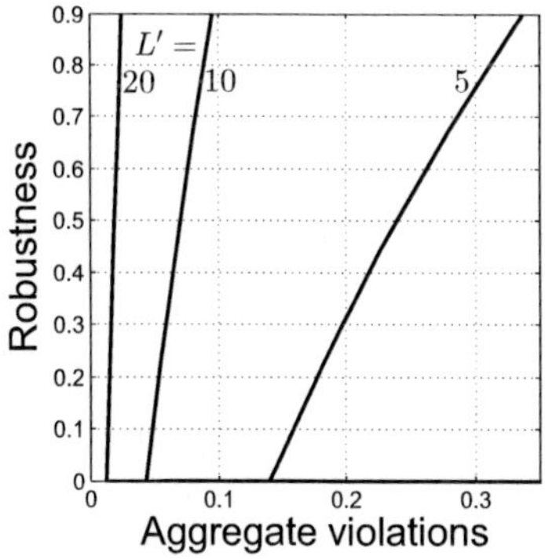

Figure 5.11: Robustness vs. critical aggregate level of violation, $\widehat{h}_{\mathrm{v}}$, for three values of L'. $\pi = (0.1, 0.1)$, $\phi = (1, 1)$.

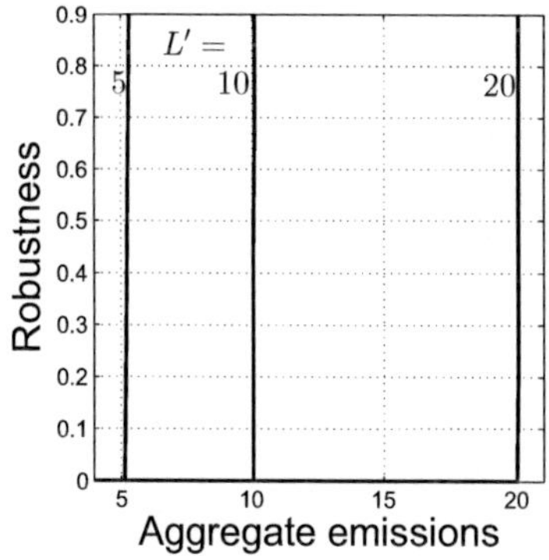

Figure 5.12: Robustness vs. critical aggregate level of emission, $\widehat{h}_{\mathrm{e}}$, for three values of L'. $\pi = (0.1, 0.1)$, $\phi = (1, 1)$.

corresponding value of L'. This is the "zeroing" property: estimated outcomes have no robustness against uncertainty. The same trade-off and zeroing properties are seen in fig. 5.12 as well, which shows robustness vs. aggregate emissions, $\widehat{h}_{\mathrm{e}}$.

The estimated level of violations decreases as the number of permits increases, as seen by the horizontal intercepts in fig. 5.11. With $L' = 5$ permits per firm on average, the estimated number of violations per firm is 0.14. When 10 or 20 permits are issued per firm, the estimated violations per firm decrease to 0.043 and 0.012 respectively. The equilibrium permit prices—based on the estimated cost functions—when $L' = 5$, 10 and 20 are 0.28, 0.0086 and 0.0024 respectively: the equilibrium price goes down as the number of permits increases. However, firms set their emission levels so that their marginal abatement costs equal the permit price, eq.(5.32). Since $c_k'(e_k) < 0$ and $c_k''(e_k) > 0$, this means that emissions rise as the number of permits increases. The estimated aggregate emissions per firm, when $L' = 5$, 10 and 20, are 5.14, 10.043 and 20.012 as expected from eq.(5.38).

This explains the reverse order of the robustness curves in figs. 5.11 and 5.12. In fig. 5.11 we saw that increasing the number of permits causes a decrease in the level of violations and, since the robustness curves do not cross one another, this makes a larger value of L' invariably more robust than a smaller value, when considering violations. But exactly the reverse is true when considering aggregate emissions in fig. 5.12: increasing the number of permits simply leads to greater emissions, and a small value of L' is now vastly more robust than a large value.

The *cost of robustness* changes significantly with L', and in the same sense for both emissions and violations. The slope of the robustness curve reflects how much it costs—in units of either emissions or violations—to increase the robustness by a given amount. For any given L', the slope of the corresponding robustness curve is the same in figs. 5.11 and 5.12. From fig. 5.11 we see that the slopes are about 70, 20 and 5 when L' equals 20, 10, or 5, respectively. Thus, a unit increase in robustness entails a much smaller increase in either emissions or violations if the number of permits is large.

This is important since we should not evaluate a choice of L' in terms of the estimated outcome (emission or violation), since the estimated outcome has zero robustness and thus cannot be confidently anticipated. The cost of robustness—slope of the robustness curve—indicates how much we must reduce our aspirations when evaluating any particular choice of L'.

Advantage of uniform audit and enforcement. We now consider a type of "profiling", in which either audit probabilities, π, or enforcement resources, ϕ, are allocated non-uniformly among the types of firms. We will compare profiling against uniform auditing and resource allocation across firms.

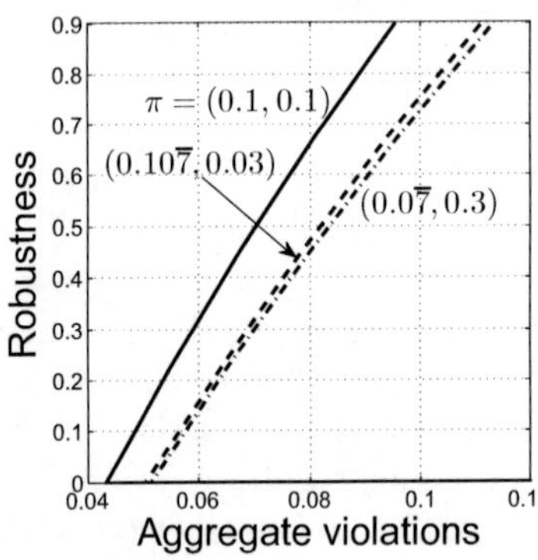

Figure 5.13: Robustness vs. critical aggregate level of violation, $\widehat{h}_{\rm v}$, for three choices of π. $\phi = (1, 1)$, $L' = 10$.

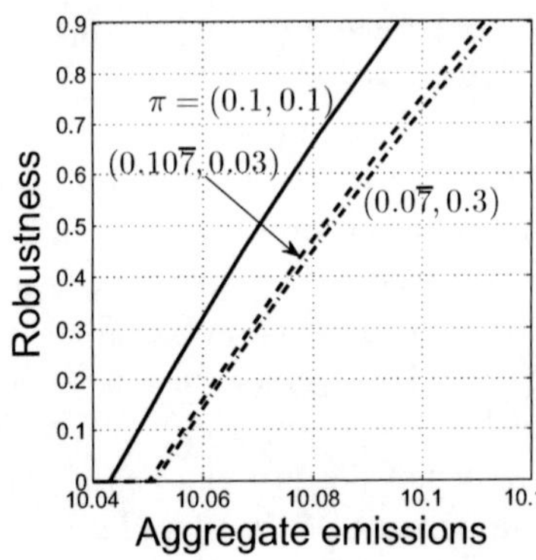

Figure 5.14: Robustness vs. critical aggregate level of emission, $\widehat{h}_{\rm e}$, for three choices of π. $\phi = (1, 1)$, $L' = 10$.

In fig. 5.13 we allocate enforcement resources uniformly, while audit probabilities are allocated in three different ways, two of which are non-uniform. The total number of audits per firm, $\pi_1 n_1' + \pi_2 n_2'$, is held constant at 0.1. That is, averaged over the entire industry, 1 out of 10 firms is audited. In the solid line this audit probability holds also for each type of firm separately. In the dashed line, however, type-1 firms are audited with probability of $0.10\overline{7}$ and type-2 firms are audited with probability of 0.03. That is, firms with low estimated abatement costs (type-1 firms) are more likely to be audited than high-cost firms. The situation is reversed in the dot-dashed curve, where audit probabilities for type-1 and type-2 firms are $0.0\overline{7}$ and 0.3 respectively.

Fig. 5.13 shows that the robustness is greater for uniform than for the two cases of non-uniform auditing. This illustrates a theorem proven by Stranlund and Dhanda (1999) which asserts that minimal estimated aggregate equilibrium violation is independent of exogenous properties of the firms (abatement costs in our example). This theorem is manifested in the curves of fig. 5.13 by the zero-robustness point being furthest to the left for uniform auditing. Since these robustness curves do not cross one another, this implies that uniform auditing is more robust than non-uniform auditing at all levels of performance, when the total number of permits is fixed.

The same effect—robustness advantage for uniform auditing probability—is seen in fig. 5.14 for aggregate emissions, whose curves are in fact simply shifted versions of the curves in fig. 5.13, as understood from eq.(5.38) on p.155.

We see in fig. 5.15 that the cost of robustness is lower for uniform auditing: the slope of the uniform-auditing curve is greatest. (This effect is evident also in fig. 5.13.) A steeper slope of the robustness curve means that the robustness can be enhanced by accepting a smaller increase in aggregate violation. Non-uniform auditing causes a lower slope of the robustness curves. In fig. 5.15 the slopes of the robustness curves for uniform and highly non-uniform auditing are about 17 and 10, respectively. A given increase in critical violation entails an increase in robustness which is about 70% higher for uniform auditing.

Fig. 5.16 shows curves of robustness of aggregate equilibrium violation, $\widehat{h}_{\text{v}}$, for three choices of the allocation of enforcement resources, ϕ, with uniform auditing probabilities π. The total quantity of enforcement resource per audited firm, $\phi_1 n_1' \pi_1 + \phi_2 n_2' \pi_2$, is constant at 0.1. As before, we see that uniform allocation is more robust than non-uniform allocation as expected from the Stranlund-Dhanda the-

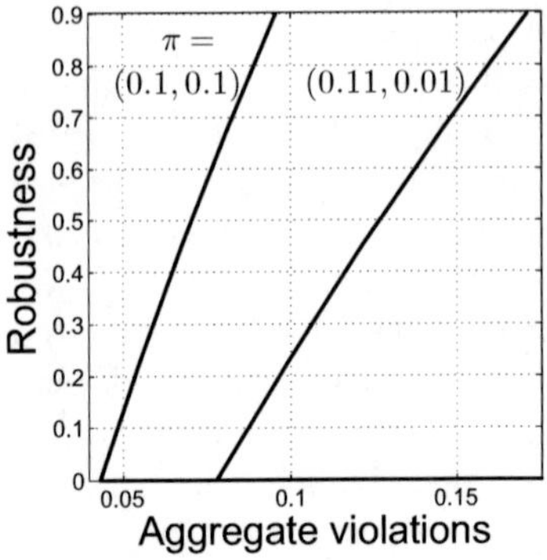

Figure 5.15: Robustness vs. critical aggregate level of violation, $\widehat{h}_{\mathrm{v}}$, for two choices of π. $\phi = (1, 1)$, $L' = 10$.

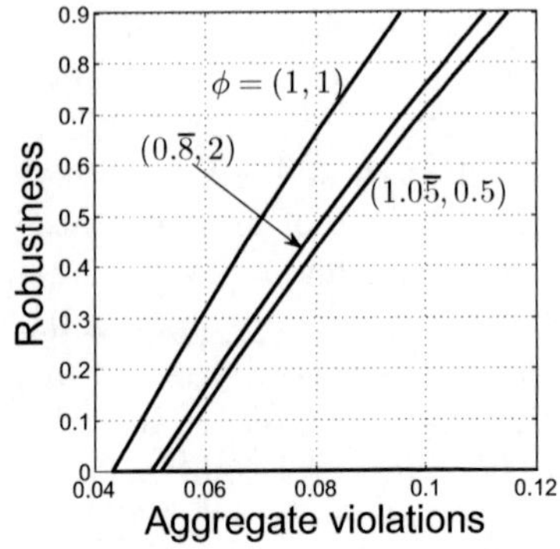

Figure 5.16: Robustness vs. critical aggregate level of emission, $\widehat{h}_{\mathrm{e}}$, for three choices of ϕ. $\pi = (0.1, 0.1)$, $L' = 10$.

orem (1999). We also note that the cost of robustness is lower for the uniform allocation (its robustness curve is steeper).

Equivalent policies. We have seen in figs. 5.11, 5.13 and 5.16 that the robustness for violations, $\widehat{h}_{\mathrm{v}}$, can be increased by increasing the number of permits, L', or by increasing the uniformity of either the audit probability π or the enforcement resource ϕ. This suggests that these three policy tools are interchangeable. We illustrate this in figs. 5.17 and 5.18.

Fig. 5.17 compares the robustness curves, $\widehat{h}_{\mathrm{v}}$ vs. the critical aggregate level of violations, for two different choices of the number of permits per firm, L', and the audit probabilities π. The dashed curve has a slightly larger number of permits per firm, $L' = 10.95$, while the audit probabilities are highly non-uniform. The solid curve, in contrast, has fewer permits, $L' = 10$, and the audit probabilities are the same for all firms in the industry. The enforcement resources are allocated uniformly among the firms in both cases. These robustness curves are the same for all practical purposes, suggesting that, as far as robustness to uncertainty is concerned, these two policy combinations are equivalent. The regulator can be indifferent between these two policies.

The example in fig. 5.17 occurs quite commonly: a non-uniform auditing policy will be practically equivalent to a uniform audit with some carefully selected alteration of the number of permits per firm. Fig. 5.17 suggests that the required change in the number of permits

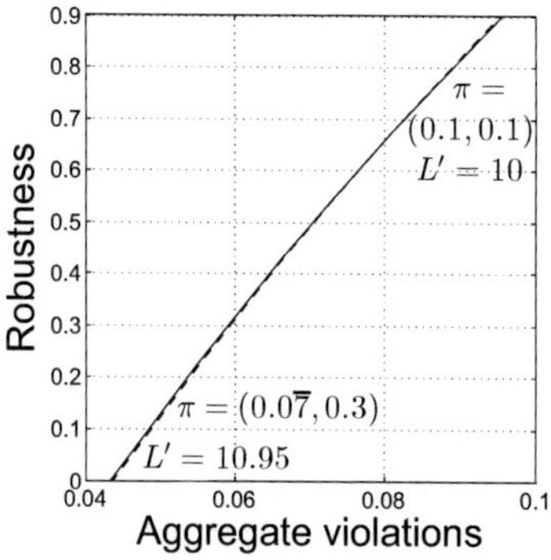

Figure 5.17: Robustness vs. critical aggregate level of violation, $\widehat{h}_v$, for two choices of L' and π. $\phi = (1, 1)$.

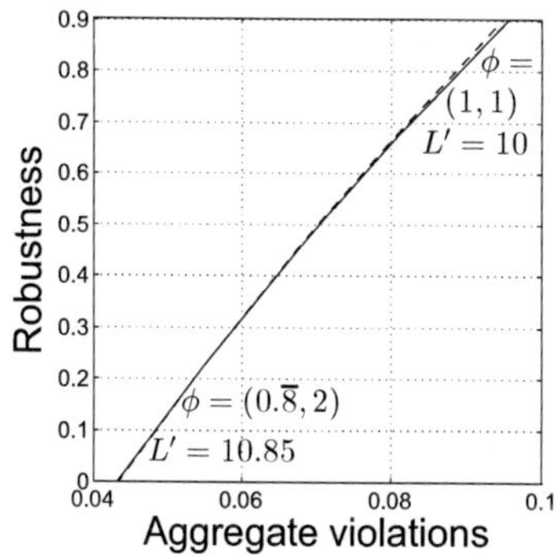

Figure 5.18: Robustness vs. critical aggregate level of violation, $\widehat{h}_v$, for two choices of L' and ϕ. $\pi = (0.1, 0.1)$.

may be quite small in order to compensate for moving from a highly non-uniform "profiling" audit to a uniform auditing strategy.

A similar effect is seen in fig. 5.18 which compares different allocations of enforcement resources and different numbers of permits. The dashed curve has a slightly larger number of permits per firm, $L' = 10.85$, and non-uniform allocation of enforcement resources, $\phi = (0.\overline{8}, 2)$, while the solid curve has fewer permits, $L' = 10$, but enforcement resources are allocated uniformly among the firms of the industry. Once again these robustness curves are nearly the same, suggesting that the corresponding policies are equivalent in practice.

Preference reversal. The robustness curves in figs. 5.17 and 5.18 are not identical and actually cross one another. Fig. 5.19 shows a clearer case of curve crossing. As discussed in section 2.2.2, intersection between robustness curves entails the possibility for reversal of preference between the corresponding policies. In fig. 5.19 we compare two very different uniform-auditing strategies, one which audits only 3% of the firms, and the other with 30% auditing. In the former case 19 permits are issued per firm and in the latter case only 5.5 permits. At low robustness and good performance—aggregate violations less than about 0.075—the intensive-auditing option is more robust. At higher robustness and poorer critical performance the low-density auditing is more robust. The choice between these two policies—if all else is the same—depends on the regulator's requirements for robustness and for equilibrium aggregate violation. (It should be noted

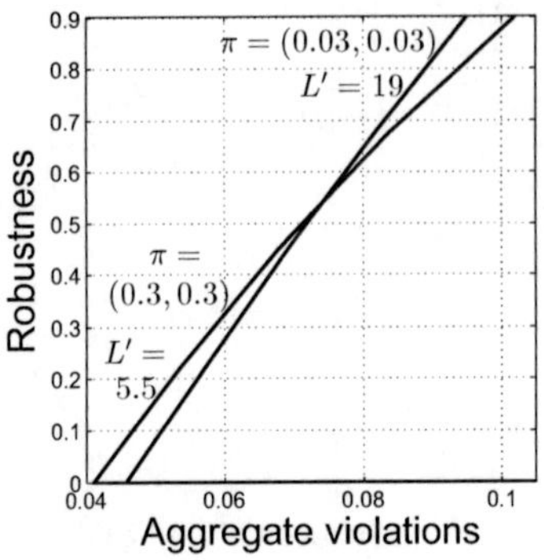

Figure 5.19: Robustness vs. critical aggregate level of violation, $\widehat{h}_{\mathrm{v}}$, for two choices of L' and π. $\phi = (1, 1)$.

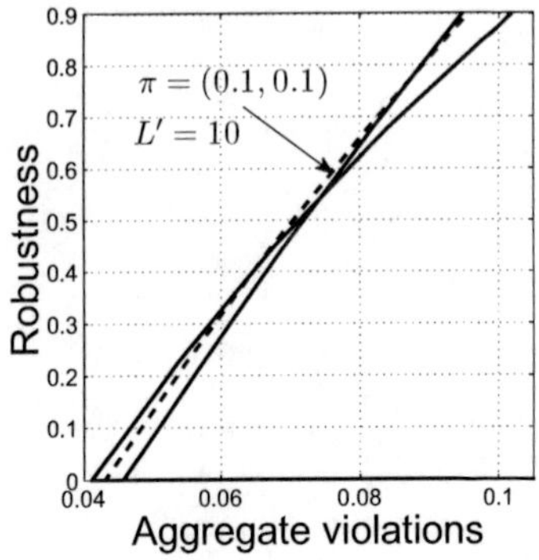

Figure 5.20: Robustness vs. critical aggregate level of violation, $\widehat{h}_{\mathrm{v}}$, for two choices of L' and ϕ. $\pi = (0.1, 0.1)$.

that all else is not the same, since the equilibrium aggregate emission, rather than violation, is much larger in the case with many pollution permits, as we learned in comparing figs. 5.11 and 5.12. In addition, the budgetary costs of these options are different.)

The solid curves in fig. 5.20 are the same as in fig. 5.19, and we have added the robustness curve (dashed) of an additional policy: uniform auditing of 10% of the firms with an initial issue of 10 permits per firm on average. Once again these curves cross one another and the preferences between them depend on the regulator's requirements.

5.2.6 Extensions

This analysis can be extended in many ways.

Cost functions. Our example is based on a specific choice of the estimated cost functions. Different choices can be studied. In addition, one can consider different models of uncertainty in the cost function.

Penalty functions. We have considered a specific choice of the penalty function, which depends on the audit probabilities and the allocation of enforcement resources. The regulator can explore different choices of the penalty function and their implications for robustness.

Probabilistic information. We have assumed that the regulator's information is non-probabilistic and uncertain. Various types of probabilistic information may be available, such as the likelihood that a type k firm will seek to violate the emissions limitation, and by how much. Such probabilistic information is valuable but also highly uncertain, so a robustness analysis is useful in reliably exploiting this information.

Interactive regulation. We have ignored the interaction over time between the regulator and the firms. Learning by both firms and the regulator, together with the impact of macro-economic dynamics, can be important in both the behavior of the firms and the policies of the regulator. Our static analysis can be extended to incorporate these interactive elements.

5.3 Climate Change

Sweeping change of the global environment as a result of human activity has been the focus of extensive scientific and economic analysis. Much work focusses on the adverse economic impact of rise in global mean temperature as a result of sustained change in the concentration of greenhouse gases such as CO_2, methane, and others.

Profound uncertainty surrounds both the transmission between change in greenhouse gas concentration and temperature rise, and in the transmission between temperature rise and economic loss. Despite these uncertainties, it is necessary to make policy choices of various sorts.

This uncertainty motivates two very different sorts of policy responses. On the one hand, the highly uncertain possibility of drastic, even catastrophic, consequences of human activity motivates precautionary abatement of greenhouse gas emission. On the other hand, the great uncertainty in our understanding of global processes in extreme conditions motivates intensive research on a wide range of environmental, biological and economic processes. Clearly, both strategies are needed.

In this section we will use simple models to illustrate the analysis of policy choices in these two categories, and trade-offs between them, when considering highly uncertain possibilities of severe scenarios. An **abatement policy** determines the extent to which the concentration of CO_2-equivalent greenhouse gases is allowed to rise. The choice of an abatement policy employs predictive models which are complex and uncertain. A **research policy** determines the extent to which the predictive models are improved by investing in scientific and economic research. We will use the robustness function to explore policy alternatives and trade-offs in these two categories. How much abatement is needed, in light of the uncertainties in the models? Large uncertainty may entail the need for precautionarily large abatement. How much research is called for to reduce this uncertainty? Can we express the abatement equivalent of an increment of model improvement?

The purpose here is not by any means to present realistic or definitive policy recommendations. The aim is to illustrate how highly uncertain data and models are incorporated in policy analysis for managing future climate change.

5.3.1 Policy Preview

The policy maker attempts to guarantee that—if an extreme scenario develops—the loss of economic output will not exceed a specified threshold. Two policies are explored: abatement of the growth of CO_2-equivalent gases in the atmosphere, and research into the scientific basis of predicting the impact of these greenhouse gases.

For any policy, the robustness to uncertainty decreases as the policy goals become more ambitious. On the other hand, policies differ in terms of the rate of this decrease as expressed as a cost of robustness: how much robustness is gained in exchange for accepting less desirable outcomes? In the context of the specific example explored here it will be seen that strengthening the research policy reduces the cost of robustness. In contrast, tightening the abatement policy leads to large improvement in robustness but does not greatly reduce the cost of robustness in units of lost economic output. This difference between the abatement and research policies underlies the trade-off between them.

5.3.2 Operational Preview

System model. The system model has two components. The first relates the change in greenhouse gas concentration, ΔCO_2, to the change in global mean temperature, ΔT, via the equilibrium climate sensitivity S, eq.(5.48). The second element of the system model is the fractional loss of GDP as a function of temperature change $f(\Delta T)$. This is an uncertain monotonically increasing function whose estimated form is eq.(5.49).

Performance requirement. The analyst is concerned to keep the fractional loss of economic output—in the case of an extreme scenario—below a specified critical value, f_c. The performance requirement is probabilistic since the climate sensitivity, S, is a random variable. Specifically, the performance requirement, eq.(5.50), is that the probability of GDP loss no greater than f_c is equal to ε.

Uncertainty models. We address two major info-gaps: the uncertain probability distribution of the equilibrium climate sensitivity S, and the uncertain functional dependence of lost GDP on temperature rise, $f(\Delta T)$. Roughly speaking, the first is a scientific uncertainty and the second is an economic uncertainty. The info-gap model $\mathcal{U}_S(h)$, eq.(5.52), is a fractional-error model for the quantiles of S, and allows for fat tails of the distribution of S. The info-gap model $\mathcal{U}_f(h)$, eq.(5.53), is an envelope-bound model for uncertain monotonically increasing functions $f(\Delta T)$.

Decision variables. We explore two different strategies. The *abatement* strategy constrains the relative growth in the concentration of CO_2-equivalent gases, ΔCO_2, which is the decision variable for this strategy. The *research* strategy focusses on the degree of scientific consensus needed in order to obtain robustness to future uncertainty in striving to achieve a specified economic goal. The decision variable for the research strategy is a target value, σ_s, for the dispersion in scientific opinion on the relevant quantile of the equilibrium climate sensitivity, S. We will not explore a research policy for consensus on the economic model of fractional GDP loss.

Robustness function. The robustness of policy $(\Delta CO_2, \sigma_s)$ is the greatest horizon of uncertainty in both S and $f(\Delta T)$ up to which the performance requirement is guaranteed. The robustness function is defined in eq.(5.54) and its inverse is specified explicitly in eq.(5.58).

5.3.3 System Model

We begin with some definitions. ΔCO_2 is the sustained relative change (ratio) in the concentration of CO_2-equivalent greenhouse gases. That is, ΔCO_2 is the ratio of the CO_2-equivalent concentration at some time in the future (e.g. a century hence) to the concentration at some prior time (e.g. today).

ΔT is the resulting change in the equilibrium global mean temperature. The temperature change is related to the change in CO_2-equivalent concentration via the equilibrium climate sensitivity coefficient, S. A widely used model is:

$$\Delta T = \frac{S \ln \Delta CO_2}{\ln 2} \tag{5.48}$$

Thus the global mean temperature rises by S degrees if the equilibrium concentration of CO_2-equivalent gases doubles. The mechanisms which underlie the relation between CO_2-equivalent concentration and temperature change are complex and incompletely understood. This uncertainty is represented by allowing S to be a random variable, and then acknowledging that the probability distribution of S—especially its upper tail—is uncertain.

f is the fractional loss of gross domestic product, $(Y^\star - Y)/Y^\star$, where $Y^\star$ is the potential future GDP and Y is the actual future GDP. f is an uncertain increasing function of ΔT.

A widely used estimated fractional GDP-loss function is (Weitzman, 2007):

$$\widetilde{f}(\Delta T) = \kappa(\Delta T)^\gamma \tag{5.49}$$

where $\kappa = 0.008$ and $\gamma = 2$ and ΔT is evaluated from eq.(5.48). This is a highly uncertain relation and may differ substantially from the true relation $f(\Delta T)$.

The **system model** is $f(\Delta T)$, whose functional form is uncertain, together with $\Delta T(S)$ in eq.(5.48) where S is a random variable whose probability distribution is uncertain.

5.3.4 Performance Requirement

The equilibrium climate sensitivity, S, is a random variable. Let S_ε denote the $1 - \varepsilon$ quantile of the distribution of S. That is, the probability is ε that S exceeds S_ε.

The fractional GDP-loss, $f(\Delta T)$, increases monotonically as ΔT increases, at fixed CO_2-equivalent concentration, and ΔT increases linearly with S, eq.(5.48). Since S is a random variable, so is f. We conclude that, at any given value of ΔCO_2-equivalent concentration, the $1 - \varepsilon$ quantile of f is $f[\Delta T(S_\varepsilon)]$. That is, at fixed ΔCO_2, the probability is ε that f exceeds $f[\Delta T(S_\varepsilon)]$.

Our performance requirement is that the $1 - \varepsilon$ quantile of the fractional GDP-loss not exceed a critical value, f_c:

$$f[\Delta T(S_\varepsilon)] \le f_c \tag{5.50}$$

For instance, we might require that the probability be 0.95 that the fractional GDP-loss not exceed 0.6. That is, for $\varepsilon = 0.05$, we require:

$$f[\Delta T(S_{0.05})] \le 0.6 \tag{5.51}$$

5.3.5 Uncertainty Models

As already indicated, we will focus on two uncertainties which beleaguer the performance requirement, eq.(5.50). First, the probability distribution of S is uncertain, and second, the functional relation between temperature rise and economic output is uncertain. We implement this with two uncertainty models, one for the quantiles of the equilibrium climate sensitivity, S, and one for the economic loss function, $f(\Delta T)$.

Equilibrium climate sensitivity. The Intergovernmental Panel on Climate Change in chapter 10 of its 2007 report (IPCC-AR4, 2007), writes that the "likely range" of values of the equilibrium climate sensitivity, S, resulting from a doubling in the concentration of CO_2-equivalent gases, is 1.5°C to 4.5°C. The report continues:

> Most of the results confirm that climate sensitivity is very unlikely below 1.5°C. The upper bound is more difficult to constrain because of a nonlinear relationship between climate sensitivity and the observed transient response, and is further hampered by the limited length of the observational record and uncertainties in the observations, which are particularly large for ocean heat uptake and for the magnitude of the aerosol radiative forcing. (p.798)
>
> There is no well-established formal way of estimating a single PDF from the individual results, taking account of the different assumptions in each study. Most studies do not account for structural uncertainty, and thus probably tend to underestimate the uncertainty. (p.799)

That S may substantially exceed 4.5°C is widely recognized. The mean of 10 different studies reported by the IPCC for the 95th quantile of S is 7.1°C, with a standard deviation of 2.8°C (IPCC-AR4, 2007, fig. 1b in Box 10.2 on p.798). That is, the average of these studies indicates that the probability is 0.05 that S will exceed 7.1°C, while one standard deviation above the mean is 9.9°C. It is very widely acknowledged that a rise of 7°C in the global mean temperature would be environmentally catastrophic, with drastic consequences for human societies.

Weitzman (2009) has shown, in a quite generic economic analysis of "uncertain catastrophes", that "there is a rigorous sense in which the relevant posterior-predictive PDF of high-impact, low-probability catastrophes has a built-in tendency to be fat tailed." By "fat tailed"

Weitzman means that "the tail probability approaches 0 more slowly than exponentially" Weitzman (2009, p.2).

We will use a fractional-error info-gap model to represent uncertainty in the $1-\varepsilon$ quantile of the distribution of S, which allows for fat-tailed distributions:

$$\mathcal{U}_S(h) = \left\{ S_\varepsilon : \left| \frac{S_\varepsilon - \widetilde{S}_\varepsilon}{\sigma_s} \right| \leq h \right\}, \quad h \geq 0 \tag{5.52}$$

σ_s is an estimate of the error of the nominal quantile, $\widetilde{S}_\varepsilon$. For instance, σ_s might be the range (e.g. standard deviation) of alternative scientifically based estimates of S_ε as discussed earlier.

Economic loss function. The estimated model of the fractional loss of GDP, eq.(5.49), is clearly a great simplification. This is a rough phenomenological model of a vastly complicated process of transmission from temperature change to loss of economic activity. Even much more sophisticated models will be accompanied by great uncertainty, especially regarding the downside risks (Tol, 2009). We will use an envelope-bound model for uncertainty in the functional form of $f(\Delta T)$, together with the assumption that economic loss increases as ΔT increases:

$$\mathcal{U}_f(h) = \left\{ f(\Delta T) : \frac{\partial f(\Delta T)}{\partial \Delta T} > 0, \left| \frac{f(\Delta T) - \widetilde{f}(\Delta T)}{\sigma_f(\Delta T)} \right| \leq h \right\}, \quad h \geq 0 \tag{5.53}$$

$\sigma_f(\Delta T)$ is an estimate of the error of the nominal function, $\widetilde{f}(\Delta T)$, for instance a range of variation among alternative models. In the absence of alternative models we might use a fractional-error model where $\sigma_f(\Delta T)$ is chosen as $\widetilde{f}(\Delta T)$, which is what we will do in section 5.3.7.

5.3.6 Robustness

As discussed at the start of this section, the policy maker must choose some combination of an abatement policy and a research policy. The abatement policy is specified by ΔCO_2, the relative change in concentration of CO_2-equivalent gases. The research policy is a mandate to the scientific community—together with an allocation of funds—to achieve a specified level of consensus on the estimate of S_ε, the $1-\varepsilon$ quantile of S. The research policy is specified by σ_s, appearing in the info-gap model of eq.(5.52). That is, the policy maker establishes a policy goal of improving the scientific consensus on a specific issue by a specified amount.

Like all policy goals, from inflation targeting to crime reduction, the costs involved are highly uncertain. In this example we will not consider the important and difficult question of the resources needed by the scientific community in order to reach the mandated consensus. We will also not consider a research policy regarding the model of economic loss, $f(\Delta T)$.

The robustness of policy $(\Delta CO_2, \sigma_s)$ is the greatest horizon of uncertainty such that the $1-\varepsilon$ quantile of $f(\Delta T)$ does not exceed the critical value, f_c:

$$\widehat{h}(\Delta CO_2, \sigma_s, f_c) = \max \left\{ h : \left(\max_{\substack{f \in \mathcal{U}_f(h) \\ S_\varepsilon \in \mathcal{U}_S(h)}} f[\Delta T(S_\varepsilon)] \right) \leq f_c \right\} \tag{5.54}$$

We now evaluate the inverse of the robustness function, assuming that $\sigma_f(\Delta T) = \widetilde{f}(\Delta T)$ in the info-gap model for uncertainty in the economic model, eq.(5.53).

Let $\mu(h)$ denote the inner maximum in the definition of the robustness, eq.(5.54). Because of the increasing monotonic dependence of f on S, this maximum occurs when S_ε and f are both as large are possible. Thus the the inner maximum occurs for:

$$S_\varepsilon = \widetilde{S}_\varepsilon + \sigma_s h \tag{5.55}$$

$$f(\Delta T) = (1+h)\widetilde{f}(\Delta T) \tag{5.56}$$

where ΔT is specified by eq.(5.48) with $S = S_\varepsilon$ as:

$$\Delta T = \frac{(\widetilde{S}_\varepsilon + \sigma_s h) \ln \Delta CO_2}{\ln 2} \tag{5.57}$$

Combining eqs.(5.56) and (5.57) with (5.49) we find:

$$\mu(h) = (1+h)\kappa \left(\frac{(\widetilde{S}_\varepsilon + \sigma_s h) \ln \Delta CO_2}{\ln 2} \right)^\gamma \tag{5.58}$$

The robustness is the greatest value of h at which $\mu(h) \leq f_c$. Since $\mu(h)$ increases monotonically as h increases (due to the nesting of the sets of the info-gap models), we see that the robustness is the greatest value of h at which $\mu(h) = f_c$. In other words, a plot of h vs. $\mu(h)$ is the same as a plot of $\widehat{h}(\Delta CO_2, \sigma_s, f_c)$ vs. f_c. In short, $\mu(h)$ is the inverse of the robustness function.

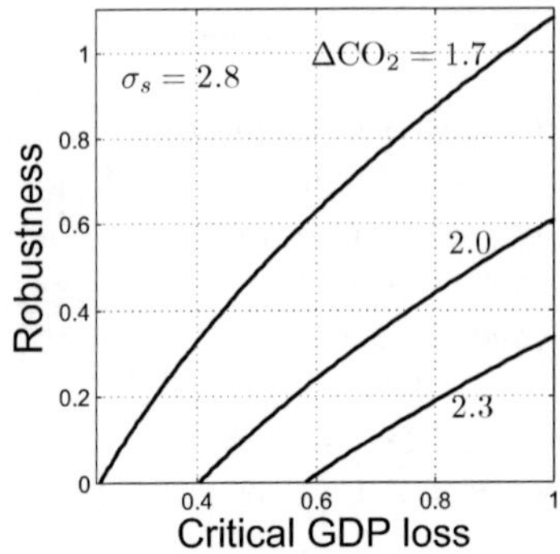

Figure 5.21: Robustness curves $\widehat{h}(\Delta CO_2, \sigma_s, f_c)$ vs. f_c for three values of ΔCO_2. $\sigma_s = 2.8$.

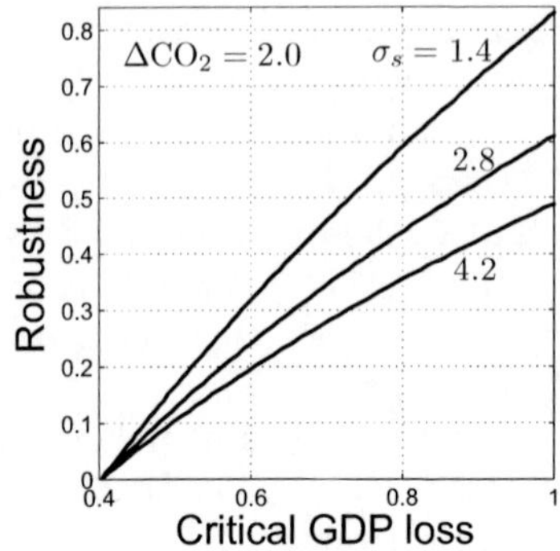

Figure 5.22: Robustness curves $\widehat{h}(\Delta CO_2, \sigma_s, f_c)$ vs. f_c for three values of σ_s. $\Delta CO_2 = 2.0$.

5.3.7 Policy Exploration

Fig. 5.21 shows curves of robustness, $\widehat{h}(\Delta CO_2, \sigma_s, f_c)$ vs. critical GDP loss, f_c.[5] The positive slope of these curves reflects the trade-off discussed in section 2.2.2: greater robustness against uncertainty (larger $\widehat{h}$) entails the potential for greater economic loss (larger f_c). Furthermore, the robustness in each case equals zero when f_c equals the estimated GDP loss: estimated outcomes have no robustness against info-gaps. That is, the value of f_c at which the robustness curve reaches the horizontal axis is precisely the estimated value of the $1 - \varepsilon$ quantile of the fractional GDP loss, $\widetilde{f}[\Delta T(\widetilde{S}_\varepsilon)]$.

The robustness curves in fig. 5.21 are for three different choices of the abatement policy, ΔCO_2, at fixed research policy, σ_s. Not surprisingly, robustness increases as abatement improves. An equilibrium increase of CO_2-equivalent gases by a factor of 1.7 entails substantially better robustness than an increase by a factor of 2.0, which in turn is better than an increase by a factor of 2.3.

For instance, suppose the policy maker requires that the fractional GDP loss not exceed 0.6 in the extreme scenario that we are considering. If the abatement policy is $\Delta CO_2 = 2.3$ and the research policy is $\sigma_s = 2.8$ (bottom curve in fig. 5.21), then robustness to uncertainty is 0.015: deviation of reality from the models by only 1.5% would allow the fractional economic loss to exceed 0.6. If the abatement policy is

[5] In all calculations in this section $\widetilde{S}_\varepsilon = 7.1$, meaning that we are considering a severe scenario. Also $\kappa = 0.008$ and $\gamma = 2$.

tightened to $\Delta CO_2 = 2.0$ (middle curve) then the robustness becomes 0.24, meaning that economic loss can exceed 0.6 only if the models err by more than 24%. Further reduction in the relative growth of greenhouse gas concentration to $\Delta CO_2 = 1.7$ (top curve) enhances the robustness to 0.63 which is nearly three times the robustness of the intermediate policy. It might be judged that robustness to 63% error is not much in light of the vast uncertainties and that even this abatement policy does not provide adequate confidence. However, fig. 5.21 shows the magnitude of change in abatement policy which causes substantial improvement in robustness to uncertainty as expressed by shifting the robustness curves to the left.

Fig. 5.22 displays robustness curves for three different research policies, at fixed abatement policy. Not surprisingly, the robustness to uncertainty increases as the scientific consensus increases (as represented by smaller values of σ_s). We note, however, that quite substantial improvements in consensus do not achieve particularly large robustness. For instance, at critical GDP loss of $f_c = 0.6$, the robustness improves from 0.20 to 0.31 as σ_s decreases from 4.2 to 1.4: a 50% increase in robustness, but still rather low robustness.

It is important to note in fig. 5.22 that the robustness curves become steeper as σ_s decreases, but they do not shift to the left. This is in contrast to the situation in fig. 5.21 where reducing ΔCO_2 primarily shifts the robustness curve to the left, and also slightly increases the slope. As explained in section 2.2.2, a large slope implies low cost of robustness. From fig. 5.22 we see that, by increasing scientific consensus, it becomes possible to augment robustness to uncertainty at reduced increment of GDP loss. This will be important when we consider trade-off between the abatement and research policies.[6]

Comparing figs. 5.21 and 5.22 shows that the abatement policy and the research policy can each enhance the robustness to uncertainty when attempting to contain the GDP loss below a specified upper bound. The figures suggest that small changes in the CO_2-equivalent concentration have greater impact on the robustness than large changes in scientific consensus. We now explore the trade-off between these policy alternatives.

Fig. 5.23 shows two different combinations of abatement and

[6] We are assuming that the value of $\widetilde{S}_\varepsilon$ will not change as scientific consensus increases. This need not be true. The middle ground of scientific dispute may change as scientific consensus improves. If $\widetilde{S}_\varepsilon$ becomes smaller then the robustness curves in fig. 5.22 would shift to the left, while an increase in $\widetilde{S}_\varepsilon$ would move the curves to the right.

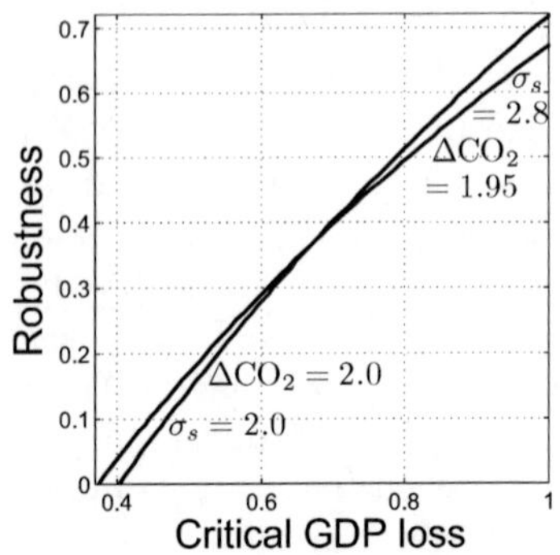

Figure 5.23: Robustness curves $\widehat{h}(\Delta CO_2, \sigma_s, f_c)$ vs. f_c for two combinations of ΔCO_2 and σ_s.

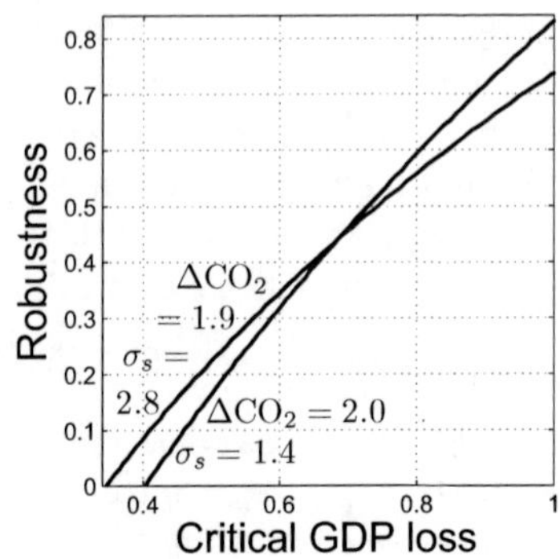

Figure 5.24: Robustness curves $\widehat{h}(\Delta CO_2, \sigma_s, f_c)$ vs. f_c for two combinations of ΔCO_2 and σ_s.

research policies, ΔCO_2 and σ_s, whose robustness curves cross one another and are nearly identical at all levels of fractional GDP loss, f_c. The figure indicates that the policy combination $(\Delta CO_2, \sigma_s) = (1.95, 2.8)$ is practically the same as $(\Delta CO_2, \sigma_s) = (2.0, 2.0)$. Increasing the relative change in CO_2-equivalent concentration from 1.95 to 2.0, and leaving everything else the same, would result in a loss of robustness at every value of f_c. However, this loss of robustness can be restored by a research policy which refines scientific consensus as expressed by reducing σ_s from 2.8 to 2.0. In this sense, then, an increase of 0.05 in relative CO_2 change is equivalent to a decrease of 0.8 in the dispersion of scientific opinion.

This analysis is predicated on the idea that it is the economic outcome—fractional change in GDP—which is of concern, and that neither ΔCO_2 nor σ_s is important in itself. This of course need not be true. The policy maker may be concerned with greenhouse gas concentration and scientific consensus themselves precisely because the future is highly uncertain. However, to the extent that the analysis views the economic outcome as dominant, our discussion of fig. 5.23 suggests how the abatement and research policies can be traded off, one against the other.

The next step might be to evaluate the direct economic benefit of allowing a 0.05 increase in ΔCO_2, as compared with the direct economic cost of financing the research needed to reduce σ_s by 0.8. We will not pursue this benefit-cost analysis.

Fig. 5.24 again shows two different combinations of abatement and research policies. The robustness curves cross one another at a fractional GDP loss of about 0.7, and are rather similar at other values of f_c, though not quite as similar as in fig. 5.23. For instance, the policy mix $(\Delta CO_2, \sigma_s) = (2.0, 1.4)$ has zero robustness for $f_c = 0.40$, while the other option, $(\Delta CO_2, \sigma_s) = (1.9, 2.8)$, has robustness of 0.09. That is, the second policy option can tolerate up to 9% deviation from the estimated loss function, $f(\Delta T)$, and equilibrium climate sensitivity, S, without resulting in fractional GDP loss greater than 0.4.

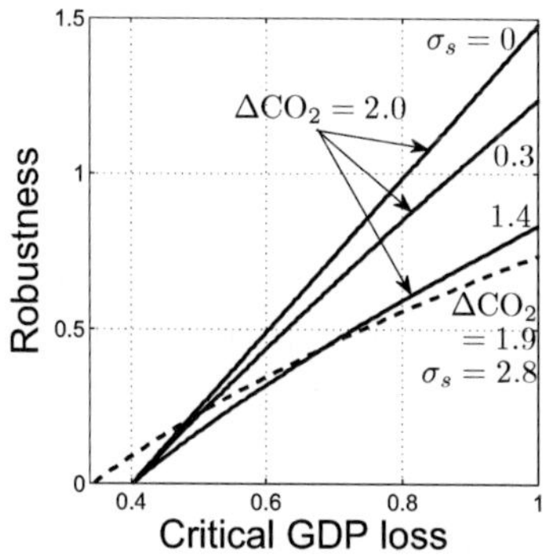

Figure 5.25: Robustness curves $\widehat{h}(\Delta CO_2, \sigma_s, f_c)$ vs. f_c for four combinations of ΔCO_2 and σ_s.

What the curves in figs. 5.21–5.24 are suggesting is that the abatement policy is far more potent than the research policy in robustly containing the loss of economic output.

This is demonstrated further in fig. 5.25 which shows increasingly small dispersion of scientific opinion, up to the extreme case of complete consensus ($\sigma_s = 0$). The dashed curve and the lowest solid curve are reproduced from fig. 5.24. The three solid curves have the same abatement policy, $\Delta CO_2 = 2.0$, and research policies with successively smaller dispersion of scientific opinion, σ_s. Increasing scientific consensus results in steepening the robustness curve—thereby reducing the cost of robustness. But the three solid curves (different research policies; same abatement policy) all have the same estimated fractional GDP loss (intersect with the horizontal axis). As a consequence, the three solid curves all cross the dashed curve, and therefore have greater robustness, for part of the f_c range, than the dashed curve. However, this robustness advantage is substantial only at very large fractional GDP loss. In contrast, a modest change in the abatement policy (e.g. from $\Delta CO_2 = 2.0$ to 1.7) would significantly reduce the estimated GDP loss and shift the entire robustness curve to the left, as seen in fig. 5.21.

This simple example is intended to demonstrate the sort of policy implications which can be deduced from an info-gap analysis of robustness, and the manner in which these inferences are made. The example should not be read as a specific policy recommendation.

5.3.8 Extensions

The simple illustrative example developed in this section—for the purpose of demonstrating the methodology—can be extended in various ways in order to develop more realistic policy recommendations.

Integrated assessment models. We have used simplistic models of the science and economics of climate change, outlined in section 5.3.3. Much effort has been devoted to developing richer models, as discussed in the IPCC reports (IPCC-AR4, 2007) and elsewhere. These integrated assessment models can be incorporated into an info-gap analysis of robustness.

Research policy for economics. We have considered a research policy only for the scientific component of the assessment of climate change, ignoring the possibility of improving the economic component of the system model. Disputes among economic modellers sometimes legitimately focus on issues of judgment and policy, as in the choice of inter-generational discount factors (Weitzman, 2007; Nordhaus, 2007). This makes the attainment of consensus more difficult than in natural science where the separation between judgment and model is sharper. Nonetheless, research to improve our understanding of the economic consequences of climate change is much needed, and the policy maker can address this in evaluating the robustness of alternative strategies.

Cost-benefit analysis. We have studied the trade-off between abatement of greenhouse gases and scientific research. However, we did not pursue the next step of evaluating the marginal cost and benefit of exchanging an increment of abatement for an increment of research, mentioned on p.174. While research is expensive, abatement is vastly so. The ability to identify equivalent increments in these two strategies, at constant confidence in outcomes, can have very substantial budgetary implications. In addition, substantial uncertainties accompany the estimates of economic costs and benefits

(Tol, 2009), and an info-gap analysis can assist in managing these uncertainties.

Adaptive strategies. The severe scenarios which we have studied are projected a century or more into the future. It is thus important to include the temporal dimension in a policy analysis. An adaptive strategy can emphasize research and learning from experience for an initial period, moving increasingly to preventive action—abatement for instance—as time passes and understanding increases. The adaptation can just as well be in the reverse direction, with strongly precautionary abatement until scientific understanding justifies different action. An info-gap robustness analysis can help choose between these two different adaptive strategies.

Discounting. When allocating resources over a long duration it is desirable to account for future wealth and knowledge by discounting over time. Inter-generational discounting is itself a policy issue and entails considerable uncertainty of preferences and principles. This uncertainty can be incorporated into an info-gap robustness analysis. That is, the policy maker can acknowledge the unresolved (and perhaps unresolvable) dispute over discount factors, and evaluate alternative policies in part in terms of their robustness to the choice of how the discounting is done. A policy which achieves a specified outcome over a greater range of discount values would be preferred—other things equal—over a policy with low robustness to the choice of the discount rate.

5.4 Appendix: Derivation of Eq.(5.19)

The welfare loss, eq.(5.9), in this special case is:

$$L(q, b, c) = \frac{[b_1 - c_1 - (\widetilde{b}_2 + \widetilde{c}_2)q]^2}{2(\widetilde{b}_2 + \widetilde{c}_2)} \tag{5.59}$$

Let $m(h)$ denote the maximum welfare loss at horizon of uncertainty h, which is the inner maximum in the definition of the robustness, eq.(5.18). We consider two cases.

Case 1: $\widetilde{b}_1 - \widetilde{c}_1 \geq (\widetilde{b}_2 + \widetilde{c}_2)q$. The inner maximum in eq.(5.18) occurs when $b_1 - c_1$ is as large as possible at horizon of uncertainty h, which is:

$$\begin{aligned} \max_h(b_1 - c_1) &= (\widetilde{b}_1 + hs_{b_1}) - (\widetilde{c}_1 - hs_{c_1}) && (5.60) \\ &= \widetilde{b}_1 - \widetilde{c}_1 + (s_{b_1} + s_{c_1})h && (5.61) \end{aligned}$$

Combining eqs.(5.59) and (5.61), the inner maximum in eq.(5.18) is found to be:

$$m(h) = \frac{[\widetilde{b}_1 - \widetilde{c}_1 - (\widetilde{b}_2 + \widetilde{c}_2)q + (s_{b_1} + s_{c_1})h]^2}{2(\widetilde{b}_2 + \widetilde{c}_2)} \quad (5.62)$$

Case 2: $\widetilde{b}_1 - \widetilde{c}_1 < (\widetilde{b}_2 + \widetilde{c}_2)q$. The inner maximum in eq.(5.18) occurs when $b_1 - c_1$ is as small as possible at horizon of uncertainty h which is:

$$\min_h(b_1 - c_1) = (\widetilde{b}_1 - hs_{b_1}) - (\widetilde{c}_1 + hs_{c_1}) \quad (5.63)$$

$$= \widetilde{b}_1 - \widetilde{c}_1 - (s_{b_1} + s_{c_1})h \quad (5.64)$$

Combining eqs.(5.59) and (5.64), the inner maximum in eq.(5.18) is found to be:

$$m(h) = \frac{[\widetilde{b}_1 - \widetilde{c}_1 - (\widetilde{b}_2 + \widetilde{c}_2)q - (s_{b_1} + s_{c_1})h]^2}{2(\widetilde{b}_2 + \widetilde{c}_2)} \quad (5.65)$$

These two cases can be combined by expressing eqs.(5.62) and (5.65) simultaneously as:

$$m(h) = \frac{[|\widetilde{b}_1 - \widetilde{c}_1 - (\widetilde{b}_2 + \widetilde{c}_2)q| + (s_{b_1} + s_{c_1})h]^2}{2(\widetilde{b}_2 + \widetilde{c}_2)} \quad (5.66)$$

If $m(0) > L_c$, then the estimated welfare loss—which occurs even in the absence of uncertainty—exceeds the critical value and the robustness to uncertainty is zero. If $m(h) \leq L_c$ then the robustness is obtained by equating eq.(5.66) to L_c and solving for h, which yields eq.(5.19).

5.5 Appendix: Derivation of Eq.(5.22)

The welfare loss, eq.(5.14), in this special case is:

$$L(t, b, c) = \frac{[b_1\widetilde{c}_2 + c_1\widetilde{b}_2 - (\widetilde{b}_2 + \widetilde{c}_2)t]^2}{2(\widetilde{b}_2 + \widetilde{c}_2)\widetilde{c}_2^2} \quad (5.67)$$

Arguing in a manner analogous to appendix 5.4 one can show that the inner maximum in the definition of the robustness, eq.(5.18), which we denote $m(h)$, is:

$$m(h) = \frac{[|\widetilde{b}_1\widetilde{c}_2 + \widetilde{c}_1\widetilde{b}_2 - (\widetilde{b}_2 + \widetilde{c}_2)t| + (s_{b_1}\widetilde{c}_2 + s_{c_1}\widetilde{b}_2)h]^2}{2(\widetilde{b}_2 + \widetilde{c}_2)\widetilde{c}_2^2} \quad (5.68)$$

Equating this to L_c and solving for h yields the robustness, eq.(5.22).

Chapter 6

Estimation and Forecasting

We illustrate the combination of statistical estimation and forecasting with info-gap robust-satisficing in three examples. In all cases the data are not only statistically random, but also subject to non-random info-gaps. Info-gaps in economic data may arise due to delay between the initiation of a systemic change and its manifestation in data. In addition, current best-estimates of economic data are info-gap-uncertain because these data may be substantially revised in the future as new information becomes available and new definitions and classifications are adopted. Section 6.1 considers a regression of serial data and the use of that regression to predict the next outcome. Section 6.2 discusses an auto-regression, and section 6.3 studies the confidence interval of the least squares estimate of a variable.

~ ~ ~

6.1 Regression Prediction

Fig. 6.1 shows US inflation for the years 1961–1965. The data look roughly linear. But if we add one more year to the graph, as in fig. 6.2, we now discern a clear non-linear trend over at least the four years starting in 1963.

Data like these raise several questions. How should we model uncertain economic processes? How can we formulate and calibrate

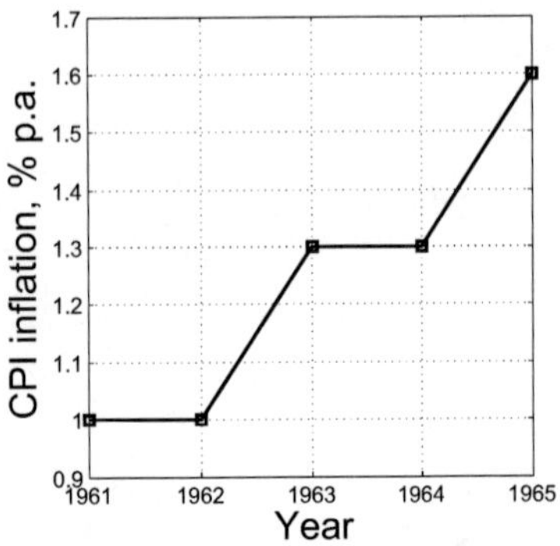

Figure 6.1: US inflation vs. year, 1961–1965.

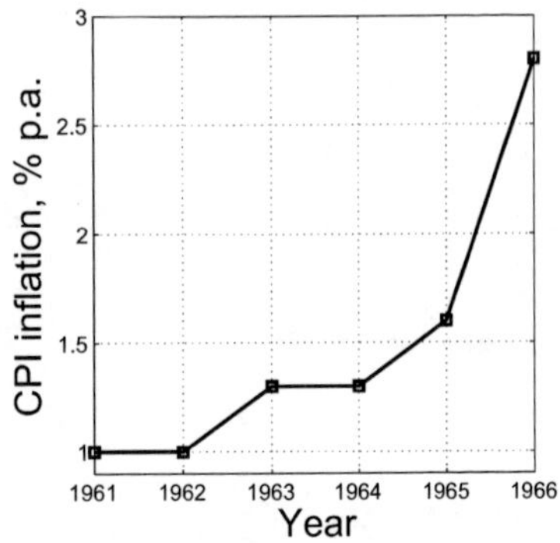

Figure 6.2: US inflation vs. year, 1961–1966.

models from historical data to meaningfully predict or anticipate future behavior? How do we combine contextual economic understanding with quantitative data? There is of course no single answer to these questions. In this section we will discuss one info-gap approach.

The inflation data from 1961 to 1965 show no indication of the subsequent rapid rise in inflation, but the astute economist might have attained contextual understanding of markets, institutions and the society at large which suggests that the inflation regime will change in a particular direction. This economist might agree to statements such as "inflation growth is accelerating" and "future inflation is likely to substantially exceed historical projections", but be unable to say how large an increase in inflation will occur or what might be the greatest reasonable inflation. A glance at the inflation chart though 1970, fig. 6.3, shows that the rise can be quite precipitous, and the chart up to 1993, fig. 6.4, shows that inflation can also be erratic.

Three points are central in attempting to understand and anticipate the future: current and recent historical data are critical; "soft" linguistic understanding is useful; things can change rapidly.

We will study an info-gap approach to quadratic regression of a serial scalar variable in which contextual information suggests that the next-in-series variable will be larger than expected. The aim is both to project into the future and to incorporate the new information—which is linguistic and contextual but not yet manifested in observations—in revising the historical regression. The contextual information is quite limited so we cannot expect to get too far with it.

Nor should we rely on it too heavily, hence the need to anchor the prediction in the historical regression. Nonetheless we can usefully incorporate contextual understanding in a systematic quantitative analysis which augments the strictly historical regression.

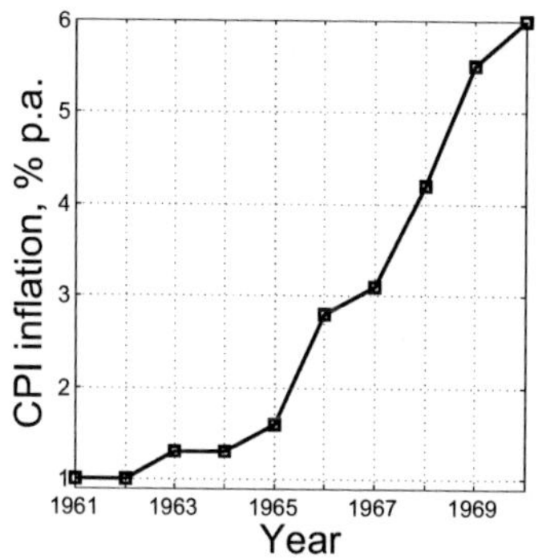

Figure 6.3: US inflation vs. year, 1961–1970.

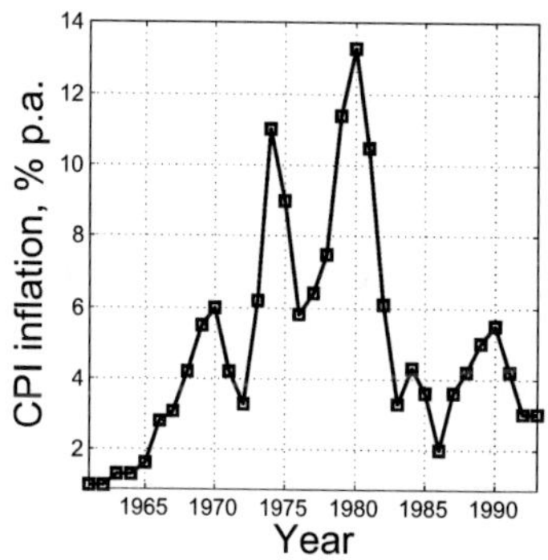

Figure 6.4: US inflation vs. year, 1961–1993.

6.1.1 Policy Preview

Given quantitative observations of economic outcomes, together with linguistic and contextual understanding of economic processes and trends, we wish to forecast a future outcome. The contextual information is highly uncertain and much less informative than future observations which are not yet available. However, we can improve our forecast in a systematic manner by incorporating this contextual understanding in a regression analysis of the observations.

6.1.2 Operational Preview

System model. Our system model is the root mean squared (RMS) error of a regression, evaluated over the data and the uncertain future outcome, eq.(6.4). This system model depends on the choice of regression coefficients and on the uncertain future outcome.

Uncertainty model. The available economic understanding indicates that the future outcome will exceed anticipations based on historical projections. However, the magnitude of the outcome is unknown. This is represented by an asymmetric interval info-gap model, eq.(6.5).

Performance requirement. We require that the RMS error not exceed a critical value, eq.(6.6).

Robustness and decision. The decision is the choice of the regression coefficients and the robustness of any such choice is the greatest horizon of uncertainty at which the RMS error does not exceed a critical value, eq.(6.7). Eq.(6.12) is an explicit expression for the inverse of the robustness function.

6.1.3 Regression and Robustness

Regression. Consider N serial data points $y_1, \ldots, y_N$, such as inflation data over N sequential years as in fig. 6.1. Suppose also that economic understanding suggests that the next outcome—e.g. inflation in 1966—will be substantially higher than would be projected from the current data. For concreteness we will refer to annual inflation data, though of course the method can be applied to other situations.

We wish to choose a quadratic regression for the serial variable (e.g. inflation) which accounts both for the data (e.g. inflation during 1961–1965) and the additional contextual economic understanding about the future (greater than anticipated inflation in 1966). The quadratic regression is:

$$y_i^{\mathrm{r}} = c_0 + c_1 t_i + c_2 t_i^2 \tag{6.1}$$

The choice of the coefficients c_0, c_1, c_2 will be based on data (t_i, y_i) for $i = 1, \ldots, N$ and the understanding that y_{N+1} will probably exceed anticipations.

System model: root mean squared error. Define the mean squared error of the regression of the N data points:

$$S_N^2(c) = \frac{1}{N} \sum_{i=1}^{N} (y_i - y_i^{\mathrm{r}})^2 \tag{6.2}$$

where c is the vector of regression coefficients which define y_i^{r} in eq.(6.1).

Let $\widetilde{c}$ denote the regression coefficients which minimize the mean squared error of the observations, $S_N^2(c)$, and let $\widetilde{y}_i^{\mathrm{r}}$ denote the corresponding regression predictions. That is, $\widetilde{y}_i^{\mathrm{r}}$ is obtained from eq.(6.1) with the coefficients $\widetilde{c}$. The least squares regression coefficients are presented in appendix 6.4.

If we knew the inflation in year t_{N+1} we could define the mean squared error as in eq.(6.2):

$$S_{N+1}^2(c) = \frac{1}{N+1}\sum_{i=1}^{N+1}(y_i - y_i^{\mathrm{r}})^2 \tag{6.3}$$

$$= \frac{N}{N+1}S_N^2(c) + \frac{\left(y_{N+1} - y_{N+1}^{\mathrm{r}}\right)^2}{N+1} \tag{6.4}$$

Our system model is the RMS error for the period including the next time step, $S_{N+1}(c)$. This of course depends on a datum, y_{N+1}, about which we have only fragmentary and uncertain information.

Uncertainty model. Our contextual information strongly indicates that the inflation in year t_{N+1} will exceed the least-squares prediction $\widetilde{y}_{N+1}^{\mathrm{r}}$, but we don't know by how much. We express this with the following asymmetric info-gap model for uncertainty in y_{N+1}:

$$\mathcal{U}(h) = \left\{y_{N+1} :\ 0 \le y_{N+1} - \widetilde{y}_{N+1}^{\mathrm{r}} \le h\right\}, \quad h \ge 0 \tag{6.5}$$

Like all info-gap models, this is an unbounded family of nested sets. At any horizon of uncertainty, h, the set $\mathcal{U}(h)$ contains all values of next year's inflation, y_{N+1}, which exceed the RMS prediction by no more than h. When there is no uncertainty (namely, $h = 0$), the set contains only the RMS prediction. As the horizon of uncertainty increases the sets become more inclusive.

Performance requirement. We would like the predicted inflation, y_{N+1}^{r}, to be close to the unknown future value, y_{N+1}. The info-gap model expresses what we know (and don't know) about the future. Since the uncertainty in y_{N+1} is considerable, we will anchor our prediction in the historical data, without limiting ourselves to the strict historical projection. Thus our performance requirement is that the RMS error of the historical and projected regression not exceed a critical value:

$$S_{N+1}(c) \le S_{\mathrm{c}} \tag{6.6}$$

Robustness function. The robustness of regression coefficients c is the greatest horizon of uncertainty h up to which the root mean squared error $S_{N+1}(c)$, including next year's inflation, is no greater than the critical value S_{c}:

$$\widehat{h}(c, S_{\mathrm{c}}) = \max\left\{h :\ \left(\max_{y_{N+1}\in\mathcal{U}(h)} S_{N+1}(c)\right) \le S_{\mathrm{c}}\right\} \tag{6.7}$$

If $\widehat{h}(c, S_{\rm c})$ is large then the RMS error will be acceptable (less than $S_{\rm c}$) even though we are very uncertain about the next outcome. A small value of robustness means that the regression is highly vulnerable to the uncertainty in the next inflation datum.

Deriving the robustness function. Let $\mu(h)$ denote the inner maximum in the definition of the robustness, eq.(6.7). The robustness is the greatest value of h at which $\mu(h) \le S_{\rm c}$. $\mu(h)$ increases as h increases because the sets of the info-gap model are nested. Consequently, the robustness is the greatest h at which $\mu(h) = S_{\rm c}$. In other words, a plot of $\mu(h)$ vs. h is the same as a plot of $S_{\rm c}$ vs. $\widehat{h}(c, S_{\rm c})$. In short, $\mu(h)$ is the inverse of $\widehat{h}(c, S_{\rm c})$.

From the expression for S_{N+1} in eq.(6.4) we see that $\mu(h)$ occurs when y_{N+1} equals one of its extreme values at horizon of uncertainty h: either $\widetilde{y}^{\rm r}_{N+1}$ or $\widetilde{y}^{\rm r}_{N+1} + h$. These two extreme values are:

$$\mu_1(h) = \sqrt{\frac{N}{N+1} S_N^2 + \frac{\left(\widetilde{y}^{\rm r}_{N+1} - y^{\rm r}_{N+1}\right)^2}{N+1}} \qquad (6.8)$$

$$\mu_2(h) = \sqrt{\frac{N}{N+1} S_N^2 + \frac{\left(\widetilde{y}^{\rm r}_{N+1} + h - y^{\rm r}_{N+1}\right)^2}{N+1}} \qquad (6.9)$$

The inner maximum is the greater of these two expressions:

$$\mu(h) = \max\left[\mu_1(h),\ \mu_2(h)\right] \qquad (6.10)$$

Recall our economic understanding that the actual inflation, y_{N+1}, will exceed the least-squares anticipated value, $\widetilde{y}^{\rm r}_{N+1}$. In light of this we will only consider regressions $y^{\rm r}_i$ for which the prediction, $y^{\rm r}_{N+1}$, is no less than the least-squares anticipation:

$$\widetilde{y}^{\rm r}_{N+1} \le y^{\rm r}_{N+1} \qquad (6.11)$$

With this restriction eq.(6.10) becomes:

$$\mu(h) = \begin{cases} \sqrt{\frac{N}{N+1} S_N^2 + \frac{\left(\widetilde{y}^{\rm r}_{N+1} - y^{\rm r}_{N+1}\right)^2}{N+1}} & \text{if } h < 2\left(y^{\rm r}_{N+1} - \widetilde{y}^{\rm r}_{N+1}\right) \\ \sqrt{\frac{N}{N+1} S_N^2 + \frac{\left(\widetilde{y}^{\rm r}_{N+1} + h - y^{\rm r}_{N+1}\right)^2}{N+1}} & \text{if } h \ge 2\left(y^{\rm r}_{N+1} - \widetilde{y}^{\rm r}_{N+1}\right) \end{cases} \qquad (6.12)$$

This is the inverse of the robustness function, as noted earlier.

6.1.4 Policy Exploration

We illustrate these ideas with a quadratic regression of US inflation data for the years 1961–1965.[1]

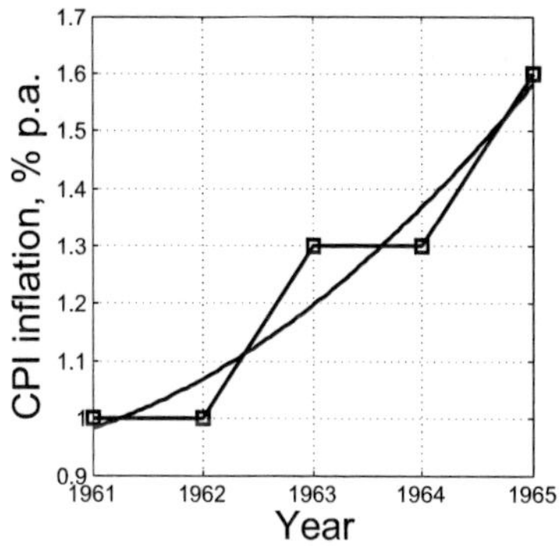

Figure 6.5: US inflation vs. year, 1961–1965, and least squares fit.

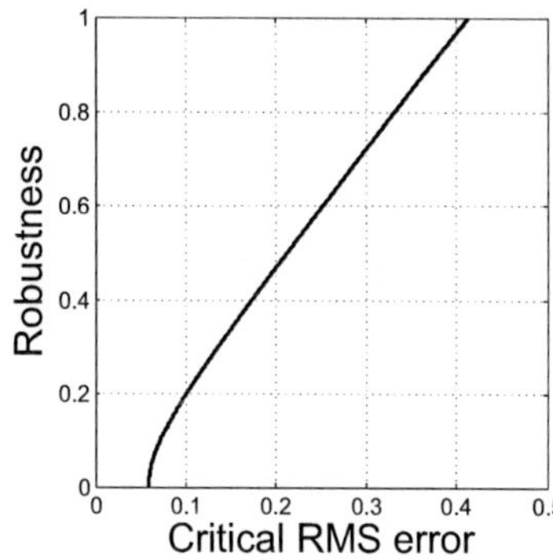

Figure 6.6: Robustness vs. critical root mean squared error for inflation 1961–1965.

Least squares regression. Fig. 6.5 shows the 1961–1965 data again, together with the least squares best fit.[2] Not quite linear after all: the coefficients $(\widetilde{c}_0, \widetilde{c}_1, \widetilde{c}_2)$ are (0.9400, 0.0214, 0.0214). The root mean squared error is 0.064: a bit more than half of one-tenth of a percentage point of inflation.

Robustness. We now consider the robustness of this least squares (LS) regression. There are 5 data points, so $N = 5$, and one unknown future value.

The robustness curve for the LS coefficients, $\widetilde{c}$, is shown in fig. 6.6, in which $\mu(h)$ from eq.(6.12) is plotted along the horizontal axis as h runs up the vertical axis. Since the regression, y_i^{r}, whose robustness is plotted is the least squares regression, $\widetilde{y}_i^{\mathrm{r}}$, the difference $y_i^{\mathrm{r}} - \widetilde{y}_i^{\mathrm{r}}$ vanishes and only the bottom row of eq.(6.12) is operative.

The robustness curve sprouts off the critical RMS axis at the value of the estimated RMS error, 0.064, which is the **zeroing property** discussed in section 2.2.2: one has no robustness against uncertainty when striving to achieve the estimated error.

[1]The CPI inflation data shown in fig. 6.1 are: 1.0, 1.0, 1.3, 1.3, 1.6.

[2]The regression is done with years shifted by 1960, so the first datum is at time $t_1 = 1$, etc.

The positive slope of the robustness curve expresses the **trade-off** between robustness and RMS error: large robustness is achieved by accepting large error, as explained in section 2.2.2.

The slope of the curve represents the **cost of robustness.** The curve has very high slope near the S_c axis, indicating that robustness can be increased at very low cost of increased RMS error. Subsequently the robustness curve is nearly linear with slope about 2.6, meaning that a unit increase in RMS error achieves an increase of 2.6 in robustness. This pattern—low cost of robustness at low robustness, higher cost at higher robustness—will be very important in comparing alternative regressions.

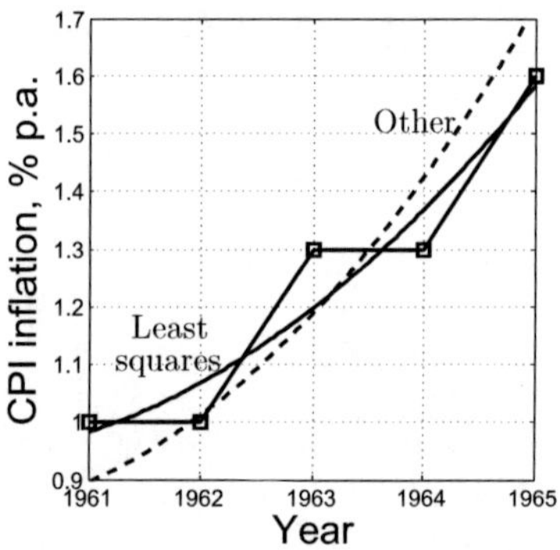

Figure 6.7: US inflation vs. year, 1961–1965, and least squares fit (solid) and other fit (dash).

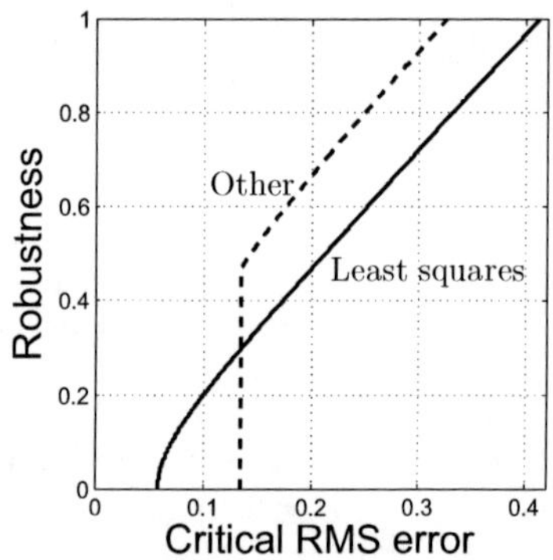

Figure 6.8: Robustness vs. critical root mean squared error for inflation 1961–1965 for least squares fit (solid) and other fit (dash).

Comparing regressions. Fig. 6.7 shows the 1961–1965 inflation data again together with the least squares regression $\widetilde{c}$ and another regression whose coefficients (c_0, c_1, c_2) are (0.84, 0.026, 0.03). This other regression is clearly a sub-optimal representation of the historical data; the LS regression is, not surprisingly, a better fit. The root mean square errors of the least squares and alternative regressions are 0.064 and 0.13 respectively. The non-LS regression misses the data, on average, by 0.13 percentage points of inflation, as compared with 0.064 for the least squares fit. On the other hand, it is seen from the curves that the non-LS regression will predict a larger inflation for year 1966 than the LS regression.

The robustness curves for these regressions are shown in fig. 6.8, where we see that the curves intersect one another. The non-LS regression $y_i^{\rm r}$, differs from the LS regression $\widetilde{y}_i^{\rm r}$, so both lines in eq.(6.12) are "activated" in the non-LS case, which explains the kink in the dashed robustness curve. This pattern of two different robustness-cost domains is accentuated in the robustness curve of $y_i^{\rm r}$. The vertical zero-cost domain extends up to robustness of 0.48, which exceeds the robustness of the LS regression at that value of RMS error. The subsequent cost of robustness—slope of the curve—is essentially the same for the two regressions.

These two regressions differ in two respects. $\widetilde{y}_i^{\rm r}$ has smaller estimated RMS error than $y_i^{\rm r}$. However, the cost of robustness is lower for $y_i^{\rm r}$ than for $\widetilde{y}_i^{\rm r}$ over a significant range of robustness. These two attributes—RMS error and cost of robustness—are different, and there is no reason to expect that optimizing one of them will necessarily optimize the other. It is precisely this difference which causes their robustness curves to cross one another.

The intersection between the robustness curves implies the potential for a reversal of preference between these two regressions, as explained in section 2.2.3. If the analyst is willing to accept an RMS error as large as 0.13, then the non-LS regression is more robust to the uncertain future and thus preferable to the LS regression.

The non-LS regression, $y_i^{\rm r}$, has robustness of 0.48 at RMS error of 0.13, while the robustness of the least squares regression, $\widetilde{y}_i^{\rm r}$, is only 0.28. Referring to the info-gap model in eq.(6.5), we see that $y_i^{\rm r}$ can err by as much as 0.48 percentage points in predicting the next inflation, and the overall RMS error will not exceed 0.13. The least squares regression $\widetilde{y}_i^{\rm r}$ exceeds this RMS error when its prediction errs by 0.28. In other words, $y_i^{\rm r}$ retains overall fidelity to the data and the auxiliary information for a wider range of uncertainty in the future outcome.

As often happens in predicting inflation, neither predictor does very well in forecasting the sharp rise in 1966 inflation. The least squares regression predicts 1.8% inflation, the robust projection is 2.1%, while the inflation actually was 2.8%. The robust regression is using the contextual information that future inflation will exceed the historical projection by an unknown amount. The robust regression misses the historical data more than the least squares regression, but it is a slightly better predictor of the future than the least squares regression.

6.1.5 Extensions

This simple example can be extended in many directions, including the following.

Multiple predictions. Contextual information may extend beyond the first period in the future, and forecasts may likewise extend further into the future. Contextual information may also relate to past data. Revisions of past economic statistics are sometimes very substantial, and the analyst may have economic insight which suggests the direction in which revisions may occur. (We will consider uncertain data revision in section 6.2.) This then allows the formulation of an info-gap model, like eq.(6.5), which describes info-gap uncertainty in future outcomes and in past statistical data. Other info-gap models can also be formulated for robustness analysis of regressions; Zacksenhouse *et al.* (2009) use ellipsoidal info-gap models.

Probabilistic judgments. The analyst may be willing to use economic understanding to make probability judgments about the future, such as "inflation above 5% is highly unlikely". Such judgments, while meaningful and useful, are quite uncertain and their translation into a specific probability distribution is also uncertain. An info-gap model can incorporate these probabilistic judgments together with their uncertainties. This info-gap model can then underlie a robustness analysis similar to the one we have explored in this section.

Multi-dimensionality. We have considered a single scalar variable, but our analysis is readily extended to vectors. We have assumed that only the serial data (e.g. inflation) is uncertain, and that the index variable (e.g. year) is known. Our analysis can be extended to situations where both variables are uncertain, as in a Phillips curve of inflation vs. unemployment.

Other estimation strategies. Our example has used least squares estimation as the core upon which the robustness analysis is built. Any estimation strategy—maximum likelihood, Bayesian estimation, etc.—could be used instead.

Tikhonov regularization. Another estimation strategy is motivated by the method of Tikhonov regularization (Tikhonov and Arsenin, 1977), in which we weight next year's error term, $(y_{N+1} - y^{\mathrm{r}}_{N+1})^2$, differently from the historical terms, $(y_i - y^{\mathrm{r}}_i)^2$ for $i = 1, \ldots, N$ (see eq.(6.3)). For instance, instead of eq.(6.4), one might use the following system model:

$$S^2(c) = S^2_N(c) + \gamma \left(y_{N+1} - y^{\mathrm{r}}_{N+1}\right)^2 \tag{6.13}$$

where $S_N^2(c)$ is the mean squared error defined in eq.(6.2) and γ is a constant Tikhonov weight chosen by the analyst to reflect the relative importance of future accuracy as opposed to historical fidelity.

In the context of a different regression problem, Zacksenhouse *et al.* (2009) showed how to use the info-gap robustness and opportuneness functions for choosing the Tikhonov weight.

6.2 Auto-Regression and Data Revision

Policy formulation depends on knowledge of the current state of the economy as expressed by statistical indicators of growth, inflation and so on. However, Runkle (1998) notes that "Between the time that the [US Bureau of Economic Analysis] makes its initial and final estimates of real growth and inflation, the data have been revised many times." (p.4). Data are revised as more information becomes available, but also due to changes in definitions and classifications and due to fundamental renovations of the National Income Product Accounts. It is certainly possible to use probability distributions to describe the spread of these revisions *ex post.* However, *ex ante* one is unlikely to know the probability distribution for the magnitude of revision. The unknown future revisions which the economic planner or policy maker faces are an info-gap.

Also, "revision error is significant compared to forecast error for the key data series" (Runkle, 1998, p.5). Furthermore, these revisions can occur over a long period of time:

> For example, real GNP was initially thought to have dropped between the third and fourth quarters of 1974 at an annual rate of 9.1 percent, as severe a fall in output as occurred during the Great Depression. But the final estimate [20 years later] indicates that between those quarters, real GNP dropped at an annual rate of only 1.6 percent. This is an upward revision of 7.5 percentage points. (Runkle, 1998, p.5)

Of course not all revisions are that large, nor are all periods as economically turbulent as 1974. However, it is precisely in times of change that accurate knowledge of the current state of the economy is essential for policy formulation.

It is clear that, especially in times of uncertainty, policy makers must use economic data cautiously. This means judging published statistical estimates in light of the analyst's understanding of the economy as a whole. In this section we will demonstrate how caution and judgment of this sort can be incorporated in an auto-regression of statistical data.

6.2.1 Policy Preview

Economic statistics are sometimes substantially revised long after the fact. This information alone—that major revisions are possible—without any commitment about the size or direction of the revision, is sufficient to formulate an info-gap auto-regression. Some info-gap regressions are substantially more robust to uncertain future revisions than the least squares regression.

Sometimes the analyst can use contextual information and economic understanding to identify the direction in which data revisions are likely to occur, without being able to make any commitment about the magnitude of these revisions. This added information can further enhance the robustness to uncertainty in these revisions.

6.2.2 Operational Preview

System model. The system model is the root mean squared (RMS) error of the auto-regression, eq.(6.16).

Uncertainty model. The uncertainty is represented by an interval info-gap model, eq.(6.20). This uncertainty model can encode asymmetric information about the direction of possible future revisions, without requiring the analyst to state magnitudes of future revisions.

Performance and robustness. The analyst requires that the RMS error of the auto-regression not exceed a specified level. The robustness of a regression is the greatest horizon of uncertainty in the future revisions up to which the RMS error does not exceed the specified level.

6.2.3 Auto-Regression

Consider N scalar data points $y = (y_1, \ldots, y_N)'$, such as inflation data over N sequential years as in fig. 6.3 on p.181. We wish to choose the coefficients $c = (c_1, \ldots, c_J)'$ of an auto-regression of order J for these data:

$$y_n = \sum_{j=1}^{J} c_j y_{n-j} \tag{6.14}$$

$$= c' y_{n-1,n-J} \tag{6.15}$$

where $y_{n-1,n-J} = (y_{n-1}, \ldots, y_{n-J})'$.

Define the mean squared error of the auto-regression of the data:

$$S^2(c) = \frac{1}{N-J} \sum_{n=J+1}^{N} \left(y_n - c' y_{n-1,n-J}\right)^2 \tag{6.16}$$

Our **system model** is the RMS error, $S(c)$. The mean squared error can be expressed more compactly as:

$$S^2(c) = \frac{1}{N-J} y' V y \tag{6.17}$$

where V is defined in eq.(6.52) on p.210 in appendix 6.5. V depends on the regression coefficients c but not on the data.

The auto-regression coefficients which *minimize the mean squared error* are found by solving $\partial S^2 / \partial c = 0$. Differentiating eq.(6.16) and rearranging one finds:

$$\underbrace{\sum_{n=J+1}^{N} y_n y_{n-1,n-J}}_{z} = \underbrace{\left(\sum_{n=J+1}^{N} y_{n-1,n-J}\, y'_{n-1,n-J} \right)}_{Y} c \tag{6.18}$$

which defines the J-vector z and the $J \times J$ matrix Y. The least squares auto-regression coefficients are:

$$\widetilde{c} = Y^{-1} z \tag{6.19}$$

If the inverse matrix does not exist then a generalized inverse needs to be used.

6.2.4 Uncertainty and Robustness

Uncertainty model. Our best estimate of the data is denoted by the vector $\widetilde{y} = (\widetilde{y}_1, \ldots, \widetilde{y}_N)'$. For instance, $\widetilde{y}$ might be the current estimates of the percent change in the real GDP shown in table 6.1.

Table 6.1: Current and previous estimates of real GDP: percent change from preceding period. 2007q1 to 2009q2. Seasonally adjusted at annual rates. Bureau of Economic Analysis, July 31, 2009.

	7q1	7q2	7q3	7q4	8q1
current	1.2	3.2	3.6	2.1	−0.7
previous	0.1	4.8	4.8	−0.2	0.9
	8q2	8q3	8q4	9q1	9q2
current	1.5	−2.7	−5.4	−6.4	−1.0
previous	2.8	−0.5	−6.3	−5.5	

The elements of these data are subject to revision, as seen in the table, so we face a gap between what we know (the current and previous estimates) and what we would like to know (the final estimate). Furthermore, we may have asymmetric information about the relative tendency for actual values to exceed or fall short of the estimates. We use the following asymmetric info-gap model for uncertainty in the data:

$$\mathcal{U}(h) = \{y : \widetilde{y}_n - w_{n1}h \le y_n \le \widetilde{y}_n + w_{n2}h, \ n = 1, \ldots, N\}, \quad h \ge 0 \quad (6.20)$$

The uncertainty weights for each datum, w_{n1} and w_{n2}, are non-negative and express the relative tendency for deviation below and above the estimated value. If an element is known with certainty then its uncertainty weights both equal zero. Suppose that the nth estimate, $\widetilde{y}_n$, is believed to be an underestimate, but we don't know by how much. We can represent this unbounded asymmetric uncertainty by choosing $w_{n1} = 0$ and $w_{n2} = 1$. Belief that $\widetilde{y}_n$ is an over estimate is expressed by choosing $w_{n1} = 1$ and $w_{n2} = 0$. If the uncertainty is symmetric then the uncertainty weights w_{n1} and w_{n2} are equal. More refined intuition about the error of the estimate, perhaps based on statistical information about revisions, can be expressed by choosing w_{n1} and w_{n2} both to be non-zero and to differ from one another.

Robustness function. The robustness of auto-regression coefficients c is the greatest horizon of uncertainty h up to which the root mean squared error $S(c)$ is no greater than the critical value S_c:

$$\widehat{h}(c, S_c) = \max \left\{ h : \left(\max_{y \in \mathcal{U}(h)} S(c) \right) \le S_c \right\} \tag{6.21}$$

6.2.5 Policy Exploration

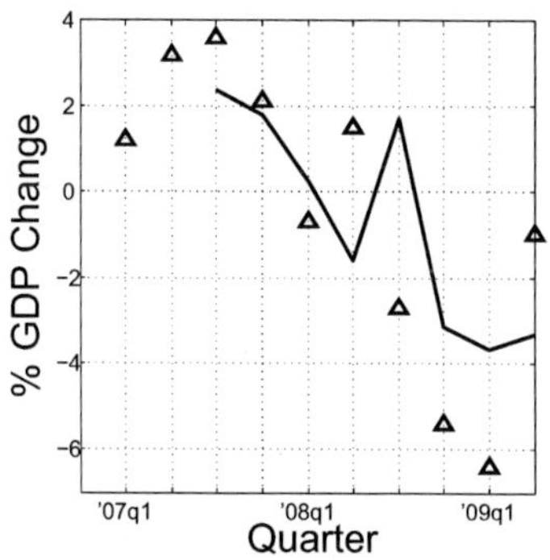

Figure 6.9: Current estimates of US real GDP change vs. quarter, and least squares auto-regression.

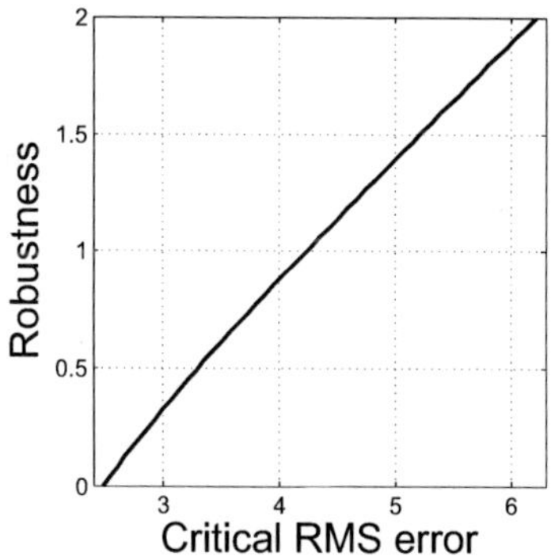

Figure 6.10: Robustness vs. critical RMS error of least squares auto-regression. Symmetric uncertainty.

We now consider some policy implications of this analysis. Our example is based on 2nd-order auto-regressions, so $J = 2$ in eq.(6.14). We use the percent change in the US GDP for 2007q1–2009q2 in table 6.1.

Symmetric uncertainty. We begin by considering a situation in which the analyst is aware that the data are subject to substantial revision in the future, but has no information to indicate either the direction or magnitude of the revision. This symmetric information about the uncertainty is represented by the info-gap model of eq.(6.20) with uncertainty weights which equal 1 for all points: $w_{n1} = w_{n2} = 1$ for $n = 1, \ldots, N$.

Fig. 6.9 shows the GDP data from table 6.1 together with the 2nd-order least-squares auto-regression, $\widetilde{c}$ from eq.(6.19). The regression coefficients are $\widetilde{c} = (0.9139, -0.4647)'$. The RMS error of this regression is $S(\widetilde{c}) = 2.49$, so the auto-regression misses the data, on average, by about 2.5 percentage points of GDP. This rather large error occurs primarily in the last 5 quarters, in which the data at '08q2 and '09q2 seem to deviate from the trend of the other data.

Zeroing and trade-off. Fig. 6.10 shows the robustness curve for the least squares (LS) auto-regression $\widetilde{c}$ with symmetric uncertainty. This figure shows the zeroing and trade-off properties discussed in section 2.2.2. The robustness of $\widetilde{c}$ vanishes when the critical error, S_c, equals the calculated error of the regression, $S(\widetilde{c})$. Only larger critical error has positive robustness, which is the trade-off property: robustness trades off against performance. Given the uncertainty in the data, the LS regression cannot be relied upon to reproduce the data as well as $S(\widetilde{c})$ once revisions occur. An RMS error no larger than 4% is guaranteed with robustness of 0.88, meaning that revisions as large as 0.88 percentage points can occur and the RMS error will not exceed 4%.

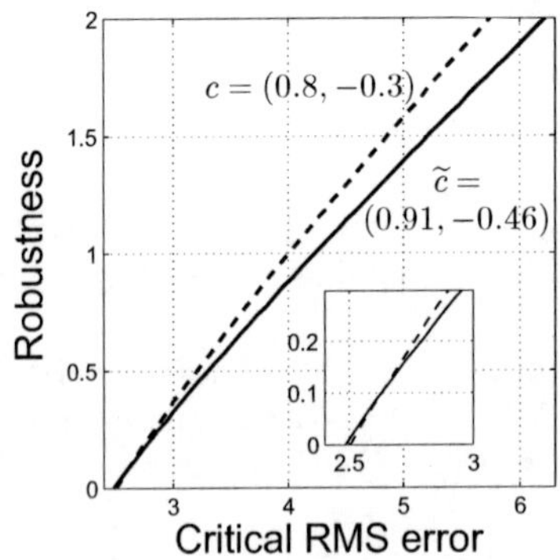

Figure 6.11: Robustness vs. critical RMS error with least squares (solid) and other (dash) auto-regression. Symmetric uncertainty.

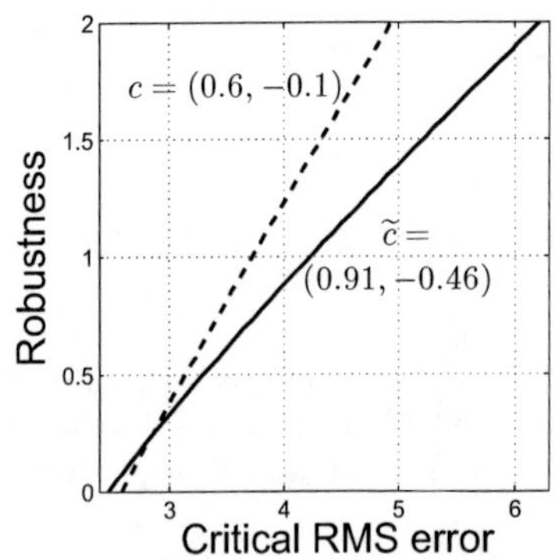

Figure 6.12: Robustness vs. critical RMS error with least squares (solid) and other (dash) auto-regression. Symmetric uncertainty.

Non-least-squares regressions and symmetric uncertainty. Figs. 6.11 and 6.12 show robustness curves for two non-least-squares auto-regressions, together with the robustness curve for the least-squares regression reproduced from fig. 6.10. In both figures the robustness curve for the non-LS regression crosses the robustness curve for the LS regression. Because of the zeroing property, the LS robustness curve reaches the S_c axis at a smaller value than the non-LS curves. However, the non-LS curves are steeper and so they cross the LS robustness curve. The slope of a robustness curve expresses the cost of robustness: the increase of RMS error which must be accepted in return for an increase of robustness. We see in figs. 6.11 and 6.12

that the cost of robustness is lower for the non-LS regressions than for the LS regression.

Intersection between robustness curves of different regressions entails the possibility for reversal of preference among the regressions, as explained in section 2.2.3. In figs. 6.11 and 6.12 the intersections occur quite near the RMS axis, so the non-LS regressions are robust-dominant over the LS regression for most of the range of critical RMS values. The robustness gain by the non-LS regression is substantial, especially in fig. 6.12.

Estimated RMS error $S(c)$ (which is the horizontal intercept of the robustness curve) is a different property from cost of robustness (which is the slope). Stated differently, we choose the regression to have small RMS error in order to manage the *statistical* uncertainty of the data. On the other hand, we choose the regression to have large robustness in order to manage the *info-gaps* in the data. These two types of uncertainty are different. When analysts are willing to accept a small increase in estimated RMS error, they are then free to search among an infinity of non-LS regressions for one with low cost of robustness. Figs. 6.11 and 6.12 show that this search for purportedly sub-optimal (non-LS) regressions can yield regressions with substantial robustness gain and with modest increase of $S(c)$.

Non-least-squares regressions: asymmetric uncertainty. We now consider a situation in which the analyst has asymmetric information about the uncertainty in the GDP data. In particular, suppose the analyst believes, based on contextual information and understanding of the economy, that the current estimates at 2008q2 and 2009q2 are over-estimates and will be revised to lower (more correct) values in the future. The analyst does not know (and cannot guess) how large these revisions will be, but believes that they will be downward revisions. We represent this asymmetric information about the uncertainty with the info-gap model of eq.(6.20) by choosing the uncertainty weights $w_{6,2} = w_{10,2} = 0$ (the 6th and 10th estimates cannot go up), $w_{6,1} = w_{10,1} = 1$ (the 6th and 10th estimates can go down), and $w_{nj} = 1$ for all other values of n and j (all other estimates can go either up or down). This encodes asymmetric uncertainty for the two data points in question, and symmetric uncertainty for all other data. In summary:

$$w_2 = [1\ 1\ 1\ 1\ 1\ \ 0\ 1\ 1\ 1\ 0] \qquad (6.22)$$

$$w_1 = [1\ 1\ 1\ 1\ 1\ \ 1\ 1\ 1\ 1\ 1] \qquad (6.23)$$

The LS auto-regression, $\widetilde{c}$, does not depend on the info-gap model,

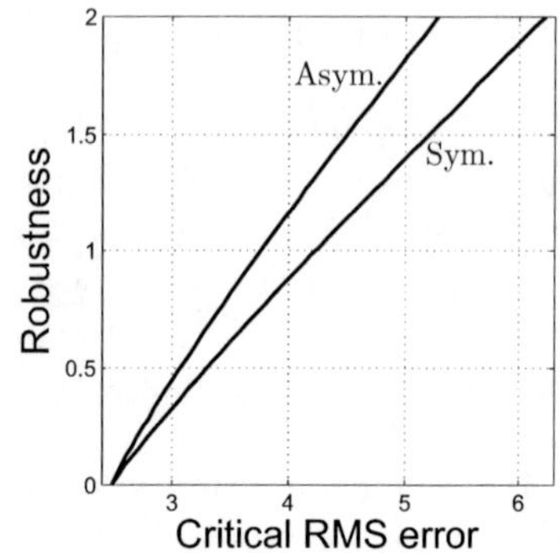

Figure 6.13: Robustness vs. critical RMS error for least squares regression with symmetric and asymmetric uncertainty.

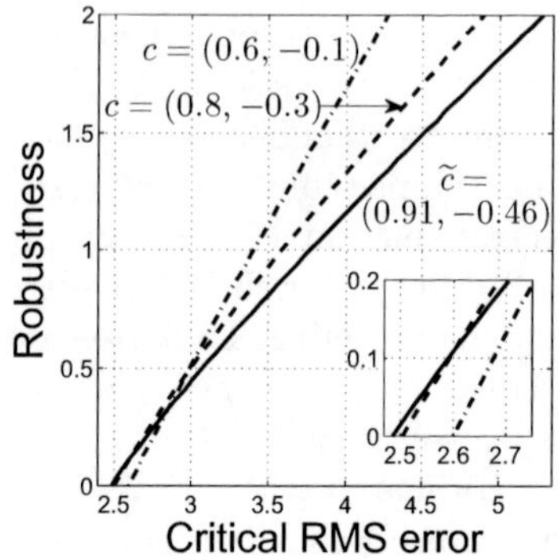

Figure 6.14: Robustness vs. critical RMS error with least squares (solid) and other (dash, dot-dash) regressions. Asymmetric uncertainty.

so $\widetilde{c}$ is the same as in the previous example: $\widetilde{c} = (0.9139, -0.4647)'$. Furthermore, the RMS error of the LS regression is the same: $S(\widetilde{c}) = 2.49$. However, the robustness of $\widetilde{c}$ *does* depend on the info-gap model.

Fig. 6.13 shows the robustness of the LS regression based on the symmetric uncertainty considered earlier, and the present asymmetric uncertainty. These curves reach the S_c axis together at the value of $S(\widetilde{c})$, due to the property of zeroing. However, we see that the additional information entailed in the asymmetric info-gap model increases the slope of the robustness curve. That is, the added information—asymmetric uncertainty in y_6 and y_{10}—reduces the cost of robustness.

Fig. 6.14 shows robustness curves for three auto-regressions with the asymmetric info-gap model. The solid curve is the LS regression: the "Asym." curve from fig. 6.13. The other two curves are for non-LS regressions, and they both cross the LS robustness curve fairly close to the S_c axis. The robustness gain by the non-LS over the LS regressions, especially the dot-dash case, is quite substantial. Comparing with figs. 6.11 and 6.12 we see that the robustness gain is greater in the current case: the added asymmetric information not only enhances the robustness of the LS regression. It also further enhances the robustness of these non-LS regressions.

6.3 Confidence Intervals

Statistical estimates of economic variables are useful in understanding the state of an economy. The confidence interval of an estimate is a valuable supplement both for assessing the accuracy of the estimate and for testing hypotheses about the economy. In this section we study a specific example of the confidence interval of a variable, illustrating the info-gap analysis of non-stochastic uncertainty in the data. We examine the linear regression of a serial scalar variable and construct a confidence interval for the slope. The data are info-gap-uncertain and we evaluate the robustness of the confidence interval.

6.3.1 Policy Preview

What is a confidence interval and how is it used? Suppose we want to estimate an economic variable, say the rate of change of the GDP. Current data give a best statistical estimate of, say, -1.0% of GDP per quarter. The data have a random element, and different data would give a different estimate. We can use the data to estimate the likely variability. For instance, our subsequent example will show that a 95% confidence interval on the -1.0% estimate would be $[-2.0, -0.17]$, indicating that the estimate has about a 95% chance of falling within this interval as the data fluctuate due to random factors. This is quite a wide range of values, and it is important to recognize that the point estimate of -1.0% per quarter is subject to considerable random variability.

But the data can vary due to non-random factors as well, such as data revisions. Furthermore, economic understanding can supplement the statistical analysis of variability. Economists often understand trends in the economy before they are evident in official numerical data. The info-gap analysis presented in this section enables the incorporation of these factors—non-random uncertainty as well as contextual information—in evaluating confidence intervals.

6.3.2 Operational Preview

System model. The system model in our example is the confidence interval for an estimated slope of a least squares regression. The estimated confidence interval is specified in eq.(6.30). This interval in turn depends on the least squares estimate and its standard error, eqs.(6.25) and (6.27).

Uncertainty model. The least squares estimate and the confidence interval depend on serial data which are info-gap-uncertain. We use an interval info-gap model, eq.(6.32). This info-gap model allows the analyst to encode information on possible revisions and other uncertainties in the data without specifying maximum changes or likelihoods.

Performance requirement. We will use current data to estimate a $1-\epsilon$ confidence interval. These data may be revised in the future—this is the info-gap we currently face. Now consider a larger confidence interval, the $1-(\epsilon+\delta)$ interval where δ is a negative number. Our performance requirement is that the revised data not imply a $1-\epsilon$ confidence interval which is larger than we would currently calculate for a $1-(\epsilon+\delta)$ confidence interval. This is formalized in eq.(6.33).

Robustness. The robustness is the greatest horizon of uncertainty in the data at which the actual $1-\epsilon$ confidence interval would not exceed the currently estimated $1-(\epsilon+\delta)$ confidence interval.

6.3.3 Formulating the Confidence Interval

Consider N serial data points $y = (y_1, \ldots, y_N)$, such as inflation data over N sequential years $x_1, \ldots, x_N$. The current best estimates of these data are $\widetilde{y}_1, \ldots, \widetilde{y}_N$. These data are subject to future revision, and we may have contextual understanding which suggests the direction—though not the magnitude—of these revisions. The x_i are known with certainty.

We will construct a linear regression for y_i vs. x_i, and evaluate a confidence interval for the slope which accounts both for the current estimates of the data and the fact that these estimates may be revised in the future.

Regression. The linear regression is:

$$y_i^{\mathrm{r}} = c_0 + c_1 x_i \tag{6.24}$$

For any data set, y, the least squares (LS) estimate of the slope and intercept are:

$$\widehat{c}_1(y) = \frac{\displaystyle\sum_{i=1}^{N}(x_i - \overline{x})(y_i - \overline{y})}{\displaystyle\sum_{i=1}^{N}(x_i - \overline{x})^2} \tag{6.25}$$

$$\widehat{c}_0(y) \;=\; \overline{y} - \widehat{c}_1(y)\overline{x} \tag{6.26}$$

where $\overline{x} = (1/N)\sum_{i=1}^{N} x_i$ and $\overline{y} = (1/N)\sum_{i=1}^{N} y_i$.

The estimated standard error of this estimate of the slope is:

$$s_{c_1}(y) = \sqrt{\frac{\dfrac{1}{N-2}\displaystyle\sum_{i=1}^{N}(y_i - y_i^{\mathrm{r}})^2}{\sum_{i=1}^{N}(x_i - \overline{x})^2}} \tag{6.27}$$

where the regression, y_i^{r}, is evaluated with the LS coefficients, $\widehat{c}_0$ and $\widehat{c}_1$.

Confidence interval. Define the statistic:

$$t = \frac{\widehat{c}_1 - c_1}{s_{c_1}} \tag{6.28}$$

If the relation between x and y is in fact linear, and if the observations $y_1, \ldots, y_N$ are independent, normal and all have the same variance, then this statistic has a t distribution with $N-2$ degrees of freedom.[3]

Since we know the distribution of the statistic in eq.(6.28) we can define a *confidence interval* for the slope, c_1. Let t_N denote a random variable with a t distribution with N degrees of freedom. Similarly, let $t_{\epsilon,N}$ denote the $1-\epsilon$ quantile of t_N:

$$\mathrm{Prob}(t_N \le t_{\epsilon,N}) = 1 - \epsilon \tag{6.29}$$

The $1-\epsilon$ confidence interval for the slope, based on observations y, is:

$$\left[\widehat{c}_1(y) - s_{c_1}(y)t_{\frac{\epsilon}{2},N-2},\;\; \widehat{c}_1(y) + s_{c_1}(y)t_{\frac{\epsilon}{2},N-2}\right] \tag{6.30}$$

Under the stated assumptions about randomness of the data, y, the slope c_1 will fall in this interval with probability approximately equal to $1-\epsilon$.

For convenience let $c_{\ell,\epsilon}(y)$ and $c_{\mathrm{u},\epsilon}(y)$ denote the lower and upper bounds of the confidence interval of the slope, eq.(6.30), where y is the set of observations with which the estimated slope and standard error are calculated, eqs.(6.25) and (6.27). Furthermore, let $I_\epsilon(y)$ denote the $1-\epsilon$ confidence interval itself. That is, a compact representation of eq.(6.30) is:

$$I_\epsilon(y) = [c_{\ell,\epsilon}(y),\; c_{\mathrm{u},\epsilon}(y)] \tag{6.31}$$

[3] The t distribution will result in some other conditions as well, such as N large enough for the central limit theorem to apply.

6.3.4 Uncertainty and Robustness

We use again the info-gap model of eq.(6.20) to represent uncertainty in the best estimate of our data, $\widetilde{y}$. We reproduce it here for convenience:

$$\mathcal{U}(h) = \{y: \widetilde{y}_n - w_{n1}h \le y_n \le \widetilde{y}_n + w_{n2}h,\ n = 1, \ldots, N\}, \quad h \ge 0 \qquad (6.32)$$

As explained on p.192, the uncertainty weights w_{n1} and w_{n2} enable the analyst to represent uncertainty in the future revisions of the data (or other sources of uncertainty). Furthermore, asymmetric contextual information about the uncertainty can be incorporated in the choice of the uncertainty weights w_{n1} and w_{n2}.

Performance requirement. The $1-\epsilon$ confidence interval for the slope in eq.(6.30) can be evaluated with any data, y. The confidence interval will vary as the data, y, vary. Conversely, when evaluated with the best available estimates, $\widetilde{y}$, the confidence interval will vary as ϵ varies. Specifically, as ϵ gets bigger, $c_{\ell,\epsilon}(\widetilde{y})$ gets smaller (or more negative) and $c_{\mathrm{u},\epsilon}(\widetilde{y})$ gets bigger (or less negative).

We will characterize the slope with the $1-\epsilon$ confidence interval based on the current estimates, $\widetilde{y}$. However, we recognize that the current estimates are likely to be substantially wrong in unknown ways. The robustness question is: how wrong can the estimates $\widetilde{y}$ be, without causing substantial change in the $1-\epsilon$ confidence interval? We can rely on the $1-\epsilon$ confidence interval if the estimates $\widetilde{y}$ can change greatly without unduly altering the confidence interval. We cannot rely on the $1-\epsilon$ confidence interval if small revision of $\widetilde{y}$ would greatly alter the confidence interval.

Let δ be a negative number, and consider the $1-(\epsilon+\delta)$ confidence interval with the current estimates, $\widetilde{y}$, denoted $I_{\epsilon+\delta}(\widetilde{y})$. This is a larger interval than the $1-\epsilon$ confidence interval evaluated with these data, $I_\epsilon(\widetilde{y})$. We will evaluate the robustness of the $1-\epsilon$ confidence interval in terms of how large an error in $\widetilde{y}$ would transform the $1-\epsilon$ confidence interval into the $1-(\epsilon+\delta)$ confidence interval.

We now state this precisely as a *performance requirement.* Our design variable is ϵ (we're calculating a $1-\epsilon$ confidence interval). Our performance requirement is that the actual $1-\epsilon$ confidence interval (after currently unknown data revisions) not exceed the current estimate of a $1-(\epsilon+\delta)$ interval:

$$I_\epsilon(y) \subseteq I_{\epsilon+\delta}(\widetilde{y}) \qquad (6.33)$$

This performance requirement embodies both a lower and an upper constraint. We manage this by first considering two robustness functions—one for the lower bound and one for the upper bound—and then combining them into a single overall robustness function.

Robustness function. The *robustness of the lower bound* of the $1-\epsilon$ confidence interval is the greatest horizon of uncertainty at which the $1-\epsilon$ lower bound is no less than $c_{\ell,\epsilon+\delta}(\widetilde{y})$. That is, the performance requirement for the lower robustness is:

$$c_{\ell,\epsilon}(y) \ge c_{\ell,\epsilon+\delta}(\widetilde{y}) \tag{6.34}$$

Note that the $1-(\epsilon+\delta)$ lower bound is evaluated with the current estimates, $\widetilde{y}$.

The lower robustness is:

$$\widehat{h}_{\ell}(\epsilon,\delta) = \max\left\{h:\ \left(\min_{y\in\mathcal{U}(h)} c_{\ell,\epsilon}(y)\right) \ge c_{\ell,\epsilon+\delta}(\widetilde{y})\right\} \tag{6.35}$$

The *robustness of the upper bound* of the $1-\epsilon$ confidence interval is the greatest horizon of uncertainty at which the $1-\epsilon$ upper bound is no greater than $c_{\mathrm{u},\epsilon+\delta}(\widetilde{y})$. That is, the performance requirement for the upper robustness is:

$$c_{\mathrm{u},\epsilon}(y) \le c_{\mathrm{u},\epsilon+\delta}(\widetilde{y}) \tag{6.36}$$

The upper robustness is:

$$\widehat{h}_{\mathrm{u}}(\epsilon,\delta) = \max\left\{h:\ \left(\max_{y\in\mathcal{U}(h)} c_{\mathrm{u},\epsilon}(y)\right) \le c_{\mathrm{u},\epsilon+\delta}(\widetilde{y})\right\} \tag{6.37}$$

Finally, the overall robustness of the $1-\epsilon$ confidence interval is the greatest horizon of uncertainty at which both performance requirements, eqs.(6.34) and (6.36), hold. This is equivalent to the overall performance requirement in eq.(6.33). The overall robustness is the minimum between the lower and upper robustnesses:

$$\widehat{h}(\epsilon,\delta) = \min\left[\widehat{h}_{\ell}(\epsilon,\delta),\ \widehat{h}_{\mathrm{u}}(\epsilon,\delta)\right] \tag{6.38}$$

Estimating the $1-\epsilon$ confidence interval with $\widetilde{y}$ is uncertain because $\widetilde{y}$ is uncertain. The $1-(\epsilon+\delta)$ confidence interval is less precise (larger) than the $1-\epsilon$ confidence interval. However, if $\widehat{h}(\epsilon,\delta)$ is large for small $|\delta|$, then the $1-\epsilon$ confidence interval can be reliably estimated with $\widetilde{y}$ despite the uncertainty. On the other hand, if the robustness is large only for large $|\delta|$ then we cannot rely on the $1-\epsilon$ confidence interval due to the uncertainty in the estimates $\widetilde{y}$.

Evaluating the robustness functions. Consider first the *lower robustness.* Let $\mu_\ell(h)$ denote the inner minimum in eq.(6.35), which is the inverse of the lower robustness function. That is, a plot of h vs. $\mu_\ell(h)$ is the same as a plot of $\widehat{h}_\ell(\epsilon, \delta)$ vs. $c_{\ell,\epsilon+\delta}(\widetilde{y})$. However, we want to plot $\widehat{h}_\ell(\epsilon, \delta)$ vs. δ: the decrement in the level of confidence. Thus, for each value of $\mu_\ell(h)$ we need to determine the value of δ from the relation:

$$c_{\ell,\epsilon+\delta}(\widetilde{y}) = \mu_\ell(h) \tag{6.39}$$

This can be re-written using the definition of the lower bound of the confidence interval in eq.(6.30):

$$\widehat{c}_1(\widetilde{y}) - s_{c_1}(\widetilde{y}) t_{\frac{\epsilon+\delta}{2}, N-2} = \mu_\ell(h) \tag{6.40}$$

Solving this for δ one finds:

$$\delta_\ell(h) = 2\left[1 - P_{N-2}\left(\frac{\widehat{c}_1(\widetilde{y}) - \mu_\ell(h)}{s_{c_1}(\widetilde{y})}\right)\right] - \epsilon \tag{6.41}$$

where $P_{N-2}(\cdot)$ is the cumulative distribution function of the t distribution with $N-2$ degrees of freedom.

To summarize, the lower robustness is calculated as follows. First $\mu_\ell(h)$ is calculated numerically. Then $\delta_\ell(h)$ is evaluated from eq.(6.41). Then h is plotted (or simply stored) vs. $\delta_\ell(h)$ to produce the plot (or table) of lower robustness, $\widehat{h}_\ell(\epsilon, \delta)$, vs. decrement of confidence, δ.

An analogous procedure is used to calculate the *upper robustness.* Let $\mu_{\rm u}(h)$ denote the inner maximum in eq.(6.37). Define:

$$\delta_{\rm u}(h) = 2\left[1 - P_{N-2}\left(\frac{\mu_{\rm u}(h) - \widehat{c}_1(\widetilde{y})}{s_{c_1}(\widetilde{y})}\right)\right] - \epsilon \tag{6.42}$$

Now $\widehat{h}_{\rm u}(\epsilon, \delta)$ vs. δ is obtained by plotting (or storing) h vs. $\delta_{\rm u}(h)$.

Finally, the overall robustness, $\widehat{h}(\epsilon, \delta)$, is evaluated from eq.(6.38).

6.3.5 Policy Exploration

Fig. 6.15 shows 2009q2 estimates of GDP change from 2007q3 to 2009q2, and a linear least squares fit.[4] The data seem to be quite

[4]The GDP data, $\widetilde{y}_n$, appear in table 6.1 on p.192. The horizontal coordinates for the linear fit are $x_n = n$ for $n = 1, \ldots, 8$.

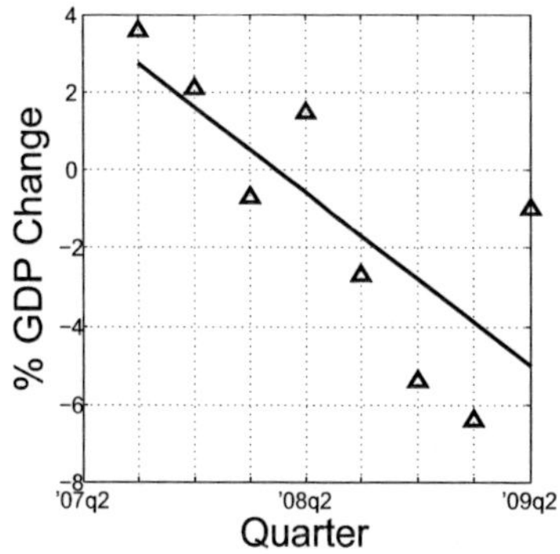

Figure 6.15: Current estimates of US real GDP change vs. quarter, and least squares linear regression.

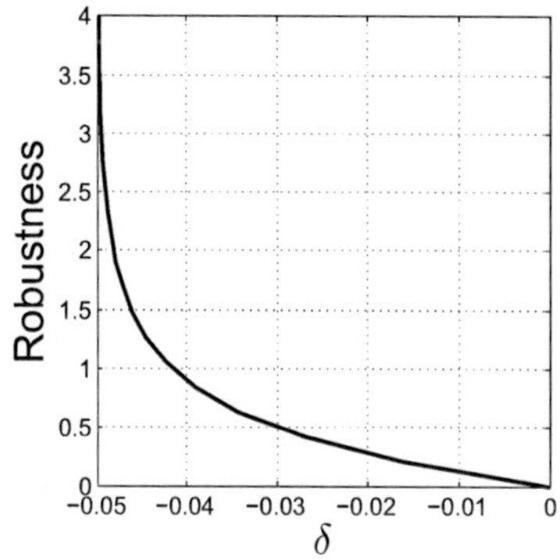

Figure 6.16: Robustness vs. confidence decrement. Symmetric uncertainty.

linear with the exceptions of the points at '08q2 and '09q2. However, all the data, and especially the more recent points, are subject to considerable uncertainty and subsequent revision as discussed in section 6.2.

The least squares estimate of the slope in fig. 6.15 is $\widehat{c}_1(\widetilde{y}) = -1.107$ percent/quarter, with a standard error of $s_{c_1} = 0.383$. Thus a 95% confidence interval of the slope, eq.(6.30) with $\epsilon = 0.05$, is $[-2.04,\ -0.17]$.

Symmetric uncertainty. How much can one rely on this estimated confidence interval, in light of the fact that the data, $\widetilde{y}$, may be substantially revised in the future? Let us suppose that we are unwilling to make any statement about which estimates might be revised nor about the magnitude or direction in which the data revisions might occur. This means that we choose all the uncertainty weights in the info-gap model of eq.(6.32) to be $w_{n1} = w_{n2} = 1$.

The resulting robustness curve, $\widehat{h}(\epsilon, \delta)$ vs. δ, is shown in fig. 6.16 for a 95% confidence interval ($\epsilon = 0.05$). For how large a horizon of uncertainty is the 95% confidence interval indistinguishable from a looser one? Fig. 6.16 helps answer this question.

At confidence decrement of $\delta = -0.01$ we are testing the 95% confidence interval against the 96% interval.[5] From fig. 6.16 we see that the robustness at $\delta = -0.01$ is $\widehat{h} = 0.12$, which means that the data points $\widetilde{y}_n$ can each err by as much as ± 0.12 and the resulting 95%

[5] $1 - (\epsilon + \delta) = 1 - (0.05 - 0.01) = 0.96$.

confidence interval is no wider than the 96% interval based on the original $\tilde{y}$. This 96% confidence interval is $[-2.11, \ -0.11]$, which is somewhat wider than the estimated 95% interval, $[-2.04, \ -0.17]$. A glance at fig. 6.15 suggests data variability—and plausible revisions—are at least as large as 0.12. The mean squared error of the linear fit to all 8 points is 2.15. If one excludes the points at '08q2 and '09q2 then the linear fit is much better and the mean squared error is 0.47. This is, however, still quite a bit larger than the 0.12 threshold of error which distinguishes the 96% confidence interval from the 95% interval. In summary, the robustness analysis strongly suggests that the current 95% confidence interval cannot be reliably distinguished from the 96% interval calculated with the same data. In other words, in light of future revisions or other uncertainties, we cannot convincingly argue that the 95% interval is not really $[-2.11, \ -0.11]$ (the 96% interval) rather than $[-2.04, \ -0.17]$ (the current estimate of the 95% interval).

Now consider confidence decrement $\delta = -0.03$, which tests the 98% confidence interval against the 95% interval. The robustness is $\widehat{h} = 0.50$ as seen in fig. 6.16. This might be larger than most reasonable revisions, with the possible exception of the points at '08q2 and '09q2. If so, then we might suggest that the 95% interval, after data revisions are obtained, would not be larger than the 98% interval evaluated with the current data. The 98% confidence interval calculated with the current data is $[-2.31, \ 0.096]$, as compared with the current estimate of the 95% confidence interval: $[-2.04, \ -0.17]$. Note that the 98% confidence interval entails a possible change in sign of the slope. Except for concern that the data points at '08q2 and '09q2 could be greatly revised, we might suggest that the 95% confidence interval would not be revised to the extent of exceeding the current estimate of the 98% interval. This is based on the judgment—which the analyst may or may not be willing to make—that robustness of 0.50 is adequate "protection" against future uncertainty.

Asymmetric uncertainty, first case, fig. 6.17. We now consider a situation in which contextual understanding leads the analyst to believe that the current estimates at '08q2 and '09q2 could in the future be revised down (but not up), without any ability to assert how large that revision will be. We encode this information in the info-gap model of eq.(6.32) by choosing $w_{4,2} = w_{8,2} = 0$ (the 4th and 8th estimates cannot go up), $w_{4,1} = w_{8,1} = 1$ (the 4th and 8th estimates can go down). Furthermore the analyst believes that the first 3 estimates will not be revised in the future, so $w_{n1} = w_{n2} = 0$

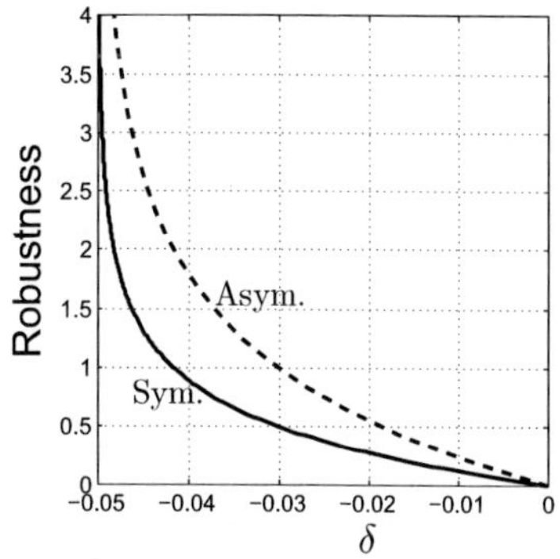

Figure 6.17: Robustness vs. confidence decrement for symmetric (solid) and asymmetric (dash) uncertainty.

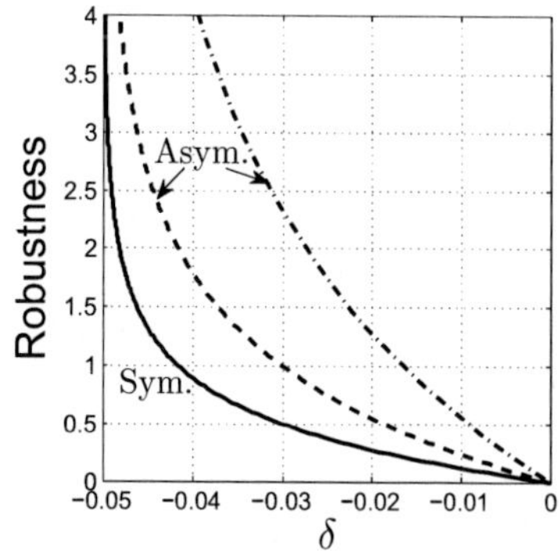

Figure 6.18: Robustness vs. confidence decrement for symmetric (solid) and asymmetric (dash, dot-dash) uncertainty.

for $n = 1, 2, 3$. The 5th, 6th and 7th estimates can go either up or down so $w_{n1} = w_{n2} = 1$ for $n = 5, 6, 7$. In short, the w vectors for the info-gap model are:

$$w_2 = [0\,0\,0\,0\;\;1\,1\,1\,0] \tag{6.43}$$
$$w_1 = [0\,0\,0\,1\;\;1\,1\,1\,1] \tag{6.44}$$

Fig. 6.17 shows the robustness curve, $\widehat{h}(\epsilon, \delta)$ vs. δ, for the asymmetric uncertainty, together with the robustness for symmetric uncertainty which is reproduced from fig. 6.16. $\epsilon = 0.05$ as before. We note a substantial increase in robustness resulting from the additional information. The robustness to uncertainty in the estimates has doubled for δ in the range from 0 to -0.03. At $\delta = -0.01$ and -0.03 the robustness now is 0.24 and 1.00, respectively. The previous robustness values at these δ's were 0.12 and 0.50.

Consider the confidence decrement $\delta = -0.01$, for which the robustness is 0.24. This is still rather small with respect to plausible revisions of the data. We are thus, as before, unable to reliably assert that the estimate of the 95% confidence interval (which is currently $[-2.04,\ -0.17]$) would not, after data revision, exceed the current estimate of the 96% interval which is $[-2.11,\ -0.11]$.

With $\delta = -0.03$, whose robustness is 1.00, the situation may look different. If data revisions larger than 1 percentage point are not plausible, then it is reliable that the 95% interval, after data revision, would not exceed the current estimate of the 98% interval. If the analyst accepts the judgment that revisions will not exceed 1 percentage point, then the analyst can assert that the 95% confidence interval, which is currently $[-2.04,\ -0.17]$, is unlikely to be revised in the future to exceed the current estimate of the 98% interval, $[-2.31,\ 0.096]$.

Asymmetric uncertainty, second case, fig. 6.18. Now consider a somewhat different situation. The analyst believes that all estimates other than at '08q2 and '09q2 will not be revised in the future, so $w_{n1} = w_{n2} = 0$ for all n other than 4 and 8. So the analyst judges that there is less uncertainty for these elements than in the previous example. However, the analyst is now more uncertain about the estimates at '08q2 and '09q2. These could be revised either up or down, but the propensity for downward revision is greater than for upward. The uncertainty weights for these elements are $w_{41} = w_{81} = 1$ while $w_{42} = w_{82} = 0.5$. In short, the uncertainty weights in the info-gap model now become:

$$w_2 = [0\ 0\ 0\ 0.5\ \ 0\ 0\ 0\ 0.5] \tag{6.45}$$

$$w_1 = [0\ 0\ 0\ 1\ \ 0\ 0\ 0\ 1] \tag{6.46}$$

The resulting robustness curve, for $\epsilon = 0.05$, is shown in fig. 6.18 (dot-dash curve), together with the first case of asymmetric uncertainty (dash) and symmetric uncertainty (solid). The increase in robustness is notable.

At confidence decrements $\delta = -0.01$ and $\delta = -0.03$ the robustnesses are $\widehat{h} = 0.56$ and $\widehat{h} = 2.33$ respectively. In the latter case for instance, $\delta = -0.03$, if the analyst judges that downward revisions will not exceed 2.33 percentage points, or upward revisions will not exceed half that amount, then the 95% confidence interval will not be revised to exceed the current estimate of the 98% interval.

The effect of confidence level, ϵ. Fig. 6.19 shows robustness curves, $\widehat{h}(\epsilon, \delta)$ vs. δ, for three different values of ϵ. The uncertainty weights are $w_{n2} = w_{n1} = 1$ for all n. The robustness curves all start at $\widehat{h} = 0$ when the confidence decrement equals 0, which is the zeroing property. Each curve then asymptotically approaches the vertical line at $-\delta = \epsilon$, which is derived from the monotonic trade-off between robustness and performance. Finally, we note that robustness increases as $1 - \epsilon$ increases. That is, a more encompassing confidence interval (large $1 - \epsilon$) is uniformly more robust than a narrow confidence interval. The effect is quite dramatic because of the shift of the asymptote as ϵ changes.

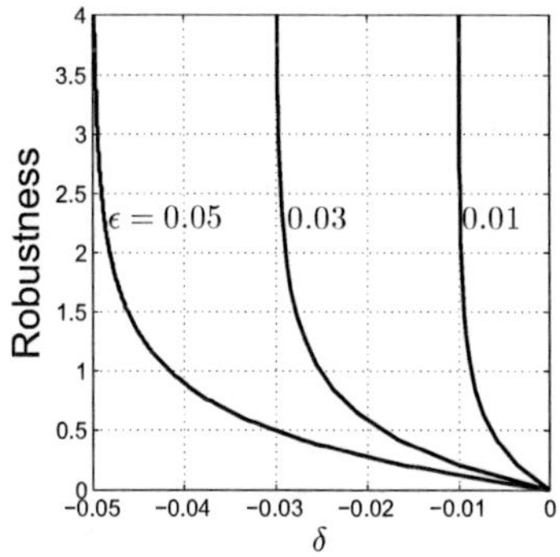

Figure 6.19: Robustness vs. confidence decrement for different confidence intervals.

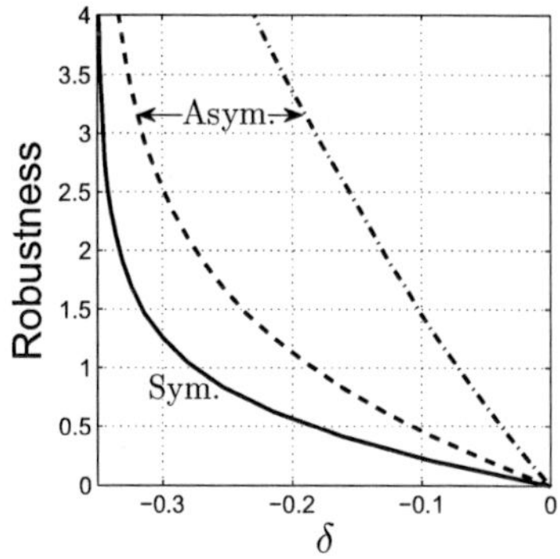

Figure 6.20: Robustness vs. confidence decrement for symmetric (solid) and asymmetric (dash, dot-dash) uncertainty. $\epsilon = 0.35$.

Fig. 6.20 shows a different aspect of the choice of ϵ. The three robustness curves are evaluated at $\epsilon = 0.35$, so we are considering 65% confidence intervals which is a much lower level of significance than we studied previously. The three curves are evaluated for the same choices of uncertainty weights, w_2 and w_1, as the corresponding curves in fig. 6.18.[6] While the estimated 95% confidence interval was $[-2.04,\ -0.17]$, the estimated 65% is much tighter: $[-1.50,\ -0.72]$. The analyst may find the tighter confidence interval more economically useful, recognizing of course that the smaller interval has lower statistical significance. On the other hand, in comparing figs. 6.18 and 6.20, for 95% and 65% confidence respectively, we note that the robustness curves are deployed similarly on their respective axes. While the statistical significance is quite different, the relative robustnesses are comparable.

Trade-off between information and confidence. In fig. 6.19 we saw that robustness increases strongly as $1-\epsilon$ increases. We reproduce the middle curve from fig. 6.19 in fig. 6.21, which has symmetric uncertainty: $w_{n2} = w_{n1} = 1$ for all n. The dot-dash curve in fig. 6.21 is reproduced from the dot-dash curve in fig. 6.18 for which the uncertainty is asymmetric, specified in eqs.(6.45) and (6.46). What has changed between figs. 6.19 and 6.21 is only that the $\epsilon = 0.05$ case in

[6]That is, the solid curve has symmetric uncertainty, the dashed curve is based on eqs.(6.43) and (6.44), and the dot-dash curve on eqs.(6.45) and (6.46).

the latter figure has asymmetric uncertainty. This added information boosts the robustness of the dot-dash curve, causing it to cross the other robustness curve in fig. 6.21.

We can understand this curve-crossing as a trade-off. On the one hand, robustness increases as ϵ decreases (as in fig. 6.19), so our robustness-based preference is for small ϵ. On the other hand, robustness increases as information is added, namely the asymmetry of the uncertainty augments the robustness (as in the dot-dash curve in figs. 6.18 and 6.21). Given purely symmetric information, consideration of robustness may lead us to use a wider confidence interval, such as $\epsilon = 0.03$ rather than $\epsilon = 0.05$. However, given more (e.g. asymmetric) information we may have adequate or even larger robustness with a tighter confidence interval such as $\epsilon = 0.05$.

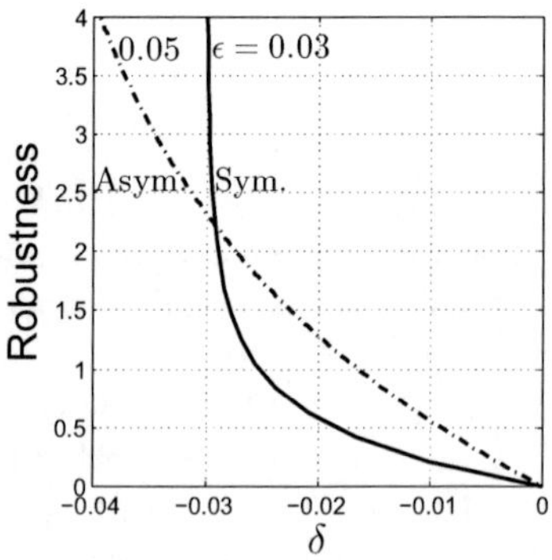

Figure 6.21: Robustness vs. confidence decrement for symmetric (solid) and asymmetric (dot-dash) uncertainty at different confidence levels ϵ.

6.3.6 Extension

Shifted confidence interval. We have evaluated the robustness of the upper and lower bounds of a $1-\epsilon$ confidence interval whose upper and lower regions have equal probability of $\epsilon/2$. A confidence interval which is shifted slightly with respect to the estimated interval may be more robust than the estimated interval. When this happens it means that we have more confidence (vis-à-vis the data uncertainty) that the estimated variable will fall in the shifted interval after data revision than that it would fall in the original interval.

6.4 Appendix: Least Squares Regression Coefficients for Section 6.1

In this appendix we formulate the regression coefficients which minimize the mean squared error, denoted $\widetilde{c}$ in section 6.1.3. Derivations can be found in many sources.

Consider a regression of order J (in eq.(6.1) $J = 2$):

$$y_i^{\mathrm{r}} = \sum_{j=0}^{J} c_j t_i^j \tag{6.47}$$

The coefficients which minimize the squared error, defined in eq.(6.2) on p.182, are denoted $\widetilde{c}$.

We define several matrices in order to conveniently express $\widetilde{c}$.

Define vectors $\theta_i' = (t_i^0, \ldots, t_i^J)$ for $i = 1, \ldots, N$. Now define the $(J+1) \times N$ matrix whose columns are the θ_i vectors: $\Theta = [\theta_1 \cdots \theta_N]$. Finally, define the $(J+1) \times (J+1)$ matrix whose jkth element is $\Xi_{jk} = \sum_{i=1}^{N} t_i^{j-1} t_i^{k-1}$.

The least-squares regression coefficients satisfy:

$$\Theta y = \Xi c \tag{6.48}$$

6.5 Appendix: Mean Squared Error for Section 6.2

The mean squared error in eq.(6.16) on p.191 can be expressed more compactly as follows. Let e_n denote the nth standard basis vector in $\Re^N$: the column N-vector with a 1 in the nth location and 0's elsewhere.

Now the mean squared error can be written:

$$S^2(c) = \frac{1}{N-J} \sum_{n=J+1}^{N} \left[e_n' y - \sum_{j=1}^{J} c_j e_{n-j}' y \right]^2 \tag{6.49}$$

$$= \frac{1}{N-J} \sum_{n=J+1}^{N} \Bigg[\underbrace{\left(e_n' - \sum_{j=1}^{J} c_j e_{n-j}' \right)}_{\zeta_n'} y \Bigg]^2 \tag{6.50}$$

$$= \frac{1}{N-J} \sum_{n=J+1}^{N} y' \zeta_n \zeta_n' y \tag{6.51}$$

$$= \frac{1}{N-J} y' \underbrace{\left(\sum_{n=J+1}^{N} \zeta_n \zeta_n' \right)}_{V} y \tag{6.52}$$

$$= \frac{1}{N-J} y' V y \tag{6.53}$$

This is eq.(6.17), where the $N \times N$ matrix V is defined in eq.(6.52) and the N-vectors ζ_n are defined in eq.(6.50).

Part III

Wrapping Up

Chapter 7

The Art of Uncertainty Modelling

We discuss a range of info-gap models for non-probabilistic quantification of uncertainty. We consider info-gap models for a single uncertain parameter and for an uncertain function. We describe how an info-gap model is formulated from limited information.

∼ ∼ ∼

Throughout this book we have used two types of models: models of the economy, and models of uncertainty. We have considered uncertainties in data, model parameters, vectors and functional relations. In the previous chapters we have encountered and employed a wide range of info-gap models of uncertainty. In this chapter we will delve more deeply into the process by which info-gap models of uncertainty are formulated, and the considerations which arise in selecting among them (Ben-Haim, 2006).

If you ask people what they know, they can tell you. But if you ask them what they *don't* know, what can they say? The art of uncertainty modelling is to find useful representations of what could be true, given what we know or believe to be true. Uncertainty is not simply the complement of knowledge. Rather, our knowledge constrains the range of contingencies which we could confront. Our task is to model what we don't know, in light of what we do know, without confusing knowledge, intuition and judgment with wishful thinking.

7.1 Uncertain Parameters

Consider a single economic variable such as inflation, unemployment, return on an investment, or any of myriad economic indicators. In the following subsections we will run through a range of different types of knowledge about this variable, and discuss the judgments involved in selecting appropriate info-gap models of uncertainty.

7.1.1 Certainty

Denote the value of our economic variable by x, and let $\widetilde{x}$ denote an estimate or projection of x. We can imagine situations—or variables—for which the estimate, $\widetilde{x}$, is known to be a highly accurate and reliable approximation to the true value, x. In such situations we make the judgment that $\widetilde{x}$ is true, or certain, and we ignore any possible uncertainty in the estimate. Such judgments are extremely important, and without the ability to say "$\widetilde{x}$ is a good (or good enough) estimate of x" we would unnecessarily impede our analysis. Certainty is an extreme situation; important, but extreme nonetheless.

7.1.2 Fractional Error

Now let's consider a different extreme. We have an estimate, $\widetilde{x}$, but we are quite sure that it is wrong. We can readily imagine that $\widetilde{x}$ differs from the true value, x, by a large margin, but we cannot say how large that margin might be. We may have asked experts and found that they disagree or have changed their minds.[1]

As an example, consider the marginal damage costs of carbon dioxide emissions. This estimate entails numerous assumptions about future economic growth and activity, discount rates, technological innovation, social preferences, and so forth. A median estimate of \$4 per metric ton of CO_2 is subject to considerable dispute (Barker, 2008). The analyst is entitled to view any estimate as possibly vastly different from the value which will emerge as the "fact of the matter" in the future.

[1] "Not only have individual financial institutions become less vulnerable to shocks from underlying risk factors, but also the financial system as a whole has become more resilient." Alan Greenspan, former Chairman of the Federal Reserve Board, 2004.

"The problem is the uncertainty that people have about doing business with banks, and banks have about doing business with each other," William Poole, former president of the Federal Reserve Bank of St. Louis, quoted in the *New York Times*, 9.10.2008.

Table 7.1: Forecasted interest rates. Source: Reserve Bank of New Zealand (2004).

Date of forecast	2001:2	2001:3	2001:4	2002:1	2002:2	2002:3
Forecast to 2003:3	6.25	6.00	6.25	5.25	6.25	7.00

As another example, consider forecasts. Table 7.1 shows forecasted interest rates for the third quarter of 2003, published quarterly by the Reserve Bank of New Zealand. The RBNZ notes that "Actual interest rates evolved very differently after many of the projections, reflecting new information that came to light after the projection was made" (RBNZ, 2004, p.18). Once again the estimate—in this case a forecast—is highly uncertain and we are quite unable to pin down a realistic or meaningful worst case. It is very likely to be true that the future interest rate is bounded by a large number, say 20. But this is not a useful bound. To base analysis on an interest rate of 20 would be meaningless.

To begin quantifying this sort of uncertainty, consider the absolute fractional deviation of an estimate $\widetilde{x}$, above or below the true value, x:

$$\left| \frac{x - \widetilde{x}}{\widetilde{x}} \right| \tag{7.1}$$

We are considering the situation in which we recognize that this error may be substantial, and we can say nothing meaningful about how large this error is. The estimate, $\widetilde{x}$, is not meaningless, but it is hardly reliable either.

This is definitely an extreme situation, and we will shortly consider the availability of further information. But let's pause to note that judgments must be distinguished from wishful thinking. We may wish that we had more information or better understanding. But the art of modelling uncertainty demands that we distinguish informed intuition from guessing. We are currently considering the situation where our informed intuition provides no guidance on the fractional error of the estimate.

Nonetheless the estimate $\widetilde{x}$ is not meaningless, and the severity of our ignorance must not stop us from proceeding in our analysis.[2]

[2] "If we will disbelieve everything, because we cannot certainly know all things;

In this situation, a fractional-error info-gap model for uncertainty in the estimate appropriately represents the limitation of our knowledge. The fractional-error model is an unbounded family of nested sets of possible realizations:

$$\mathcal{U}(h) = \left\{ x : \left| \frac{x - \widetilde{x}}{\widetilde{x}} \right| \le h \right\}, \quad h \ge 0 \tag{7.2}$$

$\mathcal{U}(h)$ is the set of all values of x which deviate fractionally from $\widetilde{x}$ by no more than h. Since h is unknown, this info-gap model (like all info-gap models) is not a single set, but rather an unbounded family of nested sets of values of x.

It is sometimes more convenient to write this info-gap model differently, by noting that the fractional-error inequality defines an interval of x values. Eq.(7.2) is equivalent to:

$$\mathcal{U}(h) = \{ x : \ \widetilde{x} - h|\widetilde{x}| \le x \le \widetilde{x} + h|\widetilde{x}| \}, \quad h \ge 0 \tag{7.3}$$

If the estimate, $\widetilde{x}$, is positive, then this takes the simpler form:

$$\mathcal{U}(h) = \{ x : \ (1-h)\widetilde{x} \le x \le (1+h)\widetilde{x} \}, \quad h \ge 0 \tag{7.4}$$

For any given value of h, we see that $\mathcal{U}(h)$ in eqs.(7.2)–(7.4) is a set of x-values: all those values for which the fractional error is no greater than h. When $h = 0$ then $\mathcal{U}(0)$ is a singleton set, containing only the estimate, $\widetilde{x}$:

$$\mathcal{U}(0) = \{ \widetilde{x} \} \tag{7.5}$$

As h increases, the sets $\mathcal{U}(h)$ become more inclusive:

$$h < h' \ \text{ implies } \ \mathcal{U}(h) \subseteq \mathcal{U}(h') \tag{7.6}$$

The fractional-error info-gap model is an unbounded family of nested sets of x values, reflecting the fact that we do not know the greatest possible error of the estimate.

All info-gap models display the properties shown in eqs.(7.5) and (7.6). The former is called the *contraction axiom,* and the latter, the *nesting axiom.* Together they endow h with its meaning as a *horizon of uncertainty.*

---

we shall do muchwhat as wisely as he, who would not use his legs, but sit still and perish, because he had no wings to fly." Locke (1706), p.57. I.i.5.

7.1.3 Fractional Error with Bounds

The info-gap model of eq.(7.2) is an unbounded family of nested sets of possible values of x. For *any* value of x, no matter how large or how greatly negative, there is a horizon of uncertainty, h, at which the uncertainty set $\mathcal{U}(h)$ contains this value of x.

The unboundedness of a fractional-error info-gap model, eq.(7.2) or (7.3), means that we are unable to commit ourselves to a most extreme value for x. The unboundedness does not necessarily imply that we believe that any and all values of x are likely to occur, or are even possible. It simply means that we lack the information to state a bounding value. The unboundedness is a statement of ignorance, not knowledge.

However, in some situations a bound is implied by the very definition of the variable. For instance, the rate of unemployment cannot, by definition, be negative. Similarly, if x represents a probability then it cannot be less than zero or greater than one. These bounds are true by definition.

In other situations one may have reliable understanding which precludes some contingencies which are nonetheless theoretical possibilities. For instance, the overnight interest rate of the European Central Bank was 5.25% on the eve of the terror attacks of September 11th, 2001. While central banks can raise interests rates, and often do so, it was certain that the ECB would lower the overnight rate after 9/11, though the magnitude of the reduction was unknown. The overnight rate was bounded above by its current value, not by definition but by basic economic understanding of how the ECB acts.

Information about bounds on an uncertain variable can be readily incorporated into fractional-error info-gap models. If prior knowledge requires that x be no greater than a known value x_1, we modify eq.(7.2) as:

$$\mathcal{U}(h) = \left\{ x : \; x \le x_1, \; \left| \frac{x - \widetilde{x}}{\widetilde{x}} \right| \le h \right\}, \quad h \ge 0 \qquad (7.7)$$

The uncertainty set, at horizon of uncertainty h, contains all values of x which are no greater than x_1 and whose fractional deviation from the estimate, $\widetilde{x}$, are no greater than h.

Eq.(7.7) is the analog of eq.(7.2). The analog of eq.(7.3) is:

$$\mathcal{U}(h) = \{ x : \; \widetilde{x} - h|\widetilde{x}| \le x \le \min[x_1, \; \widetilde{x} + h|\widetilde{x}|] \}, \quad h \ge 0 \qquad (7.8)$$

7.1.4 Calibrated Fractional Error

We now consider a situation where we have an estimate, $\widetilde{x}$, of the variable x, together with an error of this estimate, σ. Sometimes this occurs when $\widetilde{x}$ is the numerical average of data, and σ is the standard deviation of these data. We don't know the probability distribution which generated the data, and we don't even know that the data are a statistically random sample from a stationary random process. In other cases $\widetilde{x}$ and σ are somebody's guesstimate: "It's about two and a half, plus or minus, say, three-fourths." All we have is two numbers: the "estimate" $\widetilde{x}$ and its "error" σ. The quotation marks reminds us not to read into these two numbers more than is justified.

Table 7.2: Net farm income ($\$10^9$) in the U.S. Source: Council of Economic Advisors (2008).

Year	2003	2004	2005	2006	2007
NFI	59.7	85.9	77.1	59.0	87.5

As a case in point consider net farm income in the U.S. over a 5-year period, table 7.2. These data jump around quite a bit, not showing any particular trend. The mean is 73.8, with a standard deviation of 12.4. The range of these data does not preclude further excursions. For instance the NFI in 2002 was 40.1: more than a standard deviation below the lowest value in table 7.2. Nonetheless we have an estimate, $\widetilde{x} = 73.8$, and an error of this estimate, $\sigma = 12.4$.

In this situation the analog of eq.(7.2) is the calibrated fractional-error info-gap model:

$$\mathcal{U}(h) = \left\{ x : \left| \frac{x - \widetilde{x}}{\sigma} \right| \leq h \right\}, \quad h \geq 0 \tag{7.9}$$

The uncertainty set $\mathcal{U}(h)$ is the set of all x values whose deviation from the estimate, in units of the error, σ, is no greater than the horizon of uncertainty, h.

In some situations we have asymmetric information about the estimated error, in the form of three numbers: a central estimate $\widetilde{x}$, and upper and lower estimates $x_{\rm u}$ and $x_{\rm l}$. These numbers might be a mean and a confidence interval or simply somebody's assessment that "x is typically three, but might be as low as two or as large as five". We have no reason to treat these numbers as strict bounds. A

Table 7.3: Cumulative distribution function based on fan chart projections. Source: Norges Bank (2008), Chart 1.15c.

CPI	0.69	1.37	1.77	2.09	2.52	2.95	3.27	3.67	4.35
P(CPI)	0.05	0.15	0.25	0.35	0.50	0.65	0.75	0.85	0.95

simple variation of eq.(7.9) is the asymmetric fractional-error info-gap model:

$$\mathcal{U}(h) = \{x : \widetilde{x} - (\widetilde{x} - x_{\rm l})h \le x \le \widetilde{x} + (x_{\rm u} - \widetilde{x})h\}, \quad h \ge 0 \quad (7.10)$$

Like all info-gap models, this one obeys the axioms of nesting and contraction, eqs.(7.5) and (7.6). The interval in eq.(7.10) expands asymmetrically as the horizon of uncertainty grows, unlike the interval in eq.(7.3) which grows symmetrically around $\widetilde{x}$.

7.1.5 Discrete Probability Distributions

We now extend our knowledge to include probabilistic information. As an example, suppose the economic variable, x, is the percentage rate of inflation, and we consider three ranges: low ($x < 2$), medium ($2 \le x < 5$) and high ($5 \le x$). We have probability estimates for x to fall in each of these three ranges, $\widetilde{p}_1$, $\widetilde{p}_2$ and $\widetilde{p}_3$ respectively. Estimates such as these are usually based on some combination of historical data, quantitative models and professional judgment. As such, these estimates are valuable repositories of diverse knowledge, and facilitate useful insight. However, the processes which generated the historical data may change in the future, models are invariably simplifications of reality, and judgment may err. In short, the probabilities in question are often themselves highly uncertain.

As an example, consider the fan charts which some central banks use to depict uncertain forecasts in inflation and other variables. Table 7.3 shows a discrete cumulative probability distribution for CPI percent inflation for December 2011, based on data of March 2008, as inferred from a fan chart published by the Norges Bank. The baseline projection is 2.52% inflation, so the probability that CPI is no greater than 2.52 is 0.50. Similarly, $P(\text{CPI} \le 3.67) = 0.85$ and $P(\text{CPI} \le 1.77) = 0.25$. The authors write that "The projections for inflation ... and other variables are based on our assessment of the current situation and our perception of the functioning of the economy. ... The fan charts illustrate the uncertainty surrounding our projections" (Norges Bank, 2008, p.20).

The fractional-error info-gap models discussed in sections 7.1.3 and 7.1.4 can all be adapted to represent uncertainty in a discrete probability distribution.

Consider an n-dimensional probability distribution, $p = (p_1, \ldots, p_n)$, whose best estimate is $\widetilde{p} = (\widetilde{p}_1, \ldots, \widetilde{p}_n)$. A fractional-error info-gap model for p is:

$$\mathcal{U}(h) = \left\{ p : \sum_{i=1}^{n} p_i = 1, \; p_i \geq 0, \; \left| \frac{p_i - \widetilde{p}_i}{\widetilde{p}_i} \right| \leq h, \; \forall \, i \right\}, \quad h \geq 0 \tag{7.11}$$

$\mathcal{U}(h)$ is the set of all discrete probability distributions (normalized and non-negative) whose elements deviate fractionally from the corresponding estimates by no more than h.

In some situations one might have error estimates for the estimated probabilities. For instance, if $\widetilde{p}_i$ is estimated as the fraction of successes on Bernoulli trials then its error could be approximated as $\sigma_i = \sqrt{(1 - \widetilde{p}_i)\widetilde{p}_i}$. In other cases the probabilities $\widetilde{p}_i$ and their errors σ_i are expert or professional judgments. In either case we can modify the fractional-error model in eq.(7.11) to a calibrated fractional-error model:

$$\mathcal{U}(h) = \left\{ p : \sum_{i=1}^{n} p_i = 1, \; p_i \geq 0, \; \left| \frac{p_i - \widetilde{p}_i}{\sigma_i} \right| \leq h, \; \forall \, i \right\}, \quad h \geq 0 \tag{7.12}$$

7.2 Uncertain Function

In section 7.1 we considered a wide range of types of information which the analyst might have about a single parameter or variable. We now move into the rich domain of scalar-valued real functions. A function not only entails an uncountable infinity of values, it also has shape: a specific arrangement of these values. This introduces greater mathematical complexity, and brings to bear a broad class of types of information which the analyst may have about the function. For instance, we may know little about the function other than that it is monotonic, or uni-modal. Or, we may know the values of the function at specific points, but not in between. The art of modelling the uncertainty of a function will lead us to variations on info-gap models encountered earlier, but also to new sorts of models. Functional uncertainty is a rich domain which must be approached creatively.[3]

7.2.1 Envelope Bound

Let $f(x)$ be a function, such as unemployment vs. inflation, or price vs. demand. The function may also be a probability density or a cumulative probability distribution. Let $\widetilde{f}(x)$ denote our estimate of $f(x)$.

The simplest info-gap model for uncertainty in the function is the continuous analog of the fractional-error model introduced in section 7.1.2. We are once again considering a situation of severe uncertainty about the estimate, $\widetilde{f}(x)$. This estimate is not meaningless—it is perhaps our best guess—but we are unconfident that it is correct and we are unable to impose any meaningful bound on its error. The fractional-error envelope-bound info-gap model is:

$$\mathcal{U}(h) = \left\{ f(x) : \; |f(x) - \widetilde{f}(x)| \leq h|\widetilde{f}(x)|, \; \forall \, x \right\}, \quad h \geq 0 \qquad (7.13)$$

$\mathcal{U}(h)$ is the set of all functions which fractionally deviate from the estimated function, at any point x, by no more than h. This is a very rich set of functions including ones whose shape is similar to $\widetilde{f}(x)$, but also including functions with bumps, wiggles or even kinks and discontinuities not present in $\widetilde{f}(x)$. Since this is a fractional-error model, the range of variation at each value of x is proportional to the estimated function at that point.

In some situations we may have a bit more information. In addition to the estimated function $\widetilde{f}(x)$ we also know an error function, $\varepsilon(x)$, which expresses the relative error of the estimate at point x as compared to other points along the curve. The error function may come from a formal estimation process, or it may arise more informally. For instance, if $f(x)$ is demand as a function of time, we may know that fluctuations in summer are roughly 50% higher than during the rest of the year. $\varepsilon(x)$ does not constitute a maximum error; it indicates relative tendency for error along the curve. $\varepsilon(x)$ is non-negative by its definition.

[3] "And what can you imagine from being told that parallel lines intersect at infinity? It seems to me if one were to be over-conscientious there wouldn't be any such thing as mathematics at all." Musil (1906, p.90).

We can now use an analog of the calibrated fractional-error info-gap model in eq.(7.9):

$$\mathcal{U}(h) = \left\{ f(x) : \ |f(x) - \widetilde{f}(x)| \le h\varepsilon(x), \ \forall\, x \right\}, \quad h \ge 0 \qquad (7.14)$$

In some cases we have asymmetric information, suggesting greater deviation in one direction than the other. An extreme example is when deviation can only go in one direction. For instance, economic understanding might indicate that unemployment cannot exceed the estimated value at each argument, but might fall below the estimate. We express asymmetric information with non-negative lower and upper envelope functions to form an analog of eq.(7.10):

$$\mathcal{U}(h) = \left\{ f(x) : \ \widetilde{f}(x) - h\varepsilon_{\ell}(x) \le f(x) \le \widetilde{f}(x) + h\varepsilon_{\mathrm{u}}(x), \ \forall\, x \right\}, \ h \ge 0 \qquad (7.15)$$

7.2.2 Slope Bound

Uncertain slope. $f(x)$ expresses a functional relationship between two economic entities, like price and quantity, or unemployment and inflation, or GDP and time. In some situations we have an estimate of the slope of the function, we think that the actual slope will tend to follow this estimate, but we are unsure that this value is true throughout the range of the function. The actual function need not be linear and may in fact display varying slope, while our information is only sufficient to specify a linear approximation. We want to exploit both "sides" of this information: the linear estimate as well as the anticipated non-linearity of the actual function.

Let $\widetilde{s}$ be this known estimate of the slope. Suppose furthermore that we know the value of the function at a specific point, say $f(x_1) = f_1$ where x_1 and f_1 are known for sure.

Given these two pieces of information—the slope $\widetilde{s}$ and the point (x_1, f_1)—together with the contextual understanding that the function $f(x)$ will tend to have slope around $\widetilde{s}$, we can define the following envelope-bound info-gap model on the slope of the function:

$$\mathcal{U}(h) = \{ f(x) : \ f(x_1) = f_1, \ |f'(x) - \widetilde{s}| \le h|\widetilde{s}|, \ \forall\, x \}, \quad h \ge 0 \ (7.16)$$

where the prime denotes differentiation. At horizon of uncertainty h, the uncertainty set $\mathcal{U}(h)$ contains all functions which pass through the point (x_1, f_1) and whose slope differs fractionally from $\widetilde{s}$ by no more than h at any point. This is an envelope-bound info-gap model but, unlike the models in eqs.(7.13) or (7.14), no functions in the current model have sudden dips and bumps, at least until h becomes large. The functions in this info-gap model need not be linear, but they waver around the estimated linear function, or diverge away from it gradually. Of course, we don't know the horizon of uncertainty, so any function (passing though (x_1, f_1)) is contained in $\mathcal{U}(h)$ for some sufficiently large value of h.

The inequality in the definition of the info-gap model in eq.(7.16) can be expressed as:

$$\widetilde{s} - h|\widetilde{s}| \le f'(x) \le \widetilde{s} + h|\widetilde{s}| \tag{7.17}$$

From this we see that the sign of the slope of $f(x)$ can differ from the sign of the estimated slope, $\widetilde{s}$, for horizons of uncertainty greater than one.

We may have information indicating that the actual function, $f(x)$, must have the same sign of slope as the sign of $\widetilde{s}$. For instance, if economic considerations indicate that price will necessarily decrease as quantity increases, then $\widetilde{s}$ is negative and we require that $f'(x)$ be negative as well. The info-gap model in eq.(7.16) is readily modified to include this additional information. Let sgn(y) denote the algebraic sign of y. Our info-gap model becomes:

$$\mathcal{U}(h) = \left\{ \, f(x): \; f(x_1) = f_1, \;\; \mathrm{sgn}[f'(x)] = \mathrm{sgn}(\widetilde{s}), \right. \qquad (7.18)$$
$$\left. |f'(x) - \widetilde{s}| \le h|\widetilde{s}|, \; \forall \, x \, \right\}, \quad h \ge 0$$

All functions in $\mathcal{U}(h)$ pass through the point (x_1, f_1), have slope with the same sign as $\widetilde{s}$, and have slope which deviates fractionally from $\widetilde{s}$ by no more than h.

Uni-modal functions. A simple variation of the slope-bound info-gap model enables the representation of uncertain uni-modal functions. For instance, $f(t)$ might represent uncertain precipitous rise and gradual fall of the price of oil. Let $\widetilde{s}_{\mathrm{r}}$ and $\widetilde{s}_{\mathrm{f}}$ denote estimates of the rates at which $f(t)$ rises and falls, respectively, where $\widetilde{s}_{\mathrm{r}}$ is positive and $\widetilde{s}_{\mathrm{f}}$ is negative. The actual rates may differ substantially from these rates, and may also vary during the excursion. Let $\widetilde{t}_{\mathrm{p}}$ denote the time at which the peak is estimated to occur, though the actual time of the peak, t_{p}, is unknown. The initial price, at time $t = 0$, is known and denoted f_0. The following info-gap model is one representation of uncertainty in the time evolution of the price excursion. Let us define a "ramp" function: $r(x) = x$ if $x > 0$, and $r(x) = 0$ if $x \le 0$. The derivative of $f(t)$ is denoted $f'(t)$. The info-gap model is:

$$\mathcal{U}(h) = \left\{ f(t) : \; r(1-h)\widetilde{s}_{\rm r} \le f'(t) \le (1+h)\widetilde{s}_{\rm r}, \; 0 \le t \le t_{\rm p} \right.$$
$$(1+h)\widetilde{s}_{\rm f} \le f'(t) \le r(1-h)\widetilde{s}_{\rm f}, \; t > t_{\rm p} \qquad (7.19)$$
$$\left. f(0) = f_0, \; t_{\rm p} > 0, \; \left| \frac{t_{\rm p} - \widetilde{t}_{\rm p}}{\widetilde{t}_{\rm p}} \right| \le h \right\}, \quad h \ge 0$$

The first line indicates that, at horizon of uncertainty h, the rising slope before the peak is no greater than $(1+h)\widetilde{s}_{\rm r}$, and no smaller than $(1-h)\widetilde{s}_{\rm r}$ or zero, whichever is greater. The second line states that the falling slope is no more negative than $(1+h)\widetilde{s}_{\rm f}$ and no less negative than $(1-h)\widetilde{s}_{\rm f}$ or zero, whichever is less. The third line states the initial value of $f(t)$ and that the fractional error of the estimated time of occurrence of the peak is no greater than the horizon of uncertainty, h. The value of h is not known.

Sets of sets. The info-gap model in eq.(7.19) obeys the nesting and contraction properties identified in eqs.(7.5) and (7.6) on p.216. When $h = 0$ the set $\mathcal{U}(0)$ contains only a single triangular function: starting at f_0 with positive slope slope $\widetilde{s}_{\rm r}$, peaking at $t = \widetilde{t}_{\rm p}$, and then falling with negative slope $\widetilde{s}_{\rm f}$. As h gets larger the sets become more inclusive.

However, if we remove the condition that the initial value is known, $f(0) = f_0$, then, when $h = 0$, we have a set of functions: all triangular functions with slopes $\widetilde{s}_{\rm r}$ and $\widetilde{s}_{\rm f}$ which peak at $\widetilde{t}_{\rm p}$. In other words, the model now violates the contraction axiom of eq.(7.5).

Nonetheless, we can still formulate this as a proper info-gap model if we think of the elements of $\mathcal{U}(h)$ as *sets* of functions rather than as *single* functions. Thus, in the absence of uncertainty ($h = 0$) we have a single set: the set of all triangular functions with slopes $\widetilde{s}_{\rm r}$ and $\widetilde{s}_{\rm f}$ peaking at $\widetilde{t}_{\rm p}$. At any positive horizon of uncertainty, $h > 0$, we have many sets: all the sets formed by allowing slope uncertainty in each function in the initial set. The contraction axiom now holds, when applied to elements which are sets of functions. The nesting axiom also holds.

Other modifications of the original info-gap model would also lead to an info-gap model whose elements are sets of functions rather than single functions.

7.2.3 Auto-Regressive Functions

Sometimes an uncertain function is represented by an auto-regression of known order. For instance, a monotonically decaying discrete-time function, f_t, can be represented as:

$$f_t = \rho f_{t-1} \tag{7.20}$$

(Random shocks may be appended to the right-hand side, but that does not concern us here.) The value of f_t will decrease steadily if $0 < \rho < 1$, however the value of ρ may be uncertain or entirely unknown.

If an estimate of ρ is known then one of the info-gap models for uncertain parameters in section 7.1 can be used to represent uncertainty in this estimate.

If no estimate of the decay constant, ρ, is available, then a different approach can be taken. Suppose that the uncertain function f_t is part of a wider modelling and analysis problem in which a scalar loss function is important.[4] This loss function may depend on many other elements, but let's denote its dependence on ρ by $L(\rho)$. Furthermore, let's suppose that there is some value of ρ for which $L(\rho)$ is a minimum (and not negative infinity). Denote this minimum value of the loss function by L_0.

Our uncertainty concerning ρ and the resulting process f_t can be expressed by asking: how much will the loss exceed the lowest possible value? We of course don't know the answer to this question. However, an info-gap model can now be defined. The uncertainty set at horizon of uncertainty h contains all ρ-values for which the loss exceeds the minimum by no more than h:

$$\mathcal{U}(h) = \{\rho : \ \rho \in (0, 1), \ L(\rho) - L_0 \le h\}, \quad h \ge 0 \tag{7.21}$$

Two distinctive features of this info-gap model must be noted.

First, the formulation of the model is linked to the broader problem definition. Different problems, e.g. different loss functions $L(\rho)$, will generate different info-gap models. Typically, an info-gap model represents uncertainty which is prior to the formulation of an analysis. However, we see in this example that this is not a necessary property of an info-gap model. In fact, the info-gap model may even depend on the decision variables via the loss function.

The second distinctive feature of the info-gap model in eq.(7.21) is that the uncertainty sets, $\mathcal{U}(h)$, need not be continuous intervals.

[4] Modification for the case of gain rather than loss will be obvious.

If the loss function, $L(\rho)$, has multiple minima in a plot vs. ρ, then some of the sets $\mathcal{U}(h)$ will contain non-connected intervals of ρ values. This is an example of an info-gap model whose sets are not convex. The info-gap model will nonetheless obey the nesting and contraction properties identified in eqs.(7.5) and (7.6) on p.216.

7.3 Extensions

There are many other types of info-gap models of uncertainty, motivated by different types of information and different types of gaps in our information (Ben-Haim, 2006). We have encountered variations on some of these info-gap models in previous chapters. A few other classes of info-gap models of uncertainty are mentioned here.

Moment constrained. Sometimes we consider uncertain functions for which we know the value of one or several moments. One example we have already encountered is uncertain probability distributions whose zeroth moment—the sum—must equal one, eqs.(7.11) and (7.12). In other circumstances we may know the value of the mean or centroid of the function. For instance, we may be interested in income-distribution functions with a given mean income which which are otherwise uncertain. In other situations we may be interested in functions whose variance is known.

Data constrained. Data often constrain the shape of a function, but do not determine the function entirely. An example we have considered previously is the slope-bound info-gap model in eq.(7.16). The constraint that the function pass through the point (x_1, f_1) may be a datum. We may have additional information, such as an estimated slope, but beyond that, we are uncertain.

Spectral information. All functions (subject to some technical conditions) can be represented as sums of orthogonal functions such as sines and cosines. We may have estimates of these Fourier coefficients but be uncertain of their true values. An important class of info-gap models represents this uncertainty in various different ways (Ben-Haim, 2006, section 2.5).

Uncertain vectors. We have considered uncertainty in a single parameter in section 7.1 and in an entire function in section 7.2. Sometimes the uncertainty resides in a vector of parameters, or in a vector-valued function. The info-gap models we have encountered can all be adapted to the case of vectors.

Chapter 8

Positivism, F-twist, and Robust-Satisficing

We consider Friedman's positive economics, and Samuelson's scientific response, in the light of info-gap robust-satisficing.

∼ ∼ ∼

We began chapter 1 with a question: can models help? The short answer is yes, and this book is part of an attempt to describe how models, data, and human judgment can be combined in the quantitative support of economic decisions.

The central issues of this book—how to formulate and evaluate policy and how to model economic behavior—are methodological, and touch the hoary debate over positivism in economics. Without wishing to enter the fray (positive economics: right or wrong?), I will use the clash between Friedman (1953) and Samuelson (1963) to illuminate the methodological distinctiveness of info-gap robust-satisficing.

In a nutshell, the argument in this chapter is this:

- Friedman is right that good theories depend on axioms which capture an essential truth, while usually violating a messier reality.[1]

[1] "Your bait of falsehood takes this carp of truth;" Shakespeare, *Hamlet,* act II, sc.1, *l*.69.

- Samuelson is right that factual inaccuracy of a theory detracts from its validity in prediction and policy formulation.[2]
- Both Samuelson and Friedman agree that economic science, like natural science, improves over time and progresses towards truth.[3]
- However, there is an inherent indeterminism in economic systems which precludes the shared belief of Samuelson and Friedman.[4]
- Hence optimization—of models or of policy outcomes—is fatuous (or serendipitious).[5] Nonetheless, satisficing can sometimes be done reliably.[6]

8.1 Friedman and Samuelson

Friedman was undoubtedly right when he wrote (Friedman, 1953, p.14):

> Truly important and significant hypotheses will be found to have "assumptions" that are wildly inaccurate descriptive representations of reality, and, in general, the more significant the theory, the more unrealistic the assumptions (in this sense). The reason is simple. A hypothesis is important if it "explains" much by little, that is, if it abstracts the common and crucial elements from the mass of complex and detailed circumstances surrounding the phenomena to be explained and permits valid predictions on the basis of them alone.

A first-rate illustration is Galileo's "wildly inaccurate" Law of Inertia: a body moves at constant velocity unless acted upon by a force. This is the most blatantly counter-intuitive proposition in the history of

[2] "Thanks to the negation sign, there are as many truths as falsehoods; we just can't always be sure which are which." Quine (1995, p.67).

[3] "The movement of ideas toward truth may be glacial but, like a glacier, it is hard to stop." Galbraith (1986, p.201).

[4] "For fallibilism is the doctrine that our knowledge is never absolute but always swims, as it were, in a continuum of uncertainty and of indeterminacy." Peirce (1897, 1955).

[5] "Optimization works in theory but risk management is better in practice. There is no scientific way to compute an optimal path for monetary policy." Greenspan (2005).

[6] Hence the need for "a little stodginess at the central bank." (Blinder, 1998, p.12).

science: no one has ever witnessed an instance of such perpetual motion. Things stop unless you keep pushing them, so Aristotle's hypothesis is far more realistic: a body loses speed unless acted upon by a force. And yet Galileo's hypothesis is outstripped by few others for theoretical fruitfulness and predictive power. As Friedman would explain, Galileo's Law strips away the nagging nuisance of dissipative forces and cuts to the essence of material dynamics.

Samuelson summarized Friedman's position with what he referred to as the 'F-Twist' (Samuelson, 1963, p.232):

> A theory is vindicated if (some of) its consequences are empirically valid to a useful degree of approximation; the (empirical) unrealism of the theory "itself," or of its "assumptions," is quite irrelevant to its validity and worth.

Samuelson (1963, p.233) is undoubtedly correct in focussing on the basic F-Twist, which

> is fundamentally wrong in thinking that unrealism in the sense of factual inaccuracy even to a tolerable degree of approximation is anything but a demerit for a theory or hypothesis (or set of hypotheses).

Samuelson presents logical and epistemological arguments. I suggest further support for Samuelson's position. We value successful tests of a theory because they add warrant to the belief that the theory will predict accurately even when no data are around. That is, when a theory passes a severe test of its predictions, we gain support for the inductive hypothesis that the theory will reliably predict in untested circumstances as well. The significance of successful tests of a theory derives from the fact—established by Hume—that empirical evidence can never verify the inductive hypothesis that what worked yesterday will work tomorrow, or that what worked in one circumstance will work in another. Predictive success strengthens our faith in the inductive hypothesis (Haack, 2009).

Thus Friedman is right that fruitful theories can rest on idealizations which are empirically violated, while Samuelson is right that disparity between axiom and observation detracts from the value of the theory.

8.2 Shackle-Popper Indeterminism

Having now established myself firmly in both Samuelson's and Friedman's camps, I will not attempt to resolve their conflict. Rather, I will demonstrate the methodological distinctiveness of info-gap robust-satisficing by disputing a point upon which they would both agree. Both men concur that economics is epistemologically identical to physical science. Other scholars, for instance Koopmans, would also agree (Koopmans, 1957, pp.134–135). Friedman is explicit (Friedman, 1953, pp.4–5). Samuelson is implicit, by applying the criterion of logical consistency which is the pride of the physicists (Samuelson, 1963, pp.233–234). Physicists yearn for universal unifying theories, and a collection of logically conflicting sub-theories (relativity, statistical mechanics, quantum theory, etc.) is viewed with discomfort.

In contrast, a number of scholars, such as Habermas (1970), have emphasized the non-nomological nature of social science. I will not review the rich literature, but only focus on what I will refer to as Shackle-Popper indeterminism. This idea, developed separately and in different ways by Shackle (1972) and Popper (1957, 1982), underlies the methodology of info-gap robust-satisficing.[7]

The basic idea is that the behavior of intelligent learning systems displays an element of unstructured and unpredictable indeterminism. By *intelligence* I mean: behavior is influenced by knowledge. This is surely characteristic of humans individually, of firms and households, and of society at large. By *learning* I mean a process of discovery: finding out today what was unknown yesterday. One economically important example of learning is what Keynes referred to as hearing "the news". Finally, *indeterminism* arises as follows: because tomorrow's discovery is by definition unknown today, and tomorrow's behavior will be influenced by newly discovered knowledge, tomorrow's behavior is not predictable today, at least not in its entirety. Given the richness of future discovery (or its corollary, the richness of our current ignorance), the indeterminism of future behavior is broad, deep and unstructured.

The most important domain of indeterminism, for our purposes, is mathematical modelling of social systems, in particular, economic ones. Complexity and dimensionality are severe challenges in themselves. However, here we are dealing with the limited ability of laws, derived from *past* behavior, to describe *future* behavior. Intelligent

[7]Shackle-Popper indeterminism is related to Knightian uncertainty (Knight, 1921). See also Ben-Haim (2006, chap. 12) and Ben-Haim (2007, p.157).

learning behavior, as we have defined it, entails an element of innovation which seems to explain the painful experience of social modellers. In this sense, Shackle-Popper indeterminism accounts for the partially non-nomological nature of social systems.

8.3 Methodological Implications

The point is *not* that models can never describe social or economic activity, or that there is nothing that can be called a law of behavior. Rather, models of intelligent learning systems must focus on two categories of uncertainties, which I will refer to as *statistical* and *epistemic* uncertainty.

Statistical uncertainty is the usual kind: random noise in data, bias in samples, and so on. Quite often, though not always (Fox *et al.*, 2007), statistical uncertainty can be modelled and managed with statistical tools.

Epistemic uncertainty refers to the gaps and errors in our understanding of the processes being modelled, arising in part from Shackle-Popper indeterminism. For instance, complex non-linearities are approximated with linear models, high-dimensional systems are truncated, relevant interactions are ignored or not recognized. We usually know that our understanding is deficient, and we may even be ignoring implicit knowledge for pragmatic reasons. But more profoundly, the Shackle-Popper indeterminism implies that some element of error is inevitable in describing tomorrow's behavior with today's models, and that the nature and degree of this disparity is inherently unforeseeable.

Info-gap models represent epistemic uncertainty about the behavior of the economy. For instance, consider the info-gap model for uncertainty in the coefficients of an economic model, eq.(3.9) on p.33. The coefficients of the model are uncertain not only due to measurement error, but also due to the basic inability to entirely capture future behavior with past observation. The info-gap model of uncertainty is non-probabilistic precisely because the errors are epistemic, not statistical.

One methodological implication of Shackle-Popper indeterminism is that model error must be taken very seriously. The traditional positivistic optimism that our models are improving and even converging on the truth, is untenable. Positivism was enlisted to explain the wonderful success of the science-based technology which burst on the scene in the 19th century. The strategy of scientists such as Kelvin and Raleigh was to learn nature's laws, and then to apply them to technological enterprise. This works because Peirce was right that the study of nature does converge, asymptotically, on something that can reasonably be called the truth. As much as social scientists may wish to emulate this strategy, it will founder on the shoals of Shackle-Popper indeterminism.

One way of taking model-error seriously is to use the robust-satisficing strategy which we have studied in this book. The robustness function, $\widehat{h}(q, r_c)$ in any of the numerous examples we have examined, is the robustness of decision q, to epistemic uncertainty, when the outcome is satisficed to level r_c. The robustness function evaluates the policy worthiness of decision q, given performance aspiration r_c, in light of epistemic uncertainty about the economic system. Statistical uncertainty can also be included as we have seen in many examples.

Another methodological implication touches on the process of updating a mathematical model based on measurements. The two horns of uncertainty—statistical and epistemic uncertainty—generate an irrevocable trade-off. A model with high fidelity to data will have low immunity to structural error in the model. Either type of uncertainty can be ameliorated only at the expense of exacerbating the other. The methodological response is again to use robust-satisficing. A model with maximal fidelity to data will have zero immunity to structural info-gaps, so it is best to satisfice the fidelity at a sub-optimal but acceptable level (rather than to optimize the fidelity), in order to garner some robustness to epistemic uncertainty.

So what about Friedman, Samuelson, and the helpfulness of models? Logical consistency is essential for the success of deductive reasoning; mathematics depends on it. However, our mathematical models must make sense. They must submit to scrutiny by the mental models and intuitions which underlie human judgment. Far from being a restriction, this relation between math and mind enables the fruitful application of logical analysis to systems whose underlying logic eludes us. Quantitative models can help if we remember that they are rough-hewn approximations to reality, if we deal realistically with uncertainty, and if human judgment does not get lost among the equations.

References

Akram, Q.F., Yakov Ben-Haim, and Ø. Eitrheim, 2006, Managing uncertainty through robust-satisficing monetary policy. Norges Bank Working Papers, ANO 2006/10. Oslo: Norges Bank.

Andersen, Henrik, Tor O. Berge, Eivind Bernhardsen, Kjersti-Gro Lindquist and Bjørn Helge Vatne, 2008, A suite-of-models approach to stress-testing financial stability, Norges Bank Staff Memo, 2008/2, Oslo, 3 June 2008.

Barker, Terry, 2008, The economics of avoiding dangerous climate change. An editorial essay on The Stern Review, *Climatic Change,* 89: 173–194.

Ben-Haim, Yakov, 1996, *Robust Reliability in the Mechanical Sciences,* Springer-Verlag, Berlin.

Ben-Haim, Yakov, 2005, Info-Gap Decision Theory For Engineering Design. Or: Why "Good" is Preferable to "Best", chapter 11 in *Engineering Design Reliability Handbook,* E. Nikolaides, D. Ghiocel & Surendra Singhal, eds., CRC Press.

Ben-Haim, Yakov, 2006, *Info-Gap Decision Theory: Decisions Under Severe Uncertainty,* 2nd ed., Academic Press, London.

Ben-Haim, Yakov, 2007, Peirce, Haack and Info-Gaps, pp.150–164 in *Susan Haack, A Lady of Distinctions: The Philosopher Responds to Her Critics,* edited by Cornelis de Waal, Prometheus Books, New York.

Ben-Haim, Yakov, 2009, Info-gap forecasting and the advantage of sub-optimal models, *European Journal of Operational Research,* 197: 203–213.

Ben-Haim, Yakov and Maria Demertzis, 2008, Confidence in Monetary Policy, De Nederlandsche Bank Working Paper Series, No.192/2008.

Ben-Haim, Yakov and Keith W. Hipel, 2002, The graph model for conflict resolution with information-gap uncertainty in preferences, *Applied Mathematics and Computation, 126,* 319–340.

Ben-Haim, Yakov and Karsten Jeske, 2003, Home-bias in financial markets: Robust satisficing with info-gaps, Federal Reserve Bank of Atlanta, Working Paper Series, 2003-35, Dec. 2003, pdf file on the

Federal Reserve Bank website. SSRN abstract and full paper at: http://ssrn.com/abstract=487585.

Ben-Haim, Yakov and A. Laufer, 1998, Robust reliability of projects with activity-duration uncertainty, *ASCE Journal of Construction Engineering and Management, 124,* 125–132.

Beresford-Smith, Bryan and Colin J. Thompson, 2007, Managing credit risk with info-gap uncertainty, *Journal of Risk Finance,* vol.8, issue 1, pp.24–34.

Berleant, D., L. Andrieu, J.-P. Argaud, F. Barjon, M.-P. Cheong, M. Dancre, G. Sheble and C.-C. Teoh, 2008, Portfolio management under epistemic uncertainty using stochastic dominance and information-gap theory, *International Journal of Approximate Reasoning,* vol.49, #1, pp.101–116.

Bindseil, Ulrich, 2009, Central banks and other public institutions as financial investors, pp.3–48 in Bindseil, González and Tabakis, eds., 2009; see next.

Bindseil, Ulrich, Fernando González and Evangelos Tabakis, eds., 2009, *Risk Management for Central Banks and Other Public Investors,* Cambridge University Press.

Blanchard, Olivier, 2009, Guest article, *The Economist,* 29 Jan 2009.

Blinder, Alan S., 1998, *Central Banking in Theory and Practice,* Lionel Robbins Lecture, MIT Press, Cambridge.

Blinder, Alan S., Michael Ehrmann, Marcel Fratzscher, Jakob De Haan and David-Jan Jansen, 2008, Central bank communication and monetary policy: A survey of theory and evidence, *Journal of Economic Literature,* vol. 46, no. 4, pp.910–945.

Boudoukh, Jacob, Matthew Richardson and Robert Whitelaw, 1995, Expect the Worst, *Risk,* 1995, pp.100–101.

Bureau of Economic Analysis, US Dept of Commerce, National Income and Product Accounts Gross Domestic Product: Second Quarter 2009 (Advance Estimate) July 31, 2009.

Burgman, Mark, 2005, *Risks and Decisions for Conservation and Environmental Management,* Cambridge University Press, Cambridge.

Carmel, Yohay and Yakov Ben-Haim, 2005, Info-gap robust-satisficing model of foraging behavior: Do foragers optimize or satisfice?, *American Naturalist, 166,* 633–641.

Cheong, M.-P., D. Berleant, and G.B. Sheblé, 2004, Information Gap Decision Theory as a tool for Strategic Bidding in Competitive Electricity Markets, 8th International Conference on Probabilistic Methods Applied to Power Systems, Iowa State University, Ames, lowa, September 12–16, 2004.

Clarida, Richard, Jordi Galí and Mark Gertler, 1999, The Science of Monetary Policy: A New Keynesian Perspective, *Journal of Economic Literature,* vol. XXXVII, no.4, pp.1661–1707.

Council of Economic Advisors, 2008, *Economic Indicators,* U.S. Govt. Printing Office, Washington.

Coval, Joshua, Jakub Jurek and Erik Stafford, 2009, The economics of structured finance, *The Journal of Economic Perspectives,* vol. 23, #1, pp.3–25.

Crone, Elizabeth E., Debbie Pickering and Cheryl B. Schultz, 2007, Can captive rearing promote recovery of endangered butterflies? An assessment in the face of uncertainty, *Biological Conservation,* vol.139, #1–2, pp.103–112.

DeGroot, Morris H., 1986, *Probability and Statistics,* 2nd ed., Addison-Wesley, Reading, MA.

Demertzis, Maria and Nicola Viegi, 2008, Inflation targets as focal points, *Intl. J. Central Banking,* vol. 4, #1, pp.55–87.

Dowd, Kevin, 1998, *Beyond Value at Risk: The New Science of Risk Management,* Wiley, New York.

Duncan, S.J., C.J.J.Paredis and B.Bras, 2007, Applying info-gap theory to remanufacturing process selection affected by severe uncertainty, Proceedings of IMECE2007, 2007 ASME International Mechanical Engineering Congress and Exposition, November 11–15, 2007, Seattle.

Duncan, S.J., B.Bras and C.J.J.Paredis, 2008, An approach to robust decision making under severe uncertainty in life cycle design, *Int. J. Sustainable Design,* Vol. 1, No. 1, pp.45–59.

Evans, George W. and Seppo Honkapohja, 2001, *Learning and Expectations in Macroeconomics,* Princeton University Press, Princeton.

Fox, David R., Yakov Ben-Haim, Keith R. Hayes, Michael McCarthy, Brendan Wintle and Piers Dunstan, 2007, An info-gap approach to power and sample size calculations, *Environmetrics,* vol. 18, pp.189–203.

Friedman, Milton, 1953, On the methodology of positive economics, In: Friedman, Milton, *Essays in Positive Economics,* University of Chicago Press, 1953.

Galbraith, John Kenneth, 1986, *The New Industrial State,* 4th ed., Mentor Book.

Ganzerli, Sara and Chris P. Pantelides, 2000, Optimum structural design via convex model superposition, *Comput Struct,* 74, #6, pp. 639–647.

González, Fernando and Phillipe Molitor, 2009, Risk mitigation measures and credit risk assessment in central bank policy operations, pp.303–339 in Bindseil, González and Tabakis, eds., 2009; see above.

Greenspan, Alan, 2005, *Financial Times,* 27–28 August.

Haack, Susan, 2009, *Evidence and Inquiry: A Pragmatist Reconstruction of Epistemology,* 2nd, expanded edition, Prometheus Books, Amherst NY.

Habermas, Jürgen, 1970, *On the Logic of the Social Sciences,* trans. by Shierry Weber Nicholsen and Jerry A. Stark, 1990, MIT Press.

Hall, Jim and Dimitri Solomatine, 2008, A framework for uncertainty analysis in flood risk management decisions, *Int. J. of River Basin Management,* vol. 6, no. 2, pp.85–98.

Halpern, Benjamin S., Helen M. Regan, Hugh P. Possingham and Michael A. McCarthy, 2006, Accounting for uncertainty in marine reserve design, *Ecology Letters,* 9: 2–11.

Härdle, Wolfgang, 1990, *Applied Nonparametric Regression,* Cambridge University Press, Cambridge, U.K.

Hendricks, Darryll, 1996, Evaluation of value-at-risk models using historical data, *Economic Policy Review,* Federal Reserve Bank of New York, April 1996, Vol. 2, no. 1.

Hildebrandt, Patrick and Thomas Knoke, 2009, Optimizing the shares of native tree species in forest plantations with biased financial parameters, *Ecological Economics,* vol.68, issue 11, pp. 2825–2833.

IPCC-AR4, 2007, Global Climate Projections. In: *Climate Change 2007: The Physical Science Basis, Contribution of Working Group I to the Fourth Assessment Report of the Intergovernmental Panel on Climate Change,* Cambridge University Press, http://www.ipcc.ch.

Jorion, Philippe, 2001, *Value at Risk: The New Benchmark for Managing Financial Risk,* McGraw-Hill, New York.

Kanno Y. and Izuru Takewaki, 2006a, Robustness analysis of trusses with separable load and structural uncertainties, *International Journal of Solids and Structures, 43,* #9, 2646–2669.

Kanno, Y. and Izuru Takewaki, 2006b, Sequential semidefinite program for maximum robustness design of structures under load uncertainty, *Journal of Optimization Theory and Applications, 130,* #2, 265–287.

Kendall, Maurice, Alan Stuart and J. Keith Ord, 1979, *The Advanced Theory of Statistics.* Vol. 2: *Inference and Relationship,* 4th ed., Charles Griffin & Co., London.

Kendall, Maurice, Alan Stuart and J. Keith Ord, 1987, *The Advanced Theory of Statistics.* Vol. 1: *Distribution Theory,* 5th ed., Oxford University Press, New York.

Klir, George J., 2006, *Uncertainty and Information: Foundations of Generalized Information Theory,* New York: Wiley Publishers.

Knight, Frank H., 1921, *Risk, Uncertainty and Profit,* Hart, Schaffner and Marx. Re-issued by Harper Torchbooks, New York, 1965.

Knoke, T., 2008, Mixed forests and finance — Methodological approaches, *Ecological Economics,* Vol.65, Issue 3, pp.590–601.

Koivu, Matti, Fernando Monar Lora and Ken Nyholm, 2009, Strategic asset allocation for fixed-income investors, pp.49–116, in Bindseil, González and Tabakis, eds., 2009; see above.

Koopmans, Tjalling C., 1957, *Three Essays on the State of Economic Science,* McGraw-Hill Book Co., New York.

Levy, Jason K., Keith W. Hipel and D. Marc Kilgour, 2000, Using environmental indicators to quantify the robustness of policy alternatives to uncertainty, *Ecological Modelling,* Volume 130, Issues 1–3, 1 June 2000, Pages 79–86.

Locke, John, 1706, *An Essay Concerning Human Understanding.* 5th edition. Roger Woolhouse, ed. Penquin Books, 1997.

Longin, François M., 1996, The asymptotic distribution of extreme stock market returns, *The Journal of Business,* Vol. 69, #3, pp.383–408.

Mas-Colell, Andreu, Michael D. Whinston and Jerry R. Green, 1995, *Microeconomic Theory.* Oxford University Press.

Matsuda, Y. and Y. Kanno, 2008, Robustness analysis of structures based on plastic limit analysis with uncertain loads, *Journal of Mechanics of Materials and Structures,* vol.3, pp.213–242.

McCarthy, M.A. and D.B. Lindenmayer, 2007, Info-gap decision theory for assessing the management of catchments for timber production and urban water supply, *Environmental Management, 39,* #4, 553–562.

Mehra, Rajnish and Edward C. Prescott, 1985, The equity premium: A puzzle, *Journal of Monetary Economics,* 15: 145–161.

Metcalf, Gilbert E., 2009, Market-based policy options to control US greenhouse gas emissions, *Journal of Economic Perspectives,* vol. 23, #2, pp.5–27.

Miller, John H. and Scott E. Page, 2007, *Complex Adaptive Systems: An Introduction to Computational Models of Social Life,* Princeton University Press.

Moffitt, L. Joe, John K. Stranlund and Barry C. Field, 2005, Inspections to avert terrorism: Robustness under severe uncertainty, *Journal of Homeland Security and Emergency Management,* Vol.2, #3. http://www.bepress.com/jhsem/vol2/iss3/3

Moffitt, L. Joe, John K. Stranlund and Craig D. Osteen, 2008, Robust detection protocols for uncertain introductions of invasive species, *Journal of Environmental Management,* vol.89, pp.293–299.

Moilanen, Atte, Michael C. Runge, Jane Elith, Andrew Tyre, Yohay Carmel, Eric Fegraus, Brendan Wintle, Mark Burgman and Yakov Ben-Haim, 2006a, Planning for robust reserve networks using uncertainty analysis, *Ecological Modelling,* vol. 199, issue 1, pp.115–124.

Moilanen, Atte and B.A. Wintle, 2006b, Uncertainty analysis favours selection of spatially aggregated reserve structures. *Biological Conservation,* Volume 129, Issue 3, May 2006, Pages 427–434.

Moilanen, Atte, B.A. Wintle., J. Elith and M. Burgman, 2006c, Uncertainty analysis for regional-scale reserve selection. *Conservation Biology,* Vol.20, No. 6, 1688-1697.

Moilanen, Atte, Astrid van Teeffelen, Yakov Ben-Haim and Simon Ferrier, 2009, How much compensation is enough? A framework for incorporating uncertainty and time discounting when calculating offset ratios for impacted habitat, *Restoration Ecology,* Vol.17, issue 4, pp.470–478.

Morris, S. and H.S. Shin, 2002, Social value of public information, *American Economic Review,* vol. 92, #5, December, 1521–1534.

Murphy, James J. and John K. Stranlund, 2006, Direct and market effects of enforcing emissions trading programs: An experimental analysis, *Journal of Economic Behavior and Organization,* vol. 61, pp.217–233.

Musil, Robert, 1906, *Young Törless,* New American Library, 1964.

Nicholson, Emily and Hugh P. Possingham, 2007, Conservation planning for the persistence of multiple species under uncertainty: an application of info-gap decision theory, *Ecological Applications,* 17: 251–265

Nordhaus, William D., 2007, A Review of the Stern Review on the economics of climate change, *Journal of Economic Literature,* 45: 686–702.

Norges Bank, 2008, *Monetary Policy Report,* report #3/2008.

Onatski, Alexei and James H. Stock, 2000, Robust monetary policy under model uncertainty in a small model of the U.S. economy, National Bureau of Economic Research, Working Paper 7490.

Pantelides, Chris P. and Sara Ganzerli, 1998, Design of trusses under uncertain loads using convex models, *ASCE J. Structural Engineering, 124,* #3, 318–329.

Peirce, Charles Sanders, 1897, *Collected Papers,* 1.170, 171–175. Reprinted in Peirce (1955) pp.355–358.

Peirce, Charles Sanders, 1955, *Philosophical Writings of Peirce.* Justus Buchler, editor. Dover reprint of *The Philosophy of Peirce: Selected Writings,* Routledge and Kegan Paul, 1940, p.356.

Pierce, S.Gareth, Keith Worden and Graeme Manson, 2006a, A novel information-gap technique to assess reliability of neural network-based damage detection, *Journal of Sound and Vibration,* 293: Issues 1–2, pp.96–111.

Pierce, S.Gareth, Yakov Ben-Haim, Keith Worden and Graeme Manson, 2006b, Evaluation of neural network robust reliability using information-gap theory, *IEEE Transactions on Neural Networks, 17,* #6, 1349–1361.

Poole, William, 2004, Best guesses and surprises, *Federal Reserve Bank of St. Louis Review,* Jan/Feb 2004, 86(3), pp.1–7.

Popper, Karl R., 1957, *The Poverty of Historicism.* Harper Torchbooks edition 1964.

Popper, Karl, 1982, *The Open Universe: An Argument for Indeterminism.* From the Postscript to *The Logic of Scientific Discovery.* Routledge.

Quine, Williard V., 1995, *From Stimulus to Science.* Harvard University Press.

Regan, Helen M., Yakov Ben-Haim, Bill Langford, Will G. Wilson, Per Lundberg, Sandy J. Andelman, and Mark A. Burgman, 2005, Robust decision making under severe uncertainty for conservation management, *Ecological Applications, 15,* #4,: 1471–1477.

Regev, Sary, Avraham Shtub and Yakov Ben-Haim, 2006, Managing project risks as knowledge gaps, *Project Management Journal,* vol.37, issue #5, pp.17–25.

Reserve Bank of New Zealand, 2004, *The Reserve Bank's Forecasting and Policy System,* www.rbnz.govt.nz.

Rockafellar, R. Tyrrell and Stanislav Uryasev, 2000, Optimization of conditional value-at-risk, *J. of Risk,* vol.2, #3, pp.21–41.

Rockafellar, R. Tyrrell and Stanislav Uryasev, 2002, Conditional value-at-risk for general loss distributions, *J. Banking & Finance,* 26: 1443–1471.

Rudebusch, G.D. and L.E.O. Svensson, 1999, Policy rules for inflation targeting, in J. Taylor, ed., *Policy Rules for Inflation Targeting,* University of Chicago Press for NBER, pp.203–246.

Runkle, David E., 1998, Revisionist history: How data revisions distort economic policy research, *Federal Reserve Bank of Minneapolis Quarterly Review,* Vol. 22, No. 4, pp.3–12.

Samuelson, P.A., 1963, Problems of methodology — discussion. *American Economic Review,* Papers and Proceedings of the 75th Meeting of the American Economic Association, May 1963, 53: 231–236.

Shackle, G.L.S., 1972, *Epistemics and Economics: A Critique of Economic Doctrines,* Transaction Publishers, 1992, originally published by Cambridge University Press.

Shakespeare, William, *The Tragedy of Hamlet, Prince of Denmark.*

Stranlund, John K. and Yakov Ben-Haim, 2008, Price-based vs. quantity-based environmental regulation under Knightian uncertainty: An info-gap robust satisficing perspective, *Journal of Environmental Management,* 87: 443–449.

Stranlund, John K. and Kanwalroop Kathy Dhanda, 1999, Endogenous monitoring and enforcement of a transferable emissions permit system, *Journal of Environmental Economics and Management,* vol. 38, pp.267–282.

Tahan, Meir and Joseph Z. Ben-Asher, 2005, Modeling and analysis of integration processes for engineering systems, *Systems Engineering,* Vol. 8, No. 1, pp.62–77.

Tikhonov, Andrey N. and Vasiliy Y. Arsenin, 1977, *Solutions of Ill-posed Problems,* translated by Fritz John, Wiley, New York.

Tol, Richard S.J., 2009, The economic effects of climate change, *Journal of Economic Perspectives,* vol.23, #2, pp.29–51.

University of Newcastle upon Tyne and Halcrow. *Early Conceptual Options, A Framework for Uncertainty Analysis in TE2100,* Environment Agency ECO Report R10X, June 2006, 42pp.

Vinot, P., S.Cogan and V.Cipolla, 2005, A robust model-based test planning procedure, *Journal of Sound and Vibration,* Volume 288, Issue 3, pp.571–585.

Wang, Kaihong, 2005, Vibration analysis of cracked composite bending-torsion beams for damage diagnosis, PhD thesis, Virginia Tech, USA.

Weitzman, Martin L., 1974, Prices vs. quantities, *Review of Economic Studies,* vol. 41, #4, pp.477–491.

Weitzman, Martin L., 2007, A Review of the Stern Review on the economics of climate change, *Journal of Economic Literature*, 45: 703–724.

Weitzman, Martin L., 2009, On modeling and interpreting the economics of catastrophic climate change, *The Review of Economics and Statistics*, vol. 91, #1, pp.1–19.

Zacksenhouse, Miriam, Simona Nemets, Miikhail A.Lebedev and Miguel A.Nicolelis, 2009, Robust satisficing linear regression: performance/robustness trade-off and consistency criterion, *Mechanical Systems and Signal Processing*, vol.23, pp.1954–1964.

Zare, Kazem, Antonio J. Conejo, Miguel Carrion, and Mohsen Parsa Moghaddam, 2010, Multi-market energy procurement for a large consumer using a risk-aversion procedure, *Electric Power Systems Research*, vol.80, pp.63–70.

Author Index

Subject Index